THE LAST GENTLEMAN OF THE SAS

THE LAST
GENTLEMAN
– OF THE –
SAS

JOHN RANDALL AND **M J TROW**

MAINSTREAM
PUBLISHING

EDINBURGH AND LONDON

TRANSWORLD PUBLISHERS
61–63 Uxbridge Road, London W5 5SA
www.penguin.co.uk

Transworld is part of the Penguin Random House group of companies
whose addresses can be found at global.penguinrandomhouse.com

First published in Great Britain in 2014 by Mainstream Publishing Company,
an imprint of Transworld Publishers
This Mainstream paperback edition published 2016

A CIP catalogue record for this book is
available from the British Library.

ISBN
9781780575278

Offset in 9.66/12.73pt Sabon by Jouve (UK), Milton Keynes
Printed and bound in Great Britain by Clays Ltd, Bungay, Suffolk

Penguin Random House is committed to a sustainable
future for our business, our readers and our planet. This book is
made from Forest Stewardship Council® certified paper.

1 3 5 7 9 10 8 6 4 2

Acknowledgements

The authors would like to thank everyone who has helped in the creation of this book.

For John Randall, in particular, for the love and support of his family, the Special Air Service Regiment, Jason Amber and the staff of the Special Forces Club.

For Mei Trow, in particular, the invaluable support of his wife Carol, his agent Andrew Lownie and Bill Campbell and his team at Mainstream.

Contents

The Gates of Hell

An ordinary road. A warm spring day, 'Somewhere in Germany'. Lieutenant John Randall was actually 30 miles south of Luneburg Heath and forests of pines and silver birch clothed the road. There was something terrible about riding ahead of a main army, even though Randall and his driver, Corporal Brown, had been effectively doing this for months and all their training had been directed towards it. Like the horsed Light Cavalry of 50 years earlier, they were the eyes and ears of the main army, the van, the front line, the Forlorn Hope, whatever analogy military men have used over time. To say that they were exposed, alone and vulnerable does not begin to describe it. At any moment, behind any tree in those thousands of trees, there could have been a sniper, a Waffen SS unit, someone who had these two men of 1 SAS in the cross-hairs of his sights. It was April 1945 and Hitler's Third Reich was falling apart. That made some Germans desperate, bent on revenge, determined to take as many Allies as they could with them when they went down.

There were just the two of the Allies that day in an open-topped, khaki and green painted jeep, complete with twin Browning machine guns and a bazooka. The thing jolted in every rutted pot hole and jarred a man's spine to buggery. Of course, there were rumours of where the Germans were, confirmed or not confirmed by aerial reconnaissance. But the retreat was happening so fast now that reconnaissance of the conventional type became pointless. They had chased the Wehrmacht all the way from the beaches of Normandy, through the long months of a French autumn and winter, and were now deep inside the invincible Reich itself. It had not been easy and anybody who thought taking on Hitler in his own backyard would be child's play was deeply deluded.

With Brown's eyes pinned on the road, it was Randall who saw them first, a pair of huge gates to the right, the sunshine dappling on the curling wrought iron. They were wide open and beyond them a rutted path curved into the trees. He did not know what this was; some country house, perhaps, which the Wehrmacht had probably occupied long ago just as the British Army had tended to do back home. Randall told Brown to spin the wheel; they would take a look.

For the rest of his life, John Randall wished he had not made that decision. Because what he saw was the stuff of nightmare. And anybody who witnessed what these men did would have their lives changed by it. Everybody who saw what lay beyond those gates in the hours and days ahead was brought face to face with the most unimaginable evil. The Russian Red Army had seen it already as they drove into the Reich from the east, but at that stage the British had nothing to do with them and, anyway, their tales would not have been believed. No, a man had to see this place for himself. It had to be confronted – *they* had to confront it because this was what they had gone to war for in the first place. What had Neville Chamberlain said in his speech to the nation on 3 September 1939? 'It is the evil things that we will be fighting against; brute force, bad faith, injustice, oppression and persecution.' In essence, of course, he was right. But he had no idea.

From the day John Randall decided to turn into that gateway, the British perception of Germany and the Germans would never be the same again.

The first thing he noticed was the potential danger. It became instinctive in a unit like 1 SAS; men developed a nose for it. The drone of an engine, the snap of a twig, a passing civilian with a weapon-shaped bulge under his coat. This particular danger was more obvious; SS guards in their field grey and caps with death's head badges, watching them. Brown drove slowly, at perhaps three miles an hour. Randall had his pistol in his hand, but already he could count more than the clip held. Would he have time to reload in the event of a firefight? Could he swing the Brownings into action or even grab the bazooka in time? The peculiar thing was that the guards showed no sign of fight at all. The gates and the barbed wire told the men of 1 SAS that this was some sort of camp, so perhaps the men they met were not the fanatical Waffen SS who had been ordered by their Führer to sell every foot of ground with their lives. They were armed, certainly, but their rifles and machine guns lay idly by and they almost ignored the newcomers.

The whole thing was surreal. Randall had seen beaten men before, trudging columns of the vanquished on the road, now their prisoners. Men with blank stares and empty eyes, shot to hell and back and not knowing what day it was. In France, in Germany, in North Africa – the look was the same. But these men were not like that. They were fit and well. It was just that the fight had gone out of them and there were not many of them there.

The jeep had travelled perhaps 30 yards. Randall noticed the low wooden buildings beyond some sort of gatehouse, huts extending row upon row, like makeshift army barracks anywhere in Europe. He was aware of a strange smell. A smell that became overpowering as that surreal journey continued. It was sickly sweet, a smell of decay. A smell of death.

First one, then two, then a handful of people came towards the jeep. Corporal Brown jammed on his brakes and they both sat there, motionless, with the engine idling. The hair on Randall's scalp was crawling and he could not look at the man beside him.

That was because he could not take his eyes off the swarm of humanity now threatening to engulf the jeep; a tide of human beings as Dante or Hieronymus Bosch imagined them, in print and on canvas. Some of them were wearing striped uniforms, once black and white and now a sickly grey. Some wore odd scraps of clothing, rags wrapped round bleeding feet or hanging off sores. Some were stark naked, men, women and children, utterly unconcerned about their nakedness. Their eyes were sunk into their heads, the bones of their skulls jutting under skin as yellow and fragile as old parchment. Their hands reached out to the SAS men, grabbing at their sleeves, their trousers, anything they could reach.

The crescendo of noise from them was like nothing Randall had ever heard. A babble of every language in Europe, all of them asking for food, for clothes, for bandages, for help. They clearly recognised the newcomers as something different from their guards. The vehicle, the uniforms, the sudden unannounced arrival and the lack of a swastika. They did not recognise the winged dagger on their cap badges, but they knew they were not German. There was a crescendo of smell too that rose like a wave. Randall could not find a word for it. The best he could do was the slurry pit of some God-forsaken farmyard. The hands began to tug at his Denison smock and there were hundreds of them by now.

It all sounds like a scene from an over-the-top science-fiction film of the 1970s, the undead rising from their graves. In 1945, Randall and Brown had seen nothing like that on their cinema screens, but they had to tell themselves over and over again in those moments that these were people, human beings who desperately needed help.

John Randall stood up in the jeep and told them that he was a British officer, that there were others behind him, thousands of them, and they would bring food and medicine and freedom for them all. Not many of them could have heard him in that noise. Probably not many of them understood what he was saying even if they did hear. English was an alien tongue. And freedom more alien still.

Randall hissed at Brown to move on or they would have dragged them from the jeep. He gunned the engine and blasted his horn, forcing the ragged crowd to break for long enough for them to outrun them. Still the SS did nothing, just watched the scene as if it was newsreel stuff back home, an inverted sort of propaganda that Leni Riefenstahl, Hitler's film-maker, might have made. Behind them, the crowd was surging, swarming as if it had a mind of its own, but, on its edges, individuals began to break away, walking like the lost souls they were. Randall had just told them that he was a British officer. So what? Where had the British been for so long? Now they were here, standard bearers of the greatest empire in history, they were two men and a jeep, with no food, no medicine, no help at all. They hadn't even killed a guard.

About 30 yards further on, the SAS men drove to the edge of what Randall could only describe as a grotesque potato patch. Except it was not potatoes lying in the shallow earth; it was people and they were dead. Had he thought about it, he would have been grateful that this was April and not the height of summer or the scene would have been made more ghastly by the flies, black and heavy on their human feast. They lay in heaps, bleached white, caked with their own excrement, arms and legs interlocked like some appalling Dance of Death. Durer would have known scenes like this, so would any survivor of the Black Death, standing on the edge of the plague pits they once dug beyond cities when the pestilence was at its worst. So decomposed were some of the bodies it was no longer possible to tell their sex. Breasts had deflated, long empty of milk for dead babies. Hair was matted to scalps. Genitals had disappeared into the fatty slush they call adipocere.

And over them squatted human vultures. They were picking over the corpses, tearing off a striped jacket here, a cap there, a pair of ripped, ragged trousers and a shapeless pair of clogs. Dead men's shoes. They didn't notice the SAS patrol, fresh, young, healthy, aliens from a different world where things like this didn't

13

happen. Randall couldn't find any words now, so he motioned his driver on. About 50 yards further into the camp, they came across a pit from hell. It was perhaps 50 feet square and 20 feet deep, the bottom littered with more corpses, older than the 'potato patch' they had left behind. If the stench so far had been appalling, now it was unbelievable. They both fought down the need to retch and did their best to keep themselves, somehow, together. Gases expand in bloated bodies and the whole pit twitched like a dying animal as first one corpse, then another, twisted and rolled. Eyes sunken and dead. Mouths hanging open. Beyond all help. Beyond all care. Beyond all belief.

It could not have been more than half an hour, yet it seemed like years. Randall and Brown stayed with the jeep, their guns at the ready, just in case any of the SS remembered they were supposed to be fighting the British. There was a snarl of an engine behind them and another SAS jeep was following them through the camp. Randall had never been so glad to see 'reinforcements' in his life, even though there were only two of them. At the wheel was Sergeant Reg Seekings, one of the most formidable of the 'Originals' who had fought with L Detachment all across North Africa and into Italy. He should have won a VC for that. Randall knew his look of old; the one he had on his face now as he sat behind the wheel of his jeep; a look that said, 'Somebody's going to pay for this.' Next to him was Randall's squadron leader, Major John Tonkin, and he was a handy man to have at your side too. In one mission earlier in the year, he had got cut off in a cornfield. His orders had been to capture SS cipher books and, in the excitement of a firefight, he had had to go back to get them. Crawling through needle-sharp corn stalks, he came so close to the SS while planting bombs near them that their discarded chocolate wrappers fluttered down on his head. However, standing in that camp required courage of a different kind and all four men of the SAS hoped they had it.

They stood beside their jeeps staring at the horror in front of them. As they watched, a knot of Germans walked warily towards them. All the SAS guns were out now, nobody knowing quite what to expect. In the centre stood a stocky man with deep-set glittering eyes, his hair oily black and uncombed, his scarred cheeks covered in a few days' beard growth. His eyebrows were thick and beetling, and he looked a nasty piece of work. So did the blonde woman standing alongside him, wearing a dark-blue prison-guard uniform. She was younger than Randall, with large ice-blue eyes and thin lips twisted in a permanent sneer.

The man's lips parted in a half smile, the one he no doubt showed to all visitors. And he introduced himself. 'I am Josef Kramer,' he said. 'Welcome to KL Bergen-Belsen.'

1

A Chip Off the Old Block

The Allied officer who was first into Bergen-Belsen was born on 21 February 1920 into a world very different from today. In that month, the League of Nations was launched in London in the pious hope that there would never be another war in Europe. That seemed unlikely, because, also in that month, Leon Trotsky's Red Army was driving back the Whites along the Trans-Siberian railway. Their leader, Admiral Kolchak, had been executed in Irkutsk and his body thrown into a frozen river. He died, according to an eyewitness, 'like an Englishman'. In Germany, Left and Right continued to contend for control of the city streets, with violence in Berlin being directed against the Jews, who, Right-wingers said, had started the war in the first place.

The cost of the Great War, both in terms of human casualties and materiel, was staggering. At sea, where the world had learned the terrible reality of U-boat warfare, Britain had lost over 900,000 tonnes of shipping, easily the heaviest loss of any combatant country. Three-quarters of a million Britons died and 200,000 from the British Empire. Men spoke of the 'lost generation' and poets such as Wilfred Owen, Edmund Blunden and Siegfried Sassoon spoke for them.

John Randall's father, also John, was part of the generation of young men who went to war in 1914, with flags flying and drums beating. It was infamously a war that would be over by Christmas and it was one of the most pointless ever fought. Randall's father was a captain in the King's Royal Rifle Corps, an elite regiment originally raised in 1755. Its motto was *Celer et Audax*, swift and bold, and its battle honours are impressive. In the Great War alone, it saw action everywhere on the Western Front, from Mons to Courtrai. It also fought in Italy and Macedonia, but John Randall Senior fought in Flanders.

His mother, Margaret May Newman, was training to be an opera singer in Brussels under the tutelage of Elizabeth Lehmann, and she would have a huge impact on John Hugh, born to her in Hampstead that February. The letters he wrote during the war in which he fought, and the numerous entries in his diaries, make it clear that she was a very important person in his life and there is no embarrassment at all in the fact that to the end of her days he called her 'Mummie'.

Hampstead, in 1920, was still, essentially, a village in suburbia where little had changed, despite the upheaval of war. The heath nearby was originally a medieval hunting ground and the village itself became a fashionable spa in the 18th century, where various politicians and men-about-town met to take the chalybeate waters. Samuel Johnson lived there for a while, as did the poet Keats and the artist John Constable. In 1906, a Garden Suburb had been set up with rules established by Henrietta Barnett. Every class of society was welcome, roads would be tree-lined and 40 feet wide, and there was a strong emphasis on quiet – even church bells were prohibited. Architects like Edward Lutyens and C.A. Voysey were brought in to build imaginative, beautiful cottages. It did not *quite* work out, however, because the roads were too narrow for public transport and the working class found the place artificial and decamped to the East End where they felt more at home. When the tube arrived in 1907, its platforms were 192 feet down – the deepest on the entire Underground system.

If middle-class Hampstead muddled on as before, the same could not be said of the Randalls. John's father, rather unusually for an Englishman, had been a 'Mountie' in Canada before the Great War, and it may be that there was a wanderlust in his blood. Alternatively, for many men with experiences of the trenches, settling down to life in post-war Britain was not that easy. There were serious strikes among coal miners, which were a forerunner of the altogether more spectacular General Strike of 1926. Ireland was in the grip of virtual civil war with Black and Tans on the streets of Dublin and there were 94 attacks on police stations in May 1921 alone. So John Randall Senior decided to take his family out to Kenya to try his hand at farming.

The disappearance of the British Empire is one of the most bewildering episodes of recent history, not because it happened but because of the speed at which it happened. What John Randall's father chose to do in 1921 was what many restless and ambitious young men had done in various remote hill stations of the Empire for 200 years. Today, it would be unthinkable. Even the pronunciation of 'Kenya' has changed.

In 1921, British East Africa comprised Kenya, Uganda and Tanganyika, and was the living legacy of the 'Scramble for Africa' that had dominated the last quarter of the 19th century. Germany and Italy, both new states jockeying for power and pre-eminence, had challenged Britain as the owner of the largest empire the world had ever known, and the 'dark continent', at once so mysterious[1] and so potentially rich, seemed the obvious hunting ground. Kenya had been a British Protectorate until July 1920 when it was annexed to the Crown. The lowland areas were fertile, producing flax, coffee, wheat, maize, sisal, tea and pyrethrum, and the uplands grew sugar, coconuts and cotton. There was a lively trade in hides and skins, with large sheep and ostrich farms and cattle ranches.

While his father was running a coffee plantation up-country, little John spent his first years toddling with Masai and 'Loombier' tribesmen. In fact, when the Randall family came home two years later, he spoke as many Bantu words as he did English. The Masai tribesmen in particular, with their red-dyed hair, their tall imposing figures and their long-horned cattle, must have had an incredible effect on a little boy from far-away Hampstead. The 'Loombier' (John's memory of the name) were the Luhya tribe, people of the clan or those of the same hearth. From the 1890s until the Mau-Mau troubles 60 years later, both tribes lived peacefully with the British.

It may be that Randall's father realised that farming was not for him or perhaps the Kenyan episode was only ever intended to be short-lived. Either way, the Randalls were back in England by 1923, this time in Maida Vale. Young John was sent to Arnold House School where the headmistress was the daunting Miss Hanson who had established the place in 1905. Beginning with a mere nine boys, she had set out to rival the men in preparing suitable lads for public school. To get the attention of prospective parents, she had borrowed a carriage and pair from a local doctor before the Great War and made sure she was seen riding around in it.

Randall was not a natural academic, but he was a good all-round sportsman, naturally strong and with a surprising turn of speed. He won prizes on that score and his particular friend in those years was Reid Dick, the son of the famous sculptor who made the magnificent stone lions on the Menin Gate. At the age of nine, young John was sent away to boarding school as so many of his generation were and he entered the Preparatory School of St Lawrence College in Ramsgate. This was not mere chance; it was his father's *alma mater*.

The town itself of course – not that a 'new bug' would have had much chance to see it – was already a popular holiday resort by the late 1920s, made possible by the railways. It was seventy-four miles from London, and to a nine-year-old boy that must have seemed the far side of the moon. Steamers set out from here to various Channel ports and the town had been one of those hit by Zeppelin raids in the Great War. There was a promenade bustling from May to September and wide sandy beaches.

St Lawrence College was founded in 1879 as South Eastern College as a single house, like so many Victorian educational establishments. The buildings that Randall would have known, in imposing Gothic red brick, were established five years later but the chapel was still new when he arrived. Because of the risk of aerial bombing, the school had been evacuated to Chester in 1915, well out of range of any aircraft that the Kaiser's Germany could send over.

John Randall hated it. He had not actually learned very much at Arnold House and non-academics got no sympathy from gowned masters who all had degrees from Oxford and Cambridge. There was a rigorous system of competition in place, which would make educationalists wince today. Marks in tests were read out in morning prayers in the new chapel every Friday. Three poor results meant detention and Randall achieved a school record once of thirteen in one week! The headmaster was a bully of the old school – Randall disliked him intensely and on one occasion he was ordered to the man's study for the usual 'six of the best'. While John waited in the dismal corridor outside, listening to the hiss and thump of the cane, the headmaster suddenly popped his head out of the door and said to him, 'Are you the last?'

'No, sir,' Randall said. 'Two more.'

'I told you,' the headmaster said, a sadist to the last, 'to go to the end of the queue.' And so the torture continued.

Because of his mother's musicality, she inevitably wanted the boy to learn the piano. But the instrument owned by St Lawrence Junior School was a clapped-out, honky-tonk one that refused to stay in tune. Like everything else he was to do in his life, John Randall gave it 100 per cent, but in the end a career as a concert pianist was not for him!

The one saving grace at St Lawrence Junior School actually came in the form of two people. One was the matron, a kindly lady who was everybody's fairy godmother and who remembered John's father when he had been there. The other was the odd-job man, 'Boots', a wonderful old boy who would go into Ramsgate with John's pocket money and buy birthday presents for the lad's parents.

Moving to the senior school at 14 was like a breath of fresh air. Young Randall was a member of Tower House, the oldest of the boarding houses set up in 1889. Once the College had been the academic home of doctors' and clergymen's sons, but now the boys came from all walks of life. Many of the staff were clerics, however, and John got his head down as well as he could to cope with the rigours of History, French, Maths and Science. Where he really excelled was on the sports field. The school was built on two sides of a road, linked by an underground passage, and there were extensive playing fields beyond that. He loved cricket, football, rugby, hockey and athletics, and played for the First XI and First XV. He was also captain of boxing and always remembered the stern advice his father had given him: 'I'll teach you to box; and never let me hear about you bullying another boy.' It was a lesson for life and the attitudes that young Randall learned on the playing field stayed with him too.

I have in front of me three pieces of John Randall's life from this period. One is a photograph of him in his striped rugger shirt. It was a present to his parents dated half term, summer 1937, and must have been one of the last taken before he left school. The second is, in effect, his passport to the adult world. It is a postcard, posted exactly one year before the outbreak of the Second World War and addressed to John at the Old Cottage, Riverhead, Kent, to where the family had moved by this time. On the back are the results of his school certificate examination. He was not bad on the Acts of the Apostles, better on the New Testament. His Chaucer and Shakespeare were on a par and his History and Geography stood finely balanced too. His French was impressive, as was his Maths, and the master sending through the results wrote 'Well done!' on the bottom.

T.G. Mallinson, John's housemaster who had taught him French, was even more forthcoming three days later. 'Magnificent!' he wrote on another postcard. 'Delighted at your French credit. So Private Tuition was not in vain! Hearty congratulations on your school certificate with the three credits. Please tell your father how pleased I am – I don't suppose you'll forget to tell those relations who so much despised your chances.' Knowing John Randall as I do, I am sure he was modesty itself about that!

The late 1930s may have been an inauspicious time to enter the world of business, but it was where John Randall went anyway. His mother and various friends with connections got him an interview at Shell Mex House and, as an 18 year old with clear management potential, he started work as an office boy!

That summer, a pair of slacks would cost a nattily attired gent 30 shillings;[2] shorts would be 17/6d. He would have to pay one penny for a fresh peach and the same amount would get him two oranges. Perhaps John Randall had gone into the wrong business; in August, footballer Bryn Jones transferred from Wolves to Arsenal for a record fee of £13,000. And no doubt Randall was delighted that Len Hutton and England's cricketers annihilated Australia by an innings and 578 runs at the Oval.

In September, the news that dominated Europe and covered the front pages of British newspapers was the Munich crisis. As Nazi Germany sought to add yet more territory to the Reich in its policy of *lebensraum* (living space), the Chancellor Adolf Hitler had already effectively annexed Austria and was now claiming that the Czech Sudetenland should be added too. The Prime Minister, Neville Chamberlain, became a footnote in history as the first occupant of Number 10 to fly, and he obtained a promise in writing from Hitler that the Sudetenland would be the last of his conquests.

Chamberlain has become synonymous with appeasement. 'I am a man of peace to the depths of my soul,' he once said. 'Armed conflict between nations is a nightmare to me.' He was briefly the hero of the hour at Heston Aerodrome, waving Hitler's infamous 'scrap of paper' and promising, 'I believe it is peace for our time.'

It was not. And John Randall's generation paid the price.

2

The Phoniest of Wars

John Randall had only been at Shell Mex House a few months when war broke out.

'I am speaking to you from the Cabinet Room at 10 Downing Street,' the Prime Minister, Neville Chamberlain, broadcast to the nation. It was Sunday, 3 September, and thousands of very worried people sat huddled around their wireless sets to hear Chamberlain explain, 'This morning the British Ambassador in Berlin handed the German government a final note stating that, unless we heard from them by eleven o'clock that they were prepared at once to withdraw their troops from Poland, a state of war would exist between us. I have to tell you now that no such undertaking has been received and that, consequently, this country is at war with Germany.'

And so Britain embarked on the People's War, a unique experience in which the streets of cities and even country lanes would become the front line. Everybody was expected to put on a uniform and 'do their bit'. The first bomb had already gone off – not dropped by the Luftwaffe, but planted by the IRA in Broadgate, Coventry, nine days *before* Chamberlain's announcement. Five people had died and scores more were injured.

Even so, the Mass-Observation Unit[1] reported that only one Briton in five actually expected war, and those few who had television sets must have been astounded when the BBC's service shut down in the middle of a Mickey Mouse cartoon and most of the football matches scheduled for 2 September were cancelled. Most of the West Ham team were already in uncomfortable, itchy khaki battledress by the next day.

At 11.27 a.m. on that 'Chamberlain Sunday', the air-raid sirens wailed over London for the first time. Men in tin hats with the initials ARP stencilled on them herded people into the Underground stations. Worshippers in St Paul's Cathedral hurried down to the crypt. But it was all a false alarm. A single French fighter had flown into British airspace and triggered the early-warning radar system.

Then followed a long lull before the storm. In France, they called it *drôle de guerre* (the funny war); in Germany, *Sitzkrieg* (the armchair war) because nothing (except in Poland) seemed to be happening. There was no patriotic rush to join the colours as there had been in the summer of 1914, when every young man of John Randall's age had queued outside their local recruitment office and been shipped off, with the minimum of training, to halt the German advance through Belgium. Randall's father had fought in that war; his uncle George had been killed at Ypres. John's was a wiser and more circumspect generation, made more so by the fact that *some* men who fought in the People's War had fought in the Great War too.

Chamberlain's government had decided that, in the event of war, the conscription introduced in 1916 should be brought into immediate effect. That did not mean that the dreaded buff envelope of the call-up fell on the morning mats of every male aged 18 to 41 immediately and simultaneously. In keeping with the spirit of the times, however, Shell Mex gave relevant employees the option. Randall received a courteous letter – if he wished to join the forces, he was to feel free to do so. It was good advice and he took it. The truth was that John was bored at home – 'browned off' was the phrase of the '40s – and itching for some excitement. He wanted to be a fighter pilot. His parents' reaction was predictable. His mother fretted about her only son, as mothers will; his father expected it.

'The Few' would not become iconic heroes until the summer of 1940 when dog-fights took place in the skies over southern England and the new Prime Minister, Winston Churchill, immortalised them in his famous speech.[2] But they were already the 'Brylcreem boys', with a swagger and élan that might be expected of the newest branch of the services. The training of pilots took time, however, and John Randall, like many 19 year olds, was a young man in a hurry. He contacted his local unit, the 83rd Light Aircraft Battery of the Royal Artillery, with its headquarters in Sevenoaks, just up the road from his home. The town was a quiet quarter of what J.B. Priestley called the 'old England' of leafy lanes and a traditional way of life. It boasted the Vine, one of the oldest cricket clubs in the country. And, perhaps in keeping with Sevenoaks' air of gentility, the commanding officer of the 83rd was Major Victor Cazalet.

Cazalet was a fascinating character, one of many whom Randall would meet over the next five years. He was a gentleman of the old school, 44 years old at the outbreak of war and MP for Chippenham in Wiltshire. He had been commissioned into the Queen's Own West Kent Yeomanry in 1915, at a time when the regiment still had its horses, and had won the Military Cross two years later. He had won the Chippenham seat as a Conservative in 1924, the year in which the Right shuddered because Ramsay MacDonald became the first Labour Prime Minister. His sister, Thelma Cazalet-Keir, was also a Tory MP and a leading feminist at a time when women were still campaigning for voting equality with men.[3]

Cazalet was out of step with his time in the sense that he was a member of the Ninth Church of Christ Scientist, in London, then a rather shadowy cult with a small following. His political leanings, however, were more conventional. The Spanish Civil War polarised Europe's stance on the Left–Right political spectrum. Thinking men took sides, either to stop the threat of Fascism or to stem the rising tide of Communism – exactly the same dilemma that had led to the rise of Mussolini in Italy and Hitler in Germany. Cazalet backed Franco's Phalange and served on the Friends of National Spain committee.

In the Commons, Cazalet often spoke in support of his friend Winston Churchill, in the wilderness in the 1930s and at times almost a lone voice against the appeasement of Neville Chamberlain. It was Churchill who had given Cazalet the green light to set up the 83rd and this spoke volumes not only for the mindset of the man who would become the dogged hero of Number 10 but also for the whole quasi-amateur spirit of 1939–40. Country gentlemen had defended their hearths and homes for centuries; in fact, units like the West Kent Yeomanry had been specifically set up for that purpose in the 1790s to guard against attack from Revolutionary France. Throughout his wartime leadership as Prime Minister, Churchill delighted in the unconventional and approved wholeheartedly of both the elite units John Randall was later to join – Phantom and the SAS.

Cazalet lived in the grounds of Cranbrook School, 25 miles from Sevenoaks, one of the few in the vulnerable county of Kent that did not evacuate its pupils. It was here that Randall, as a mere 19-year-old gunner in the Royal Artillery, shook the hand of the soon-to-be-great, and already famous, Winston Churchill. People either loved Churchill or hated him, and Randall was in the first camp from that very first meeting. Branded a failure so often in his life, early in 1940 Churchill was First Lord of the Admiralty (a post he had held in the Great War) and a member of Chamberlain's War Cabinet. The homburg, the spotted bow tie and the cigar were to become the visible icons of dogged Britishness in the months ahead.

John Randall was less enthusiastic about Cazalet's other friends. Many of them were thespians from the London stage and, since at the time Cazalet's unit had no uniforms and no guns, they spent their time putting on concert parties. If you ask John Randall today about this, he will say, 'You can guess what sort of shows they were.' Several of these men were quite openly homosexual, at a time when such activity was illegal. Henry Labouchere's 'blackmailers' charter', the Criminal Law Amendment Act of 1884, which had outlawed homosexuality, was still current and would stay on the statute books until 1967.

The drill Randall learned was basic. Marching (which he grew to hate) in hob-nailed boots; how to load, strip and fire a .303 rifle and a short course on the gas attacks that everybody expected any minute.[4] He was also taught how to handle a Lewis gun.[5]

Promotion to sergeant did not just give John Randall stripes on the sleeves of his battledress; it also gave him a chance to manage men. To be fair, he had already had a taste of that at school, with his captaincy of various teams, but this was different. This was the outside world. And this was war. Even so, there was again an amateurishness about this time. 'I managed to get away with it,' he says today about his role in man-management. 'If anybody disagreed with me, I thumped them.' The thirty-five men of the 83rd were photographed in three ranks outside the makeshift Mess hut sometime in 1940. John Randall is standing at the back, second from the left, looking grim and determined, at ease with his hands behind his back, his white-banded field cap tucked under his right shoulder strap. He is clearly one of the youngest men there, 20 when this photograph was taken, and that fact alone must have given him problems.

By May 1940, Sergeant Randall found himself on duty guarding Chatham Docks, one of the oldest naval bases in the country and the birthplace of Nelson's HMS *Victory*. It was not a victory that Randall was witnessing now, however. It was a defeat. Neville Chamberlain had resigned after three days of agonising, and the reins of government passed to Churchill on 10 May. That was the day Hitler's Wehrmacht struck west and the phoney war was phoney no more. By the end of the month, the British Expeditionary Force had been effectively surrounded and the only means of escape was off the beaches at Dunkirk. Belgium had surrendered, and 750,000 Germans were forcing the British back into the sea.

The roads were choked with refugees, clogging troop movements; survivors came back with stories of British heroism and German atrocities in equal number. Men, women and children were mown down on the roads, their bodies flung into ditches, but wave after wave of the Wehrmacht kept on coming, taking terrible punishment from the beleaguered British, but coming on nonetheless.

On 4 June, Operation Dynamo was launched. Every ship and boat available – the navy's destroyers and mine-sweepers, Channel ferries, river-launches, even fishing vessels – risked the sea crossing to get the troops off. The lines of battered, exhausted men waited patiently and waded up to their necks out to sea to reach the boats, some of which went back again and again. This was the army that John Randall saw limping home via Chatham. They were 'poor wretched fellows', he remembers, walking half asleep, with wounds under filthy bandages. Although 338,226 men were saved at Dunkirk, thousands had surrendered and had to be left behind. As did most of the guns, tanks and ammunition of an army that could ill afford to lose anything at all.

Churchill's rhetoric in the Commons reached new heights. That same day, he promised that 'We shall fight on the beaches, we shall fight on the landing grounds, we shall fight in the fields and in the streets; we shall never surrender.'[6] Anthony Eden, Churchill's Minister of War, sitting near him on the Treasury benches, muttered to a colleague, 'Fight? What with? Broken bottles?' In time, the defeat would become the 'miracle' of Dunkirk and today it is celebrated almost as a victory. J.B. Priestley, broadcasting the day after Dynamo, began the turn-around propaganda:

> Our great-grandchildren, when they learn how we began this war by snatching glory out of defeat, and swept on to victory, may also learn how the little holiday steamers made an excursion to hell and came back victorious.[7]

At least, by the time he saw the shell-shocked columns hobbling home at Chatham, John Randall had a gun.

He had one, too, three months later and this time he was guarding Detling Aerodrome. Luftwaffe reconnaissance photographs showed quite clearly that British fighter planes, Spitfires and Hurricanes, were on the tarmac at Detling so it was the target for a major raid on 13 August. In fact, the airfield was used by Coastal Command only for the occasional refuel, unlike the nearby bases of Hawkinge and Biggin Hill. The attack on Detling was a classic example of the right hand not knowing what the left was doing. The Observer Corps had seen a huge bomber squadron coming in over the Kent coast but they had no direct telephone link to Detling. The information had to be relayed via their headquarters at Maidstone who believed the target was actually the Shorts-Pobjoys factory in Rochester further north. A delivery boy in the nearby village of Bredhurst saw the hangars burn and the ammunition dump go up like a vast firework display. Smoke drifted for miles. Sixty-seven people were killed and ninety-four injured.

When Randall got there, the place was a shambles. There was debris everywhere and rumour had it that there were policemen put on board the double-decker buses passing the airfield who gave orders to passengers to look the other way rather than witness the demoralising sight. Five days later, Fighter Command's airfields all over the south-east were hit in what would become known, nostalgically, as the 'Spitfire Summer'. Churchill delivered his famous speech praising 'the Few' on 20 August and the Battle of Britain roared over the south-east.

By 7 September, with Randall's battery constantly on the alert in Sevenoaks, Goering's Luftwaffe changed tactics and bombed London. The Blitz had begun.

In Sevenoaks, someone, perhaps even Major Cazalet himself, had noticed that John Randall had officer potential. And that meant a posting to the Officer Training School at Llandrindod Wells in central Wales. Travelling in wartime was extraordinarily difficult. Randall's later diaries are full of the crowded trains, the lack of petrol, the hours spent walking when he had missed the last bus home or to the barracks. From Sevenoaks, he would have had to have negotiated disrupted rail services to London, with its bombed docks and shattered East End, before heading west. There would inevitably have been a change at Swindon and the likeliest method of transport from Llandrindod Wells station would have been via a pair of army boots, size 8.

Randall had formally enlisted in the Royal Artillery in January 1940. In that month, there were, according to official figures, 14,202 officers and 312,309 Other Ranks in that branch of the service. The National Service Act had merged the regular army, the Territorial Army, reserves and militia, and choice of branch of the service was left up to the individual with guidance from the Ministry for Labour based on a very superficial assessment.

One of the biggest problems in the first two years of war was the selection of officers, the process through which John Randall now went. There was almost a subconscious perception that the best officers came from the landed classes (however minor and impoverished by 1940) and those who had been to public or private school, in that most of them, like St Lawrence College itself, had a Combined Cadet Force and had taught their boys at least the rudiments of soldiering. The Duke of Wellington never claimed that the battle of Waterloo was won on the playing fields of Eton,[8] but the sentiment was cherished by the Horse Guards and the War Office that replaced it. The notion of colonels and their ladies, officers and their wives, and Other Ranks and their women had not disappeared by the start of the Second World War.

The Royal Military Academy at Woolwich, known to generations as 'The Shop', was closed at the outbreak of war. The Artillery, the Engineers and some signalling units had been trained there since the 1860s. In its place, a number of Officer Cadet Training Units (OCTU) were set up to train potential officers in field artillery work; 124 OCTU Llandrindod Wells was one of these. Officially, John Randall should have undergone a six-month training period here, but a shortage of instructors led to its being reduced to three.

The town of Llandrindod was known as 'the queen of the Welsh watering places' and had been a spa since the 18th century. Tucked away in a rural idyll in what was then Radnorshire, the Pump House Hotel was typical of the large, elegant buildings the army commandeered for war use. It was part of the Lady Honeywood chain of hotels by 1929, and boasted that it could rival any establishment on the French Riviera. It was far enough away from any bombing zone for training to be carried on without interruption.

John Randall did well, passing all the exams with flying colours and emerged as number-one officer cadet at the end of his three months. It was a proud day when he led the march past at the passing-out parade and he was now second lieutenant in the Royal Artillery, with a single pip on the shoulder tab of his tunic and the famous grenade and 'Ubique' badges on his lapels. He was 21 and the war beckoned.

3

An Officer and a Gentleman

A key turning point in John Randall's life was his meeting with Colonel George Hopkinson in early 1941. This had been arranged by Bill Newman, Randall's uncle, who had already served with the colonel. Hopkinson in many ways was the epitome of the slightly eccentric officer who fought Hitler's War. His nickname, 'Hoppy', almost certainly came from his surname, but he did have a spring in his step, which was part of his boundless energy, and he also had a habit, in peacetime, of 'hopping' in and out of the army.

Before the Great War, Hopkinson had been an engineer and on its outbreak he enlisted in the North Staffordshire Regiment. He won the Military Cross during the last German offensive early in 1918. In the light of the unit that Randall was to join under his auspices, the citation for Hopkinson's award is interesting: '. . . His services in maintaining communication between brigade headquarters and the front line were most valuable.' He had also saved the life of a lost and wounded soldier by lifting him onto his motorbike and taking him to safety.

After the war, Hopkinson resigned his commission and enrolled as a rather mature student at Gonville and Caius College, Cambridge, the university being home to the oldest engineering school in the country. His mischievous reputation as a practical joker was born here with memorable Rag stunts carried out as military operations, for example, stealing the Jesus College gun. But the army was in Hopkinson's blood and he rejoined the Staffordshires in 1923, taking up hunting and riding with the county hunt at the same time. Typical of the man was his founding of the Bachelors' Club while Adjutant of his regiment. Appalled at the number of his fellow officers who were falling prey to matrimony, Hopkinson set up the club to deter them. A man who became engaged had to throw a dinner party for his fellow officers, which was an expensive evening. Hopkinson had a standing bet that he would be the last bachelor left and, at £5 a time, claimed to be making a steady income from it.

In 1930, he joined the Staff College at Camberley, where ambitious officers had the chance to rise above the regimental level of operations. As Hitler came to power in Germany and John Randall was making a name for himself on the playing fields of St Lawrence, Hopkinson learned to fly and became a general staff officer attached to the School of Artillery at Larkhill. In 1937, he left the army again, to become a civil engineer in Turkey, although there is a suggestion that part of his brief here was to cosy up to the Turkish authorities in the face of growing tension in Europe. Turkey had been an ally of Germany in the Great War and, should it come to it, no one wanted another Dardanelles fiasco.[1]

On the outbreak of war, Hopkinson rejoined (again) and was sent to the Staff of the Military Representative that served on the Supreme War Council. This group, first set up by David Lloyd George in the Great War, was essentially a strategic think-tank involving senior British and French politicians. Oddly, the senior British Army officer, Lord Gort,[2] was not a member, but junior officers like Hopkinson had a chance not only to meet key people like Halifax, Chamberlain and Churchill, but also to be privy to top-level planning of the direction of the war.

Someone who knew him well was Reginald Hills, a Life Guards officer who joined Hopkinson's Phantom and became the historian of the regiment. Today, his description of Hoppy reads a little oddly, but the 1940s were different days:

> Hoppy . . . loved war and said so. In other days he would have been a soldier of fortune . . . as a commanding officer, he was blithely unorthodox. A good deal of a showman, something of a snob, he gathered his remarkable collection of people and worked on them to such an extent that those of us who served him became inevitably and finally 'Hoppy's Men'.[3]

By November 1939, events had moved on. The phoney war continued to be phoney as far as British civilians were concerned, but it would not be long before the apparently invincible Wehrmacht struck west. Hopkinson was now in command of the General Headquarters Reconnaissance Unit, and on 10 May, when General von Runstedt's Army Group A crashed into the Ardennes, 'Hoppy' found himself carrying out vital liaison work with the Belgians, whose 18 divisions were soon in trouble. His war diary reads, 'Crack went the whip and off went the horses.'

With his usual frenetic energy, Hopkinson injured himself in a motorbike accident to the extent that for the rest of his life he had to salute with his left hand, but was recovered in time to join the lines of demoralised men on the beaches of Dunkirk. On 20 August, he was given the Order of the British Empire for his liaison work and dedication to duty.

This, then, was the man who sat before John Randall in his office at Pembroke Lodge that January day. He was 43 years old, small and stocky with a round face and twinkling eyes. He was in the process of becoming a parachutist, as Randall would later. He had hurt his back on his first jump, but, undeterred and still wearing a plaster cast, carried out his second and landed in the middle of Poole Harbour. There are different accounts of this. The 'official' version is that Hopkinson was irritated by the airfield's doctor, a Pole who spoke very little English, and he drove himself to hospital, complete with fractured spine.

Hopkinson was clearly impressed by the young sergeant sitting in front of him. 'Go away and get yourself a commission,' he said, 'and we'll talk again.' And once he had got his 'pip', Randall was accepted. He was now part of an elite outfit, the 1 GHQ Reconnaissance Unit, which had been revitalised after Dunkirk. It was ground-breaking in terms of what it did, and it maintained a cachet not simply because of its mysterious and at first unofficial name of Phantom but because most of the British public had no idea of its existence until 1945. Before that, the unit had had a very shadowy history and it had to fight for acceptance for the next two years. The Great War had been the last to follow conventional strategic and tactical lines, of the three arms of the service; the cavalry, the infantry and the artillery. The Second World War was so different, in terms of scope and the men and women who fought it, that it called for more unorthodox measures. The Commandos was one such new outfit; the jungle-fighting Chindits another. The other two were the ones in which John Randall would serve – the Special Air Service and the GHQ Liaison Regiment. All these smacked of 'private armies', rather like the regiments of Irregular Cavalry raised in India to suppress the Mutiny of 1857, and there were many in the corridors of power in 1940 – and, indeed, in the army itself – who did not approve.

One definition of GHQ Liaison's role was 'to transmit vital information from the battle front, ignoring the usual channels, to the Commander able to dispose of the vital reserves'.[4] Newspapers, who had got wind of the unit's existence, defined it as the 'eyes and ears of the Commander-in-Chief'.[5] In that sense, they were nothing new. All generals in 19th-century Europe had a staff of 'gallopers', usually junior cavalry officers, who were sent to various parts of the field with orders and/or instructions to report back accurately what they saw. In fact, well after the turn of the 20th century, the ability to sketch a terrain quickly and accurately was an essential part of an officer's training. The difference in 1940 was the wireless and motorised transport, which had revolutionised communication anyway. Prior to that, communication on the battlefield was carried out by bugle and drum, and anything more long range by a flag system of semaphore or, where the sun shone, heliograph. Wireless communication based on Marconi's pioneering work was used for the first time in the Great War, although radios were temperamental and did not take kindly to damp or extremes of heat.

In the early days of the Second World War, a number of missions were set up, some of them rather vague. While the British Expeditionary Force had sailed for France very much as its predecessor had done in August 1914, various missions were being avidly discussed at the highest levels of the armed forces. Number Three Air Mission was George Hopkinson's, born of the need to communicate between the forward Belgian and British troops, the Belgian headquarters and (the marked difference from 1914) the Advanced Air Striking Force. Originally, 'Hoppy's Men' were only twenty-nine strong – seven officers and the twenty-two Other Ranks under the overall command of Wing-Commander J.M. 'Fairy' Fairweather. Hopkinson was at first attached to this unit merely as an observer but quickly took command of it. His own team, which drove out from Caserne Vincent, Valenciennes on 28 October 1939, comprised a driver, a batman, a clerk and Hopkinson, all in one car. By 2 November, a unit of the 12th Lancers joined Hopkinson and one of its captains, Tony Warre, stayed on as part of GHQ Liaison. He would later become John Randall's commanding officer in K Squadron. Based at Belgian headquarters, Hopkinson's mission came to be known as an Advanced Report Centre, codenamed Rapier. The centre consisted of a Headquarters Detachment, a 'Phantom Squadron' (the name coming from the internal reports they used) and an Intelligence section.

Hopkinson was anxious to recruit as many 'bright young men' (a phrase of the then relatively unknown General Bernard Montgomery) as possible, men with presence, dash and initiative. They came from every branch of the service. Hopkinson himself was an infantryman but by no means as blinkered as some of his fellow officers were. We have already noted the arrival of Captain Warre, and the fact that his 12th Lancers were among the first cavalry regiments to become motorised (in 1928) was a good sign of things to come. Captain John Collings was another cavalryman, from the 'Skins', the 5th Royal Inniskilling Dragoon Guards. He had lived in Belgium for years and spoke fluent French. His Intelligence section consisted of six officers and six NCOs who were equally fluent and who all rode motorbikes, at that stage of the war considered to be essential for fast reconnaissance work.

Some of the men recruited in Belgium had equally varied backgrounds. Privates Macdonald, Fournier and Lenthall were all members of the Royal Army Service Corps, the drivers of the army, and they all lived in Paris. Fournier claimed to be Canadian but was probably American,[6] and Lenthall drove a taxi in Paris before the war. The unit's motorcycle troop was made up of the Queen Victoria's Rifles, part of the London Territorial unit that had become bored guarding London's docks.[7] They were led by Second Lieutenant John Morgan.

The official history of Phantom records that the all-important Wireless Section was manned entirely by Royal Corps of Signals personnel. This may have been true of the first weeks of the unit's existence but quickly spread out. John Randall himself became a radio operator, with his background in the Royal Artillery. While Hoppy ran the mission, the word Phantom was not used, but all members were issued with the sleeve badge – a black square embroidered with a white 'P', which was unique in the army. Other officers joined – Lieutenant Lord Banbury of Southam, who would later take John Randall under his wing; John Jackson of the Intelligence Corps, Piers Edgecombe, 'Crasher' Purvis and James Spicer, also of the Intelligence Corps, who became the Adjutant.

Tony Warre walked around in his blues complete with cavalry shoulder chains, making stirring speeches and prodding the occasional man with his riding crop. Everybody was expected to join in daily Physical Training and route marches. Officers too old or distinguished were allowed to walk rather than run.

The GHQ Liaison Regiment played a full and successful part in what was otherwise largely a shambles; the fall back to Dunkirk. General Giraud of the Seventh French Army sent a telegram to the unit on 13 May 1940: 'Heartiest congratulations on most useful information with which you have kept us supplied. It has been invaluable. Please inform all concerned.'[8]

Corporal Hall drew the regiment's first blood when he used his Bren gun to bring down a Heinkel towards the end of that month, and Lieutenant Edgecombe became the first casualty two days later, hit at close range by an anti-tank gun. The regiment fell back to the seaside town of La Panne, north of Dunkirk, and Tony Warre walked along the line of his own vehicles, tossing a hand grenade into the engine of each, rather than allow them to fall into the hands of the Wehrmacht, now getting uncomfortably close. He blew off a trouser leg doing this but was otherwise unhurt. The last of the unit to go home left on 31 May.

However, disaster was to follow. Most of Number Three Mission got off from Ostend on board the SS *Aboukir*. Eight miles out from the Belgian coast, the ship was torpedoed by an E-boat (a motor torpedo launch with 2000 hp engines, known to the German Kreigsmarine as a *schellboot*) on the night of the 27th. Most of them drowned, including 'Fairy' Fairweather, a fine officer who was a great loss to the RAF and combined services. One who got away was Lieutenant Norman Reddaway, with whom John Randall would work in the months ahead. The mission had lost one officer (Fairweather), two NCOs killed in action, one officer (Edgecombe) wounded, and seven officers and twenty Other Ranks from the RAF were killed.

Back in London, Hopkinson was keen to rebuild his unit, to expunge the memories of *Aboukir* and to get the GHQ Liaison Regiment back to war. To that end, he accepted John Randall.

One of the oddest original documents among John Randall's papers is a list of officers of the GHQ Liaison Regiment 1939–46, together with their addresses. Some websites today – and even some of the better-informed books – refer to Phantom as a 'private army', with all the cloak-and-dagger elements that that implies. How odd, then, that this little notebook was printed. I can only assume it did not see the light of day until 1946, by which time the obvious security threat was over. Walter Schellenberg's Black Book of 1939 was a compilation by the SS of men very much like those in the Phantom address book; men the SS would have rounded up had Operation Sealion, the invasion of Britain, ever become reality.

There are 196 officers listed, the highest proportion from various corps like the Engineers and the Signals. John Randall was one of 27 Royal Artillery recruits and then we have the Guards and line regiments of cavalry and infantry. An Elwood Camp is listed as belonging to the US Army, so, presumably, he was a liaison officer attached to the unit. There is no regiment listed for Graeme Adair, known as Robyn, perhaps because he held an emergency commission in the Royal Berkshires. His service record rather cryptically describes him as being 'specially employed' by the spring of 1944. Miles Reid is from the General List, i.e. not attached to a specific regiment (although, as we shall see, he was an engineer), and, rather oddly, John Randall's second initial is given as A., not H. for Hugh.[9]

Randall gives his mother's address of Donnington Manor, Dunton Green, Sevenoaks, and most of the entries give their principal home addresses too. Some give their gentlemen's clubs – J.W. Birch-White specifies the Cavalry Club in Piccadilly; George Grant of the Middlesex Yeomanry was a member of Brooks' in St James's, and so on. Others give their agents or banks; the regiment's historian R.J.T. Hills, who would go on to write several regimental histories, banked with the Westminster in Victoria St, SW1. F.S. Lamb gave his contact details as the Yorkshire Insurance Co Ltd in Cornhill. A handful give their telephone numbers too – fewer digits from a simpler age. Randall's friend Harold Light could be reached on Maidenhead

826. Major J.E. Dully of the Northamptonshires could be rung on Datchet 174.

Not all the officers listed in the address book were there when Randall joined Phantom; various names will become apparent in later chapters. But they were a colourful lot, an elite, privately educated group of men, mostly wealthy – in a way, something of a vanishing breed by the 1940s.

Some, like Hugh Fraser, were of the aristocracy. He was a younger son of Lord Lovat, a Scottish nobleman who had raised a Yeomanry regiment in the Boer War comprising stalkers and ghillies from his Highland estates. Fraser joined his father's unit in 1936, having attended Ampleforth College and become President of the Union while at Balliol, Oxford. Charles Cockayne, who would go on to become the regiment's senior signals officer, took the family title of Cullen of Ashbourne in 1932, but he did not actually take his seat in the Lords until ten years later. He had been to Eton, like most of Phantom, and went straight into the City, his father having been a governor of the Bank of England.

Probably the most academic officer in the Phantom book was Michael Oakeshott. His father had been a Fabian Socialist and a friend of George Bernard Shaw, and he had attended the progressive, co-educational St George's School in Harpenden. Having read History at Gonville and Caius, Cambridge, he became a Fellow of the College and wrote an essay in 1939 called 'The Chain of Politics', which defended the right of individuals not to get involved in a war of ideologies between Right and Left. Despite this, he joined up anyway in the Artillery. Accounts differ, but Oakeshott, who was to become a major philosopher after the war, had a reputation as something of a womaniser. His nickname in the army was Dipstick!

Robert Mark was unusual in Phantom because of his middle-class background. He was three years older than Randall and had been captain of rugby at William Hulme's Grammar School in Manchester. He was not academic, however, and ended up as a carpet salesman briefly, before joining the Manchester Constabulary two years before war broke out. His father was appalled – the move was, he said, only one step away from going to prison. By 1938, he was a plainclothes man, attached to Special Branch, and had an experience two years after that that he would never forget. Under a welter of new legislation rushed through by Churchill's paranoid government, Regulation 18B was designed to weed out undesirables. That included foreign nationals like Germans, Austrians, Italians and any other ethnic group whose native country supported the Nazis. Mark had to deport an Italian waiter who had lived in Manchester for 30 years. The man was completely harmless but the boat deporting him was torpedoed with all hands by U-boats in the Channel. Mark did not join Phantom until 1943.

There is no doubt that the most high-profile member of Phantom, who gives his address as Boodles Club, St James's, was the film star David Niven. Reginald Hills calls him 'the prince of good fellows'. In many ways, the man was the epitome of the 'glamorous Phantom', if only because the lackadaisical, casual heroism of men like him and Randall was, in Niven's case, seen large on the silver screen. When leading his men into action in Normandy in 1944, he said to them, 'It's all right for you. You've only got to do this once; I've got to do it all over again with Errol Flynn.'

Niven had been expelled from his prep school at the age of ten but fared better under a kind headmaster at Stowe. He failed to get into the navy because his maths was atrocious, but he succeeded at Sandhurst. He joined the Highland Light Infantry, but did not enjoy it, largely because he hated wearing a kilt. By 1933, he was a full lieutenant but quickly fell foul of his superiors. He attended a terribly boring lecture on machine guns in modern warfare, but his mind was elsewhere, principally on a hot date. When the major-general lecturing the group finished, he asked if there were any questions. Lieutenant Niven said, 'Could you tell me the time, sir? I have a train to catch.' For that, he was arrested for insubordination, but managed to get legless with Rhoddy

Rose, later a recipient of the Military Cross and a DSO. Niven escaped and took a ship to the United States. He resigned from the army by telegram on the way.

California was already booming by 1933, the film studios making a fortune now that 'talkies' had well and truly arrived. Niven was, according to Central Casting, 'Anglo-Saxon Type No. 2008', but, in fact, he always essentially played himself – a charming officer and gentleman. In four years he made nineteen films, including *The Charge of the Light Brigade*, *The Prisoner of Zenda*, *Dawn Patrol* and *Raffles*. He became one of the 'Hollywood Raj' of British ex-pats, in the company of Boris Karloff, Rex Harrison, Ronald Colman, Leslie Howard and C. Aubrey Smith. He also became a hard-drinking buddy of Errol Flynn, sharing a house with him that came to be known as 'Cirrhosis by the Sea'.

When war broke out, Niven was the only British film star who came home to 'do his bit'. He joined the Rifle Brigade in February 1940, and met Winston Churchill at a London dinner party in the same month. 'Young man,' the First Lord said to him, 'you did a fine thing to give up your film career to fight for your country. Mark you, had you not done so – it would have been despicable.'[10] Bored by the Rifle Brigade, Niven transferred to the Commandos, where he claimed to have brought Colonel R.E. Laycock into the organisation that would prefigure in some ways the SAS (see later chapter). In Phantom, he commanded A Squadron, but was constantly elsewhere making propaganda movies with the Army Film Unit. Reginald Hills sums up his future with the regiment:

[A Squadron] had existed in almost inaccessible happiness, in a remote corner of Wiltshire, where it played with the Guards Armoured Division. Major Niven had been among our chief delights. He was the morale raiser *par excellence*. At last his fate overtook him. By inclination drawn to the more active, if irregular, forms of army adventure, he was inevitable whisked away into circles where it was considered that his very considerable and particular talents could best be employed. He became lieutenant colonel in General Eisenhower's headquarters.[11]

His last photographed appearance in the war was driving a battered German car labelled 'US NAVY' somewhere in France in 1944.

The Wireless Section had two No. 9 and two No. 11 sets, although the later types were smaller, state-of-the-art machines, developed by Captain Peter Astbury of the Royal Corps of Signals. It is perhaps a facet of the quirkiness of Phantom that Astbury, who gave his official address as Shrewsbury, was actually an active Communist who had been under surveillance by the authorities since 1936.

If John Randall had hoped for an exciting overseas posting, he was to be disappointed. To an extent, a siege mentality developed after Dunkirk. There was little realistic hope of gaining another toehold in Europe for the foreseeable future, and so the war would be fought elsewhere in the world. Phantom's HQ, now at the hub of things in St James's Park, had its own generating system in case the Blitz took out more conventional methods, so that it could keep its radios working. It also had carrier pigeons in the loft in case the generator failed. This pigeon loft was the largest in the army, run by Lance Corporal Starr who had joined the unit shortly before Dunkirk. He was one of Belgium's leading pigeon fanciers, and the whole unit soon started talking of 'backenders', 'Great North Road birds' and all the other jargon involved. 'Pigeoneer' Starr would carry his birds with him on manoeuvres and release them whenever an inspection from a general was taking place.

After Dunkirk, Phantom's home became Richmond, with Hopkinson based at St Paul's School. In the event of invasion, it was ideally placed as a headquarters and the main accommodation was the derelict Richmond Hill Hotel. This was across the road from Wick House, headquarters of the Royal Signals, so in that sense it was ideal. The hotel's garages became workshops for motor vehicles and radios, and the park, closed to civilians for the duration, was excellent mock battle terrain.

Hopkinson was convinced that the Luftwaffe knew all about Phantom's HQ because over 400 bombs fell on the park between May 1940 and May 1941, and he did not approve of his officers flinging themselves to the ground every time the sirens wailed.

Training was tough. No one could leave the area until 6 p.m. and they all had to be back by midnight. Everyone underwent Physical Training before breakfast and everyone had to become proficient in radio use. Hopkinson 'turned night into day', to instil into everybody the fact that war is not a nine-to-five business. Barracks were inspected in the small hours; vehicle maintenance was carried out by torchlight.

That said, Hoppy knew how to relax too. He liked a drink and was the life and soul of any Mess. He would always round off any evening in the same way: 'Well, gentlemen, charpoy. Schlafen.'[12] He persuaded the Astor brothers, both in Phantom, to give the officers the run of the family home in St James's Square, and Claridge's did the catering while the band of the Life Guards played. David Niven laid on concerts and serious actors like John Gielgud and Beatrice Lillie entertained on a regular basis.

But, if there was to be an invasion, it might not be via London. After Dunkirk, Phantom was scattered in units called groups (the term squadrons came later) to various parts of the country where invasion might be imminent.

Second Lieutenant Randall was sent to Belfast where he won his second 'pip'. The posting probably made little sense to the new boy, but there was a point to it. The Battle of Britain was supposed to be a prelude to Operation Sealion, the German invasion of Britain, and all troops stationed on British soil had to be ready for that. Hindsight now suggests that Hitler was loath to launch Sealion, that the scheme was over-ambitious and could never have worked, but at the time that was not how it seemed.

Some of Churchill's military advisers, men of experience like Basil Liddell Hart, had grave reservations in 1940–1 that Britain could survive at all. Information collected recently from the Mass-Observation Archive makes it clear that there were many in the country who were unimpressed by the Prime Minister's rhetoric about fighting on the beaches and believed he should strike some sort of deal with Hitler.

The Northern Ireland to which Randall was posted in the late spring of 1941 was a potential frontier war zone. Historian Angus Calder refers to it as 'part of the front line',[13] because the Six Counties were only a grenade's throw from Eire, officially neutral between 1939 and 1945. Memories of the Easter Rising of 1916, the Black and Tans and seven years of bloody civil war had not diminished much by 1941, and it did not help the situation that the first UK mainland bomb of the 'war' (which had actually exploded a week before war was declared) had been the one that killed five people in Broadgate, Coventry, and had been planted by the IRA.

However unlikely it was that Hitler would launch an invasion of Britain via Eire and with Irish help, the possibility could not be entirely ruled out.[14] The Belfast shipyards in particular were a vital source of materiel for the war effort, with 140 warships and 10 per cent of all merchant ships being constructed there between 1939 and 1945. Fifteen hundred heavy bombers were built in the city, as well as two million parachutes of the type that John Randall would later trust his life to in the SAS and a third of the rope used by all the armed forces. An astonishing 90 per cent of the shirts worn by all branches came from the area's textile industry.

Ulster also provided men. In such a politically sensitive area, with its large number of Catholics sympathetic to Eire and neutrality, there was no conscription. There were huge recruitment rallies, however, the largest in October 1939 and the following summer, shortly before Randall arrived. A total of 42,000 Ulstermen and women volunteered, with a further 60,000 working in munitions factories in mainland Britain. The egg supply from the area to the rest of the UK was huge, even if the black market flourished widely because of the impossibility of policing the border.

The Belfast shipyards, with their seven miles of docks, were a natural target for the Luftwaffe. They were the headquarters of the navy's operations against the U-boat warfare being carried out in the Atlantic, and the five air raids on the city should have come as no surprise to anyone. The worst attack, when the city was 'coventrated', took place on 15 April 1941. In all, 946 people died and over 3,000 houses were completely flattened, with extensive damage done to 50,000 more. Ships were sunk in the harbour and the biggest flax mill in the world demolished by incendiaries. About 100,000 'ditchers', as refugees were called locally, streamed out of the city on that April night, to hide in the hedgerows and the fields as Belfast burned. There were fewer air-raid shelters there than in any other British city and their quality was poor.

Given the troubled history of the province, Randall might have expected – as the authorities clearly did – problems with the IRA. In fact, it was surprisingly quiet on that score. There were four divisions of the British Army on hand, which might have acted as a deterrent but volunteer fire brigades from Eire came to tackle Belfast blazes, and Catholics and Protestants prayed together in perfect harmony at the mass funerals of the Blitz's 150 victims after 15 April. The only IRA activity that John Randall saw was a local leader once haranguing British troops in a cinema. The boys of Phantom found this hilarious.

Randall describes his posting to Northern Ireland as idyllic. Officially, this was G Group (later squadron) commanded by Major Terry Watt of the Life Guards. Randall got to know many of the local gentry, and his scrapbook today is full of newspaper cuttings of them, at weddings and engagement parties and point-to-point meetings. It may be that this social class was putting a brave face on things, trying to forget that the enemy was potentially at the gate and carry on with business as usual. He also got to know several WRENs, some of whom he would meet again in London or even North Africa.

A number of lasting friendships were made here. Eric Wright and Dugan Webb we shall meet later because Randall's diaries of 1942 and 1943 are full of them. The man who took the young subaltern under his wing in Northern Ireland was Charles, 2nd Baron Banbury of Southam, then a captain in the 12th Lancers, whose principal home was Wadley Manor, Farringdon in Berkshire. The baronetcy had been created as recently as 1924. The first baron had been Conservative MP for Peckham and a prominent stockbroker in the City. The Phantom officer was his grandson, to whom the title passed in 1936, his own son having been killed earlier in the Great War. In fact, he was an orphan. His mother died giving birth to him in 1915. The man had followed a conventional career – attending the public school at Stowe before a commission in the Coldstream Guards. In October 1939, with the impact of war, he transferred to the 12th Lancers. He had covered the withdrawal of the 144th Division from Wormhoudt shortly before Dunkirk. Banbury was one of a succession of titled officers with a great deal of money whom Randall was to meet as his war progressed. He remembers marvellous evenings out on the town in Belfast, blitzed though it was, and he never had to put his hand in his pocket once.

But the war had progressed. And Phantom was already back in it. 'A' Group under Major Miles Reid was chosen to go to Greece. Reid himself was an experienced officer with accolades from the Great War. He had joined Phantom after acting as a liaison officer with the French. The group was to travel in two sections, and the destination kept secret even from the men, and they travelled from Liverpool on 30 November 1940. No one in Alexandria where they landed had ever heard of Phantom, and Reid had to start virtually from scratch. There were serious problems with radio communication and a direct line to Richmond was not set up until January 1941. All in all, the experience was not a good one.

The second unit to go out had only two Phantom officers – Peter Forshall of the Parachute Regiment and Lieutenant Frank Thompson, a poet whose brother, E.P. Thompson, would go on to be one of the best known of the 1960s social historians. Thompson spoke fluent Greek and would be invaluable. Their party sailed on 19 March 1941 on HMT *Pasteur* from Glasgow. Reid's group had taken the dangerous route via Gibraltar and the Mediterranean, at that time crawling with German U-boats and Italian aircraft. Forshall's travelled via the Cape, longer but safer. By this time, Greece had fallen to the Germans and the unit arrived in Alexandria with nowhere specific to go and nothing specific to do.

They at least located Reid's group – 12 men in a transit camp and Lieutenant George Pinckney in hospital. As Reg Hills put it, 'Phantom was looked upon in Cairo as something between a Commando and a Signals unit.'[15] It was either both or it was neither, and nobody seemed able to find a use for it. It was part of the Phantom story – a brilliant idea sometimes badly handled and misunderstood, which had a knock-on effect of frustration of the new boys, like Randall, waiting at home for action. However, before long, John Randall was posted to a real war for the first time. Africa. Tunisia. And the killing ground of Longstop Hill.

4

'So this is War'

By the summer of 1941, Britain's fortunes in North Africa had fluctuated wildly. Ever since Benjamin Disraeli had negotiated the purchase of the lion's share of the Suez Canal in 1876, Egypt had been very much part of the British Empire. Since Palestine was also in British hands, the whole eastern end of the Mediterranean was a target for the Axis powers, in particular Benito Mussolini, the Italian dictator, who had dreams of recreating a Roman Empire based on the inland sea the Romans had called *Mare Nostrum*.[1]

Italy had declared war on 10 June 1940, when it was clear that France was finished and the British Expeditionary Force was on the run at Dunkirk. Today, the Italian army of the Second World War is often regarded as a joke,[2] but at the time it was largely an unknown quantity. British Intelligence knew that the Italians had over 200,000 troops along the narrow strip of the North African coast. Against that, Britain defended Egypt with fewer than 50,000. The Italians built up a formidable series of depots and supply bases from Benghazi to Sollum, a thousand miles apart along a new road, which was excellent for tanks and armoured vehicles.

The first clash came at the advanced British railhead at Mersa Matruh only days after the declaration of war. In fact, the attack was so swift that some Italian garrisons did not know war had been declared, and 220 prisoners were taken. In three months of fighting, Italian casualties added up to some 3,500 compared with the British 150. But nobody was writing off the Italians yet, least of all General Archibald Wavell, the General Officer Commanding in the Middle East. This poetry-loving Christian was hugely respected, even by his enemies. When Erwin Rommel faced him with the Afrika Korps, he carried a German translation of Wavell's book on *Generals and Generalship* in his pocket. Wavell had served in the Boer War, and won the Military Cross at the second battle of Ypres in 1915 when he had been wounded, losing his left eye. By the end of the Great War, he was brevet brigadier-general in Palestine and Egypt, and knew the conditions of desert warfare very well. Between the wars, he had been steadily promoted (at the same time as successive penny-pinching peacetime governments had put him on half pay) and two months before the outbreak of war he had been given the Middle East command.

Wavell's problem was that the job was vast. In fact, his successor, Claude Auchinleck, publicly stated, on replacing him, that he had had no idea how complex the task was; 40 different languages were spoken by the men under his command. At first, the Italians gained success against an outnumbered British force, but by 17 June they reached Sidi Barrani and effectively stopped for three months. Wavell took the initiative in this period of inactivity and attacked. Churchill's War Cabinet were delighted. As he himself wrote later, 'I purred like six cats.'[3] With his flair for the dramatic, the Prime Minister wrote later of 'our lean, bronzed, desert-hardened and completely mechanized army'[4] driving the Italians back by the middle of December. Tobruk fell in January 1941 with virtually no resistance, and the much-vaunted Italian campaign was in ruins.

In six weeks, the British Army had advanced over 200 miles and had taken 113,000 prisoners and more than 700 guns. The balance was changed, however, by the arrival of Erwin Rommel and his panzers. The 'Desert Fox', as he came to be known, was probably the most outstanding German general of the war. Even

Churchill said so, in the Commons in January 1942: 'We have a very daring and skilful opponent against us and, may I say across the havoc of war, a great general.'[5] He was taken to task about that by various colleagues.

By the end of March, the brilliant risk-taker launched a counter-attack at Agheila, which destroyed Wavell's western flank, driving the British back through Bardia and Sollum, which they had only recently taken from the Italians. Wavell's Cruiser tanks, called 'Matildas' by the troops, were hopelessly outclassed by the German Armour and the Luftwaffe punished the soldiers on the ground.

Wavell's problem was not merely that he was facing one of the most deadly and decisive generals that Germany possessed; he also had to keep diverting his forces, at Churchill's insistence. Expeditions were mounted to support the Greeks and to keep Syria loyal. No doubt there were sound political and strategic reasons for this, but Wavell was not convinced by them and obeyed only reluctantly. Operation Battleaxe in the middle of June began well against Rommel at Tobruk, but the attack petered out after a day and Wavell paid for it with his job.

Typically of this modest and unassuming man, he took the order from Churchill well. 'The Prime Minister is quite right,' he said on reading the telegram that relieved him of command. 'There ought to be a new eye and a new hand in this theatre.'[6]

The new eye and hand was Claude Auchinleck, who had served with the Indian army since 1903. He had won the DSO fighting the Turks at Ismailia in the Great War, and, by 1938, he was Deputy Chief of the General Staff back in India. His initial involvement in the Second World War was as commander of the Anglo-French ground forces in Norway, in a mission that was bound to fail. By the 'Spitfire Summer' of 1940, he had succeeded Wavell as General Officer Commanding in Southern Command but led the successful operation against the pro-Axis forces of the Baghdad government at RAF Habbaniya, which Wavell had been loath to send. On 5 July 1941, he replaced Wavell, effectively swapping jobs with him, and almost immediately fell foul of Churchill.

The Prime Minister wrote, 'I started my relations with the new Commander-in-Chief in high hopes, but an exchange of telegrams soon made it clear that there were serious divergences of views and values between us.'[7] Bernard Montgomery, who had been Auchinleck's second-in-command in 1940, would have understood: 'In the 5th Corps I first served under Auchinleck . . . I cannot recall that we ever agreed on anything.'[8] Wavell, Auchinleck and later, ironically, Montgomery himself were all victims of the hectoring interference of Churchill, who all his life delighted in the almost schoolboy cavalry heroics he had exhibited at the battle of Omdurman in 1898. In 1944, he had to be restrained from sailing with the transports in Operation Overlord towards the Normandy beaches on D-Day, and was nearly photographed by the Press urinating with senior officers in the Rhine some months later.

Auchinleck did not fit this 'dash and fire' mould; he accepted, as most serving soldiers did, that British tank crews going into battle faced odds of three to one against survival. As early as August, Churchill flew to Cairo for top-level discussions with all the senior officers concerned. The decision was made to split the command. Auchinleck would remain commander-in-chief of the Middle East, centred on Basra and Baghdad, but the Near East Command would be given to General Harold Alexander, focusing on Egypt, Palestine and Syria.

Under Alexander, the newly formed 8th Army, comprising British, Australian, New Zealand, Indian and South African units, was to be commanded by General William 'Strafer' Gott, but he was killed when his transport plane was shot down days later, and the command was given to Bernard Montgomery instead. On 8 August, Auchinleck was asked to stand down as he had no intention of accepting the new command.

The German advance had been halted by June, and Montgomery steadily built up his tanks and support units to smash Rommel at the second battle of El Alamein at the end of October. One of the decisive battles of history, it made Montgomery's reputation and could not have come at a better time for Churchill. The Prime Minister expected daily to be overthrown in the House in a vote of no confidence, but, to use a more modern analogy, this was his Falklands moment, and the Afrika Korps was in headlong retreat. Hitler had ordered that no such retreat should take place, but, as often before and later, he was out of touch with the reality of the situation on the ground. Whereas Churchill was a frequent visitor to the desert, Hitler never went near the place. Churchill summed up the situation years later with hindsight: 'Before Alamein, we never had a victory. After Alamein, we never had a defeat.' Hitler would lose one-eighth of his fighting men in Africa.

It was not until January 1942 that Phantom saw any action. Reid and Forshall's unit, now known as H Squadron, was commanded by Captain Graham Bell from the Cameronians, whose patrol had narrowly escaped destruction crossing a minefield. 'You can sleep all day,' he was told on arrival at a village near Benghazi. 'Damn all happens here.' That was not true because Rommel's panzers attacked the very next day, but the point was that H was the only squadron of Phantom so far involved in a war zone at all. Everybody else was still going through the motions back home in what Reg Hills describes as 'the doldrums of war'.

Where, in all this grand strategy, was Lieutenant John Randall of the GHQ Liaison Regiment? It is ironic to think that the war zone he was to sail to in a year's time was a mystery to him. With 70 years of research behind us, we can evaluate the People's War in a way that was impossible to contemporaries. Junior officers like Randall could pick up little more information than the man in the street. The paranoid Ministry of Information remained convinced that there was a 'fifth column'[9] operating in Britain, and produced posters and newspaper advertisements warning everyone that 'careless talk costs lives'. The papers themselves were war economy issue, reduced to four or five pages to save paper and print, and carried only the sketchiest outline of events that were thought suitable for public consumption. There has been a great deal of discussion in recent years covering the accuracy of this information. The consensus is that Churchill told the truth when he possibly could, but that, of course, was Churchill's version of the truth. If he lied, he did it for the best of intentions. Joseph Goebbels, Hitler's Minister for Propaganda and Enlightenment, made exactly the same claim. On the night of the heaviest blitz in London in the war – 10 May 1941 – Churchill's government claimed that 28 enemy aircraft had been shot down. In fact, the figure was seven.

Randall's diary, the first of four, begins on Saturday, 17 October 1942. Three of these are black-covered notebooks and this one contains a yellow cloth triangle, marked with a black skull and crossbones. It fluttered, along with hundreds of others, at the perimeters of minefields in Tunisia, the war zone of which John Randall as yet knew nothing.

He was leading a hectic social life and had just met a 'most charming' girl called 'Bunny' Steele. He had also met a nurse – 'Doodles' Rayment – and confided in his diary, 'What wonderful people nurses are and one in particular.' Randall's diaries and letters for 1942 and 1943 are littered with references to charming and beautiful girls. He was a strikingly handsome man himself, suave and sophisticated, in an elite regiment that boasted famous names. It is not surprising that he was something of a 'babe magnet', in today's terms, and seems to have fallen in love, to a greater or lesser extent, with a lot of them. We have to factor into all this the extraordinary circumstances of the People's War. The situation was best described by Molly Lefebure, one of the charming girls John Randall might have met if circumstances had been only slightly different, since they were both in London and of an age. Molly was 22 and had the least likely job in the country; she was secretary and general factotum to the Home Office pathologist Keith Simpson. She wrote about war-weariness: 'It was a real illness . . . and as the war went on, almost everybody fell victim to it . . . Some it made drink a lot. Others took to bed – with others – a lot. Some became hideously gay,[10] brave and hearty. Others became sardonic and bored. Some seriously depressed . . . A few took to prayer.'[11]

By the autumn of 1942, G Squadron had been transferred from Northern Ireland to Penn Woods in Buckinghamshire for training for foreign active service. 'Penn Woods,' wrote Reg Hills, 'is engraved deeply on many a Phantom heart. In this dismal camp among the dripping Buckinghamshire woods, Phantom reached its nadir . . . there are few sadder or more aimless bodies of men than military units awaiting disbandment.'[12] The wood itself is a designated site of natural beauty today and dotted with a variety of Iron Age and Roman archaeological sites. In the 1940s, it was full of Nissen huts and prefabs capable of accommodating 300 men, with ablution blocks and concrete roads. At first, the camp had been used by Canadian troops who used the obstacle course there to prepare for the raid on Dieppe (see below). Officers like Randall were billeted in local houses.

Before that, Phantom had got itself involved in a debacle: the raid on Dieppe. In his account of the war, Churchill played it down, and, in 1951, when writing his history of Phantom, Reg Hills looked for the positives, the lessons that were learned, particularly by the navy. On 19 August, the 2nd Canadian Division under General Roberts along with Nos 3 and 4 Commandos, detachments of Inter-Allied troops (essentially the Free French) and the United States Rangers, in all 6,000 men, were landed at a coastal town that was, in fact, a death trap. There were cliffs on each side of Dieppe that limited the beach-landing places and the area was heavily defended. It seems an expensive way to learn how *not* to carry out a raid.

Phantom was represented by J Squadron under Jakie Astor, with Captain Brent Hutton-Williams, originally from the Calcutta Light Horse, and Julian Fane of the Gloucesters (who would become Randall's CO and a good friend), and Sergeant Major Harrison of the 5th Inniskilling Dragoons as senior NCO. They had been selected, in fact, from various squadrons.

Rear headquarters, under Hutton-Williams, was set up on board HMS *Calpe,* which had a radio link forward to the troop positions and back to London. Alistair Sedgwick from the Tank Regiment led one patrol with No. 4 Commando on Orange Beach and had cliffs to climb. Julian Fane's went with brigade HQ and the main assault on the town itself. Lieutenant Mike Hillerns was with No. 3 Commando at Yellow Beach, which also involved scaling cliffs.

The landing craft were scattered by the sudden unexpected arrival of a German convoy, and when they got ashore the Canadians were pinned to the beaches. The Churchill tanks sent in faced a 12-foot wall of concrete that the planners seemed not to have known about – 27 of these vehicles were lost in the ensuing firefight. Julian Fane's landing craft was hit before he even reached the sand and he had to return to HMS *Fernie.* The most successful phase was that carried out by No. 4 Commando under Lord Lovat, whose son, Hugh Fraser, served with Phantom. Sedgwick did a brilliant job here, keeping up with forward movements and reporting back. Oddly, given the need for secrecy in all things military, there was a civilian war correspondent on the scene who acted as Sedgwick's runner.

Mike Hillerns was not so lucky. His unit was fired on by E-boats and lost contact with other ships in the convoy. When they got ashore, the cliffs were higher than anticipated and the Commando force was down to only 60 men. They had no mortars and the machine-gun fire from the Wehrmacht defence was so severe and continuous that Hillerns could not set up his radio. When the order to pull out came through, Corporals Craggs and Masterson and Driver Richardson were all hit by machine-gun fire, Craggs fatally. At the beach, there were no boats in sight and the unit hid in the shallow coves at the base of the cliffs. Hillerns saw a boat drifting a mile off shore and swam for it. He was machine-gunned in the water.

In all, 3,600 men died or were wounded at Dieppe; 106 aircraft were destroyed, as well as 27 tanks and 33 landing craft. Lessons for what would become Overlord nearly two years later were no doubt learned, but it was a bloody way to do it.

John Randall's diary, which begins three months after Dieppe, makes no mention of it and seems, perhaps, a little trivial by comparison. It is, however, a textbook example of the sangfroid of the British officer of 1939–45. There are losses, there is tragedy; but you have to move on. It was all about life, even in the midst of death. And that life must be lived to the full.

On Saturday, 17 October, Randall left the Eastern Command Intelligence School with various officers and had supper in the Roebuck at Richmond. He and Dugan Webb went to Joan Carter's flat at Hillbrow, and he was 'very giddy' by one in the morning; Webb was worse. The next day was a hectic social whirl. He played squash in the morning and had 'surprising news' from 'Washy' Hibbert from the Queen's Bays – although today nobody remembers what that was! He spent time with Webb and John Sadoine, and went to a cocktail party in the evening where he met the Chinese military attaché and his wife.[13] He was bored with the particular course that G Squadron was undergoing, and even night exercises under a beautiful moon did not grip him particularly. There is a sense in these early diary entries that Randall is *playing* at war, because the real thing always seems just over the horizon.

Lectures of varying quality followed. The one on German equipment was tedious; that on the Tank Regiment better. On the 23rd, Randall was in Cambridge visiting the Intelligence School and ran into two Old Laurentians. He had news of friends getting medals and was delighted. The most high profile of these was Arthur Aldridge, a squadron leader in the RAF by June 1942. He won the DFC that summer having carried out four operational flights over the besieged island of Malta and sinking the Italian heavy cruiser *Trento* despite being wounded. He was 21.

Back in London, Randall ran into Tony Warre and had written

work to do: 'Stayed in after supper to do an appreciation, blast it.' Appreciations were very much part of what a Phantom patrol officer was supposed to do. They described the position confronting a formation at a given time, and, in this mock exercise, Randall would have had to prove that he understood the situation and the role that Phantom could play in it.

Towards the end of October, the bored lieutenant visited North Weald Aerodrome to find a Norwegian air force squadron there. The airfield was built on the edge of Epping Forest and had been a vital station during the Battle of Britain. There were two American Eagle Squadrons based there flying Spitfires. The Norwegians were 'a good crowd' and, as well as Mustangs, Randall saw his first Mosquito: 'a grand-looking job'. The Mustang P51 was a long-range single-seat fighter-bomber but it was the Mosquito that drew everyone's admiration. The 'Wooden Wonder' was almost entirely timber built (unique among Second World War aircraft) and was officially the de Havilland DH 98. It had two engines and a two-man crew and had gone into production the previous year. Many experts today consider it the best warplane of the Second World War.

There were various parties going on, and 'Washy' Hibbert was out with his news again. This time, we know what it was – Randall was to be posted to Tony Warre's K Squadron. He played a great game of ruby – G Squadron v. the Signals – and partied that night with fellow Phantoms Roger Brunsdon of the Devonshires, John Hannay of the Cameronians and Tom Lambert of the Tank Regiment. The girls there were on good form and Randall staggered home at three o'clock.

That Friday, John Randall paraded with his new squadron for the first time. They all had to stand for hours and it was bitterly cold. The top brass inspecting them was General Sir B. Paget, Commander-in-Chief Home Forces, under whose vast umbrella Phantom came. The man had been in post since the previous December, having served in the Norway campaign before that. Randall was due to go to North Wales, but missed his train and could not get through on the phone. Instead, he went to the pictures and on to the Roebuck with Jane Short, whose mother put the officer up for the night.

Early in November, Randall was visiting his parents or talking to them on the phone. He had lunch with Dugan Webb and Jane at an Indian restaurant in Richmond, which must have been unusual then. 'Spent all afternoon with Jane – quite a session. I wonder if and how long that bargain will last – we will see.' Jane is one of a large number of girls whose names litter the pages of John Randall's diaries. Long before he had Formation signs to pin there, he wore his heart on his sleeve. On the 5th, he took his mother to see Noel Coward's *Blithe Spirit* at a West End theatre and had a poor dinner at the Dorchester. He had drinks at the Officers' Club but could not get a taxi to the Coconut Grove and got to bed by 2 a.m.

The next day, he got to North Wales a day late, and wandered around Pwllheli in the pouring rain: 'Good old Wales,' his diary reads. 'Such lovely weather,' and no doubt he remembered it well from his time in Llandrindod on the Officer Training Course. He visited the graves of German airmen shot down in the area and the next day heard 'rather good news – Monty doing his stuff'. This was 8 November, the beginning of Operation Torch, which was the Allied invasion of North Africa.

This was the war zone into which Randall and K Squadron would be sent four months later. Algeria, Tunisia and Morocco had been French since the 'Scramble for Africa' among European powers in the 19th century, and France's position was complicated. Most of France had been occupied by the Germans since the spring of 1940, but the south-east, known as Vichy, remained independent under the French hero of the Great War, Marshal Pétain. He was clearly head of a puppet government, but most of the French colonies around the world, including those in North Africa, paid allegiance to him. No one was quite sure, then, how the locals would react to the arrival, in force, of British and American troops. The other problem, which niggled at the back of the minds of military planners, was Gibraltar and Spain.

'The Rock' had been a prized British possession since 1713, guarding as it did the narrow Straits into the Mediterranean. North of it, however, since 1939, Spain had had a Fascist government under Francisco Franco. In fact, the Luftwaffe's Condor Legion had already tried out its Blitzkrieg aerial assault by flattening Guernica on El Caudillo's behalf, and who knew whether Franco would not try to repay the Führer by abandoning neutrality and throwing in his lot with the Axis powers?

With these misgivings, the landings went ahead. The Western Task Force under General George Patton, direct from the United States, hit the Moroccan coast at three points: Safi, Casablanca and Mehdia. The Centre Force, under General Fredendall, came from Britain and landed at Oran in Algeria. The Eastern Task Force under General Ryder concentrated on Algiers and Bougie. There was an immediate German counter-offensive as Feldmarschal Kesselring poured troops into Tunisian towns that John Randall would come to know well, from Bizerta in the north to Gabes in the south. The 78th (Battleaxe) Division of the British Army fought for weeks in the pouring rain, which made a mockery of every Englishman's idyllic picture of a desert of palm trees and sun. They lived on their packs and wore the same clothes day after day.

With General Kenneth Anderson's First Army was Major Mervyn Vernon's E Squadron from Phantom. Vernon was notorious in the regiment for his clever 'sales' at the 'Slave Market', i.e. ditching people he had no use for. His pitch was to praise such a 'dud' to the hilt – 'Very smart man, can ride and drive, cooks a bit, excellent shot, plays several instruments.'[14] E Squadron had been posted to Scotland while Randall was in Belfast, with Vernon given a semi-independent role in Edinburgh.

E Squadron landed in Algiers in two echelons, the one waiting to disembark being raked by machine-gun fire from the Luftwaffe's Stukas snarling overhead. Once ashore, they marched to the zoo and bivouacked as the rain turned everything into a sea of mud. The three patrols went east with various units. No. 1 was with the 36th Infantry Brigade at Djebira; No. 5 with the 78th Division near Qued Zaega; and No. 3 with the 56th Reconnaissance Regiment. The squadron headquarters was with V Corps at Souk-el-Khemis and a rear (Anchor) squadron at Constantine.

The rain barely stopped, and the Humber vehicles Phantom had brought were totally unusable, breaking down and sinking to their axles in the mud. Lieutenant Stileman from the Queen's Regiment led a patrol working with the French, and relations here were frosty. Since the whole area was French, most Frenchmen involved expected the command of the invasion to go to a French general. General Juin certainly led XIX Corps with style, but Eisenhower vetoed any higher command for the man. Stileman's men spent a very cold Christmas of 1942 in French company. As Phantom became more experienced in desert warfare, its ranges increased. Most patrols were 50 miles to the forward positions, 150 from Anchor.

The new vehicle for the regiment was the jeep and it quickly replaced the motorbike in terms of speed and mobility. When Lieutenant McIntosh-Reid from the Royal Artillery went to pick up some Italian prisoners of war north of Foudouk, his patrol was divebombed by Stukas. Lorries were hit and everybody was out of their vehicles, lying in a ditch with their hands over their heads. When the mayhem was over and the trucks stood burning on the road, the jeep stood without a scratch.

Working for the first time with Americans and Frenchmen caused problems. Each country had a different method of map-reading, and because Phantom men had to ask for information, they were often regarded as 'snoopers'. The First Army had its own communication system based on radios, with the codename 'J'. For a while, the two systems existed side by side, but Phantom more than proved its worth in the coming months.

By January 1943, E Squadron had four patrols – Mackinlay was with the 26th Armoured Brigade; Fraser with the 1st Guards;

McIntosh-Reid was with the 78th Division and Macdonald with the French. There was heavy fighting in the middle of the month, but the Americans and the British 8th Army were converging on the area. On the 23rd, Montgomery entered Tripoli, as Reg Hills puts it, 'the last city of the Italian Empire'.[15]

The Americans were badly mauled at the Kasserine Pass, the result of their inexperience as much as the determination of Rommel's Afrika Korps to hold their advance. In the battle for Sidi Bou Said, Lieutenant Butcher from the Reconnaissance Regiment admitted, 'It's the worst walloping we have taken in this fight.'

By Monday, 9 November, Randall was back in London after a 'shocking journey' by train (it took nine hours). 'My God,' he wrote, 'these are dreary days. A good way to spend 14 days embarkation leave – will be glad to get to duty.' Even his parents were less than helpful and his mother, unusually, 'quite neurotic'. On Wednesday, having repeated the previous week's diary entries, he wrote: 'I am suffering from a lapse of memory. I did not do this at all. I went to Richmond for a game of rugger.' And even that was cancelled.

There is a gap in Randall's diary now, but he spent Christmas at home and was back at Penn Woods by the 30th. Unlike many Phantom men, he liked the place and took part in a few 'schemes' (army slang for manoeuvres). He had met 'Bunny' Steele, a 'most charming and attractive' girl, and spent a lot of money.

Randall found time, among the leave taking and hectic packing, to play rugby at Richmond. He had 48 hours' leave and crammed them by seeing as many friends as he could. There is no hint of foreboding in any of Randall's diaries. He got 'browned off' from time to time, but the idea of premonition and death in some foreign field did not occur to him. His mother took the parting well, although Randall knew she was 'shattered'. 'She is just everything I would love a wife of my own to be,' he wrote, and noted that 'Grandy', his grandmother, was upset to see him go too. It would have been perfect to 'get hold of Betty', had he been able to, but that was not to be. He walked up Piccadilly, still sandbagged and black as pitch in the on-going blackout, with Doodles: 'I think she was sorry to see me go.' He spent too much money in these weeks and made too many lady friends; Molly Lefebure was right.

Each of Randall's diaries carries the phrase 'This diary is the property of Lieut. John Randall No. 182006 Royal Artillery . . . This diary has only sentimental value.'

The problem was the paranoia of the times. 'Days and dates are best omitted,' he wrote, 'and so too are places but I hope to fill these in by memory one day when it is safer!'

There was a lot of movement in Phantom itself before Randall set sail, and he was not happy about it. Originally, in G Squadron, his particular friends were John Sadoine, Roddy Pannell, Dugan Webb and Harold Light. The men were a 'grand crowd' too and Randall hoped to have a reunion with them all one day. Even in a new regiment like Phantom, traditions in the British Army were fiercely adhered to. David Niven[16] tells the story of having to pretend that the actor Peter Ustinov was his batman; otherwise he could not have talked to him socially at all. Niven was a major and Ustinov a humble private.

Of the four, Raymond John McCulloch Sadoine was the most colourful. Some records today claim his real name was Octave Dupont. He was definitely Belgian and the son of Baron Sadoine, who had served in the Great War. An article in the *Melbourne Argus*, 30 July 1940, refers to his mother, the former Esther McCulloch, who had left England after 'the French debacle' [Dunkirk] and was trying to locate her husband who was living in Monte Carlo. Sadoine had been commissioned in the Irish Guards in that same month and joined Phantom at the end of February 1941. Three years later, Private Adrian Bazar, serving in his platoon attached to the SAS, would remember him as a volatile and difficult officer, but totally reliable and efficient in action.

From G Squadron, Randall was to be transferred to L Squadron under Reg Hills and Michael Astor. The Honourable Michael Langhorne Astor, Royal Artillery, was a scion of the seriously wealthy Anglo-American Astor family, the fourth child of 2nd Viscount Astor and Nancy Langhorne. They were both Members of Parliament, and Michael had recently married. He was a close friend of Ian Fleming, the Naval Intelligence officer who would go on to create James Bond in the Cold War era.

However, Randall's posting to L Squadron never materialised and he found himself sailing with K Squadron under John Anthony Warre of the 12th Lancers. Oddly, Warre's name is not listed in the Phantom address book. Randall's diary reads, 'Big, big disappointment.' Such observations may seem petty, but morale plays a huge part in any war, and for men to be able to trust each other, and to like each other, was certainly an advantage.

February 1943 was unseasonably hot. Tony Warre cracked a bottle of champagne as the men lugged their heavy kitbags to the station. They reached the port at 5.30, speculating about their ship's tonnage and seaworthiness. In keeping with his need to observe secrecy, we do not know from the diary what ship this was or even which port. In fact, they left Richmond on 18 February and sailed from Glasgow on the SS *Boissevain*, a Dutch merchant ship that would later bring survivors of the Burma railway back home. They left on a Saturday and waited to join a convoy. No merchant or troopship ever left Britain without a navy escort because the U-boat menace was very serious. Only a couple of months before, the numerical superiority of Italian and German fighter aircraft made sailing through the Mediterranean highly dangerous. Where possible, alternative routes were chosen. So the reinforcements sent out to Singapore in 1941, for example, went the long way around the Cape of Good Hope rather than through the Suez Canal.

The first day was hell with rough seas and people vomiting over the side. The second was better, and Randall was enjoying the food. He saw Spitfires from 504 Squadron, the iconic fighter planes that had won, along with Hurricanes, the Battle of Britain.

He saw a Sunderland Flying Boat too, indispensable in picking up crews whose ships had been torpedoed. On board ship, it was important to keep men busy. As it was, Randall had too much time to think. 'Will I be a good officer?' he wrote in his diary. 'Can I take it the same as the others?' 'Yes,' he decided. 'I have got to! Hope I do not disgrace the squadron or myself!' He missed his mother, as all soldiers secretly do, and their little home at Westerham with the cluster of white houses around the Green. He could picture Alfred Friend, the estate agent who was keeping a kindly eye on Randall's mother, trying to light a fire and his mother getting cross about it. He even missed Sevenoaks in the rain.

To avoid too much introspection, there was daily boat drill, lectures and Morse practice. The whole point of Phantom was to send secret coded messages that the enemy could not decipher if they were intercepted; there was a lot to learn here.

The ship had an officers' Mess, as most wartime transports did, and someone was playing the piano, 'classical stuff, not boogie-woogie', on the third day. Randall spent time on the bridge, chatting to the officer of the watch and looking at charts. He gave a lecture on the US Army, although he did not know much about it, and attended one by Colonel Sandeman Allen, MP. Randall *did* learn something, his diary assures us, but not 'a new and better way to kill Germans'.

By 28 February, as the convoy moved south, it was getting warmer. There were lectures on wireless batteries, and a minor panic when unidentified aircraft were spotted. The next day, there was a concert at which Randall's friend 'Tam' Williams was the star. Hugh Williams, from the Devonshire Regiment, was a film star in the Niven mould. By the time of this sailing to North Africa, he had made over 40 films, both in America and Britain, including, in the previous year, propaganda efforts like *Ships With Wings*, *Secret Mission* and *One of Our Aircraft is Missing*.

On Wednesday, 1 March, the convoy sailed through the Straits of Gibraltar, Plato's legendary Pillars of Hercules. Randall saw the Rock for the first time, and could look to the north to see Europe and to the south to Africa. That was the day that Lieutenant Randall had a bit of a rocket from Tony Warre. He told him that he was too friendly with his men and would never truly earn their respect that way. Randall had an inferiority complex, he said, but Warre was sure he could get over it because he was a better soldier than most. Life, of course, went on; that evening, Randall played vingt-et-un in the Mess and watched a school of porpoises cavorting alongside the ship.

The port at which they arrived is left blank in the diaries. There was a sunk ship in the harbour with just the bow visible above the water line. There was a castle and little white houses dotted on the hillside. They steamed out again at 8.15, and the twinkling shore lights seemed strange after London's blackout. No U-boats in the Atlantic and marvellous food – when would they eat like this again? Randall wondered.

On Friday, 5 March, they landed at their destination, Algiers, after an early air alert that turned out to be a false alarm. Randall saw his first mosque and his first Arabs. They were 'scruffy, dirty-looking devils' and the Phantoms were immediately surrounded by them as they stepped onto dry land, scrawny children gabbling in Arabic with their hands out for chocolate or cigarettes or *anything*. There were Frenchmen there too, driving very fast in flash cars, a reminder that Algeria was still nominally free and nominally French, even if France itself was not. The French had invaded what had once been the haunt of the notorious Barbary Coast pirates in 1830, but subduing the country took 40 years and it had to be said that French 'civilisation' had had its downside. Thousands of undesirables drifted there, known as the *pieds-noirs* (black feet).

The Phantoms marched to their first billet in a local sports stadium and were given French/Algerian currency. This was a British outfit, however, so tea was served promptly at four. There was bully beef, bread, jam and tea. That first evening, a gramophone somewhere nearby was playing 'Moonlight Becomes

You', aptly enough from the Bob Hope/Bing Crosby film *The Road to Morocco*. Not that Randall was thinking of Dorothy Lamour; he remembered a slow dance to this number with Bunny Steele. His valise arrived at dusk and was still dry; several of them had become waterlogged somehow during the unloading. He sampled some very good red wine, while the lads 'kicked up a tremendous row', singing songs. 'This is the Army, Mr Jones' was a hit of 1943, so, ironically, was the German song 'Lili Marlene' (which would become the unofficial theme song of 1 SAS later). Whatever they sang, the men probably had a few improvised lyrics of their own!

That night, John Randall sat in a dusty old building in Africa, writing his diary by candlelight: 'So this is war. Now all we want is the Germans and not the mosquitoes.' That early in March, the impossible temperatures had not yet kicked in. Later entries in the diaries show how wonderful sea-bathing was at the height of the summer. When Winston Churchill visited nearby Tunisia in August, he was moved to comment: 'When I marched to Omdurman forty-four years before, the theory was that the African sun must at all costs be kept away from the skin. The rules were strict. Special spine pads were buttoned on to the back of all our khaki coats. It was a military offence to appear without a pith helmet. We were advised to wear thick underclothing, following Arab custom enjoined by a thousand years of experience. Yet now, halfway through the twentieth century, many of the white soldiers went about . . . hatless and naked except for the equal of a loin cloth. Apparently it did them no harm.'[17]

The next day, Randall inspected his men's weapons and watched the civilian street life with Oliver Edwards from the Grenadier Guards. No one walked fast, they noticed, but they all drove like maniacs. At home, of course, the Highway Code had been in existence for only 12 years, but in Algeria there seemed to be no rules at all, with battered vehicles, meandering cyclists, honking horns and flying dust. Randall put on his breeches and puttees and did the town with Hugh Cuming. Like Randall, Cuming had served in the ranks in the early phase of the war and was commissioned into the Seaforth Highlanders in August 1940. The two would become great friends in North Africa. That night, they 'did' the Hotel Alessi, not 'quite up to the Berkeley' in Knightsbridge, and had supper at La Paris. The oranges were marvellous but they had trouble with the artichokes.

Recent books written about the special forces of the Second World War concentrate on the blood and guts, the heroic actions and the flying bullets. War is not always like that. Most of it is spent waiting. Waiting for orders to move; here, there, everywhere. Waiting for the right weather conditions. Just plain waiting. So the Phantom officers carried on as usual, sampling the good life Algerian-style. Randall had never seen such an extraordinary range of clothes before as the civilians wore, but he did notice that their whites could do with a dose of Persil! He tried out his schoolboy French, but to many locals it sounded like Arabic backwards. He and Oliver went to the opera, a theatre near the cathedral – the pink ticket is still among his papers.

But there *was* a war on, and on Monday, 8 March, the unit set out on a route march in the morning. It was 'damn hot' (temperatures in March can reach 85°F), and it was important that men learned to move at speed in full pack because one day their lives might depend on it. There was a change of command – Warre and Williams left to contact Major Mervyn Vernon at 1st Army headquarters, and Norman Reddaway and Julian Fane were left in command of the squadron. The two squadrons clearly had to work together, but, since Vernon had the edge over Warre in terms of desert experience, Warre deferred to him in terms of troop placements. Reddaway was a Cambridge academic with a double first from King's College in Modern Languages. Like Randall, he had joined the ranks shortly after the outbreak of war, and had been one of the few survivors of the *Aboukir*, whose sinking had claimed the lives of so many of the original Hopkinson mission after Dunkirk. Fane had received his own baptism of fire shortly before that. His unit, the 2nd Battalion of the Gloucester

Regiment, had been ordered to hold the advance of the Wehrmacht to allow the retreat to the beaches. A shell had smashed his arm and he had been lucky to survive. We have already seen how the Dieppe raid ended for him.

There were by now two British armies in North Africa – the 8th and the 1st – and it would be Phantom's job to liaise between them. By the time Randall left England, the Afrika Korps was nearing exhaustion. It was still on the attack and had delivered a severe blow to the Americans at the Kasserine Pass. Despite the inexperience of the 'doughboys', it was obvious that their equipment was far superior to that of the Axis powers and seemed to be in limitless supply.

Tuesday, 9 March dawned wet and dull, in contrast to the previous day. The route march was carried out and there was an air raid that night: 'plenty of noise and pretty colours'. The unit might have been considerably cheered up by the fact, had they known, that Feldmarschal Rommel left Africa that day for good. On his way home, he tried to persuade both Mussolini and Hitler to withdraw from Africa entirely. His advice was not taken. Phantom had no vehicles yet, rather negating their whole purpose, and Randall took the opportunity to write home. The next day, the weather was worse and the rain bounced off tin hats, kitbags and rifle butts. 'How I hate marching,' the diary reads.

The military situation in the forward positions in Tunisia fluctuated daily while Phantom waited for its jeeps. General Patton attacked at Gafsa and E Squadron went with him. Randall's K Squadron, but not Randall himself, were in action for the first time three days later. The Afrika Korps panzer units halted George Patton's Americans at El Guettar on the 23rd, but, three days later, the German forces at the Tebaga Gap were thrown back and the American 1st Armoured Division rattled towards El Hamma under a full moon.

The Allies were sweeping towards Tunis, the ancient Carthage, which had given Rome such a headache under impressive generals like Hannibal. In his more soulful moments, General Montgomery might have echoed the words of the Roman statesman Cato. At the end of every speech he made in the Senate, he finished with the words '*Delenda Carthago est*' – 'Carthage must be destroyed'.

5

'Grin, you Bugger, grin!'

'Still I hate marching,' Randall wrote on 12 March. He and his men were wearing gas capes, uncomfortable protective cloaks that hung from the neck, and 'battle bowlers', the tin hats designed by John Brodie in the Great War. At least they were all able to have a steam bath afterwards. The previous day had been a change from routine, however, because Randall, Cuming and Pannell had been invited aboard a submarine in Jean-Bart harbour. There was also an American Red Cross show in the evening, which was excellent.

Randall met some of the local girls while waiting for orders to move to the Front. One was a 'most amusing and most attractive' girl who was probably not, in his opinion, a prostitute. The next day, he heard from Tony Warre that he would not be sent ahead with E Squadron as was originally planned, but would bring up the next wave of reinforcements. There is a sense now of a young man itching for action. He was no medal hunter but he did want to do his bit – as he would tell various commanding officers for the next two years. He was irritated by some of the officers around him who were 'too damn idle and cliquey'.

The following Monday, Randall was at the docks hoping that the long-promised vehicles had arrived but he was to be disappointed. He had lunch with a couple of RAF lads and a captain in the Free French Tank Corps. Edward Oliver found the Frenchman obnoxious, especially since he had had a few and there was nearly an embarrassing scene. So much for the *entente cordiale*! Two days later, the vehicles turned up and Phantom could at last start to move. The camp was buzzing, but for Randall there was again disappointment: 'Hugh gets a patrol. I get damn all.' To compensate perhaps, Randall accepted a 'flip' in a Beaufighter, having made good friends with the RAF 'types'.[1] This aircraft, a long-range heavy fighter with twin engines, was only three years old and was used in virtually every theatre of war between 1940 and 1945. The Japanese called it 'the whispering death' because its approach was so sudden and silent. Its maximum speed was actually only 335 mph, making it slow by fighter standards, and its first use was as a night-fighter. One hundred Beaus were about to be delivered to the American Air Force in the North African area and their squadrons used them for night attacks and daytime convoy escort. Snarling out over the Bay of Algiers and into the blue of the Mediterranean sky was an extraordinary experience for Randall. No more extraordinary perhaps than being inspected on his return during a surprise visit from Air Vice-Marshal Hugh Lloyd, a much-decorated pilot who was in command of the Allied Coastal Air Force that spring.

On the following Thursday, Randall's squadron moved to the east of Jean-Bart to a pleasant spot on the rocky coast that reminded him of North Wales. The officers were in billets and the men under canvas, spending most of the day swimming and cleaning kit. Blanco and boot polish were the constant companions of the men of the Second World War, as they had been for nearly 200 years. Spit and polish was still believed to be important for morale and it filled men's time. A week later, Randall himself was bawled out by the Adjutant for being improperly dressed: 'a most unpleasant creature'. Meanwhile, units of K Squadron were being sent forward piecemeal. Percy Pennant from the Royal Welsh Fusiliers was sent with the 34th US Infantry to attack Fondouk. Springett Demetriadi's No. 3 Patrol joined the 9th US Infantry.

No. 5 Patrol was also with the 9th but on the opposite side of the advance road. Lieutenant Dawson from the Intelligence Corps accompanied the 1st US Armoured Division from its headquarters at Maknassy.

Three hundred miles back, Randall's 'local' served an excellent muscatel and the place was jammed with French sailors. The eager young lieutenant was not impressed with his men's performance on the rifle range: 'these people are shocking duds'. On the same day, a 'whole batch of padres arrived, quite astonishing'. Towards the end of the month, Randall was both attending and giving lectures. He explained the role of Phantom, although aware that he himself was doing nothing yet, to Canadian paratroopers and thought it went quite well. He was on the range again on the 26th, supervising grenade throwing, and there was a massive thunderstorm, the heavens adding to the roar and crash on the ground. Two days later, Patton hit Gafsa and took it quickly, K Squadron installing its headquarters there. Phantom was acquitting itself well, liaising with the Americans who quickly lost their suspicion of the 'Limeys' and got on well with them.

Increasingly bored behind the lines, Randall played football for the padres' team. He does not record the score but it was the first real exercise he had had for ages. He even went with Hugh Cuming to a service that Sunday at the Catholic church in Jean-Bart. Otherwise, he slept most of the day. He chatted up the barmaids Fifi and Zezi and wrote home to his mother and Betty. What runs through Randall's diaries is the sense that just over the hill all hell was breaking loose and he was not part of it. One of the padres, Father Tuckerman, was sent to the 84th General Hospital, and Randall could only imagine what that must be like; terrified men dying and in pain, seeking the comfort of their God. He dug slit trenches with the men, since this was a standard defensive precaution and had to be done in a hurry in the event of enemy attacks. In the Great War, a similar groove in the ground had been called a foxhole and they were actually of very limited use against sustained machine-gun or mortar fire. For that reason, the Americans called them 'Ranger Graves'.

Jean-Bart boasted a cinema, and Randall saw a lot of French films during these weeks. One night, he went with Lieutenant Davis of Phantom and met Dickie Pritchard-Jones, an old chum from the 83rd Battery from what must have seemed an eternity ago. For some reason, the girl who was with them took umbrage and walked out on them. There was a great party on Sunday, 4 April and 15 letters arrived in the mail. Randall talked nostalgically about Northern Ireland to the WREN Pat O'Neill and met some 'very pleasant' American nurses. The rest of the officers, however, were 'BUM'.

Five days earlier, Springett Demetriadi had had his baptism of fire and covered himself with glory. He went on a reconnaissance with Colonel Benson of a Commando unit and knocked out two anti-tank guns. Demetriadi took forty-one Italian prisoners at the point of his revolver, no doubt hoping that no more than six of them would try to jump him at once! The man had been educated at Eton and was commissioned into the Surrey and Sussex Yeomanry Field Brigade of the Royal Artillery in 1933.

That was the week that Hugh Cuming and four of the men left to join the squadron at the Front. Cuming left Randall a letter: 'Fare thee well, old boy. It's quite a wrench saying goodbye like this. However, you'll be up with us soon and at any rate I'll keep you posted, be sure of that . . . God bless you, dear old lad – best of luck to you and Pat. Chin up! . . . grin, you bugger, grin!'

There was always the sense, in the casual and random separations of friends, that this might be forever. The huge casualty rate of Phantom aboard the *Aboukir* and an even grimmer mortality record in the SAS later was proof that there really was no safe place in any theatre of war.

So Randall took Cuming's advice and grinned at Rosemary Ames of the United States Army Reserve Command out of Fort Bragg, but spent most of his free time with Pat O'Neill, the Pat referred to in Cuming's letter. She was 'clean fresh air amid all the beastliness' and she made him laugh. By 7 April, when Demetriadi met the 12th Lancers who were forward scouts of Montgomery's 8th Army and reported back, 'The enemy is retiring fast and his front is crumbling,' Randall was admitting, at least to his diary, that 'I seem to have fallen a bit for her'. Two days later, he was fretting over his inactivity again. He wanted to have 'a crack before it finishes. Oh, why aren't we there?' On Sunday, he celebrated the fact that he had been commissioned for two years. He had tea with Pat in the officers' Mess and won a bet with the squadron's number two that all the lads would be back to camp on time. His Artillery friends, Wilkinson and Harding – 'good types' – were ordered forward on the 12th.

Information must have reached Phantom by this time that the Axis forces were on the retreat. That was why Randall was so impatient – 'before it finishes'. On the 10th, the advance units of the 8th Army entered Sfax on the Tunisian coast. Randall records in his diary the fall of Soussi, the next town to the north: 'Oh, boy how they fly!' The Axis troops took up positions in an arc around the Bay of Tunis, extending from Cape Serrat in the north to Enfidaville in the east. Randall was depressed, hanging around in his room. And his mood was not lightened two days later by attending a court martial. There were two cases, both petty, and the whole thing was a waste of time. 'Seems a pity,' he wrote, 'they have nothing better to do than to charge men for such stupid offences.' The next day, he went out for a brisk march, just to get out of the claustrophobic atmosphere of the camp.

On Saturday, again to relieve the boredom, he went to Algiers and got himself invited on board HMS *Maidstone*, which had been moored as a sort of floating headquarters since November of the previous year. She was designed as a workshop to service submarines and was equipped with a foundry, plumbers' and carpenters' shops, machine shops and plants for recharging submarine batteries. She also had a cinema, a hospital, a chapel, a bakery, a barber's shop, operating theatre and dental surgery.

Among the men Randall had lunch with, Commander Charles 'Bertie' Pizey was the most distinguished.

This was not Pizey's home patch and it is not clear what he was doing on the *Maidstone*. He had served in the Mediterranean 13 years earlier as flag lieutenant on board HMS *Revenge* but his role more recently was as staff officer protecting the Soviet convoys in the North Sea. He had seen action against the formidable German battleships the *Scharnhorst* and the *Gneisenau* as well as the heavy cruiser *Prinz Eugen*. He had been made Companion of the Bath in March 1942. With him was the submarine ace Commander Ben Bryant, whom Randall describes as 'quite a big pin'. By the time Randall met him, he had an unequalled record as a destroyer of enemy ships and only a week before had sunk three Italian merchantmen, the *Loredan*, the *Entella* and the *Isonzo* off Sardinia. A fellow officer, Commander Edmund Young, remembered Bryant with fondness years later:

> He believed in taking the game of war seriously; nevertheless it somehow always seemed a game . . . he was out to hit the enemy with all he knew, but he did it with such an air of gay bravado that half the time you had an odd feeling you were playing at pirates . . . He had that rare gift of being able to switch, without loss of dignity, from commanding officer to entertaining messmate.
> [no source given]

Not surprisingly, perhaps, Randall admits that he went to bed that night 'just a little dizzy'.

The navy impressed John Randall and compared favourably to some of the army types he met. 'What grand types they are – they are officers and gentlemen too, which seems to me to be becoming an increasingly rare thing in the Army.' As orderly officer from time to time, he had the chance to talk to the men, almost certainly ignoring Captain Warre's advice from weeks before. He found, as he supervised Mess cleaning, dental checks and bathing, that they were just as 'browned off' as he was.

'Some of the chaps here,' he wrote near the end of April, 'behave appallingly badly, which in my present state of unrest and dissatisfaction, becomes increasingly annoying . . . Self control and ordinary, decent, good manners seem to go by the board here – "On Active Service" is an excuse for almost everything.' He attended Intelligence lectures and carried out field-craft manoeuvres. The new officers who arrived now were a 'mixed bag', and he felt guiltily smug at being an old hand among the new boys. New tropical kit – shorts and open-necked shirts – were issued as were mephacine tablets to ward off malaria. There were mosquitoes and flies everywhere and, despite the glorious blue of the sky and sea and the sun glancing off the stones of ancient Carthage, all Randall wanted was 'a diverting game of cricket or tennis'.

The next day, everybody was ill with the after-effects of the tablets, but the men were in good heart, Wyatt and Plant behind the bar in the canteen dishing out all sorts of things, especially to Randall's unit. As a good junior officer, he turned a blind eye to it once he had satisfied himself that they were not breaking any military law.

On 2 May, a Sunday, Randall was orderly officer when a complaint had been made about one of the men making a nuisance of himself. The line was a fine one. Randall's diaries are full of comments about local girls, not all of them very flattering, but we must take into account the mores of the time. Officers were expected to behave and, as we have already seen, Randall could become a little puritanical about this. For the men, however, it was different, and that Sunday Lieutenant Randall found himself interviewing a woman in his best French. He does not reveal specific details, but it was all a storm in a teacup, and he was glad his own boys were not involved. The 'rather sweet' barmaid Fifi gave him a St Teresa for good luck: 'Let nothing disturb you. Let nothing make you afraid.'[2]

By 6 May, Phantom had been in Jean-Bart for seven weeks. Four of the men, including Snooks, Randall's batman, had received orders to move. This process of weeding out individuals for service at the Front can have done little for morale. Were not those left behind thinking, 'Why not me?' The next day, at last, Randall heard that he too was to move. 'We are in the streets of Bizerta. It will soon be over.'

The battle front was 300 miles away. General Omar Bradley's II US Corps were advancing along the coast towards Bizerta on the edge of a bay. The British V and IX Corps under Generals Allfrey, Crocker and Horrocks were advancing on their right flank alongside the XIX Free French of General Koeltz. The 8th Army under Bernard Montgomery completed the encircling movement and, short of a miracle, the Axis forces were doomed. The 78th Division had taken the Jebel Ahmara, known to the Allies as Longstop Hill. General Alexander wrote of these men, 'They started famous. Now they won immortality.'[3] The Gulf of Tunis and the Mediterranean beyond was safe in Royal Navy hands again, and the Afrika Korps and the Italians had nowhere to go. Only their respective air forces could make a serious impression on the Allies on the ground. The American and British Corps had met for the first time in conflict on 7 April. 'Hello, Limey' might not have been the friendliest greeting but each side was glad to see the other.

From 6 May, Air Chief Marshal Tedder's Allied aircraft were flying 2,500 sorties a day; the Axis reply was a mere 60. Two days later, as the Italians were pinned down in the Cape Bon peninsula, Randall was still orderly officer 300 miles to the rear. He went to the pictures and played cards, welcoming a new major, Storm, to the squadron. He refereed a boxing match on Monday 10th, while a rather more ferocious one was going on around Bizerta and Tunis.

'I expect all organised resistance to collapse within the next forty eight hours,' General Alexander cabled to Churchill the next day, 'and final liquidation of the whole Axis forces in the next two or three days. I calculate that prisoners up to date exceed 100,000 . . . Yesterday I saw a horse-drawn gig laden with Germans driving themselves to the prisoners' cage.[4] As they passed we could not help laughing and they laughed too. The whole affair was more like Derby Day.'[5] General Armin, Rommel's successor in the Afrika Korps, surrendered the next day.

The navy was on hand to make sure that the Tunisia campaign did not end in a Dunkirk-style evacuation. Admiral Cunningham, in charge of this exercise codenamed 'Retribution', signalled to the fleet: 'Sink, burn and destroy. Let nothing pass.' Nothing did.

'Sir,' signalled Alexander to Churchill on the 13th. 'It is my duty to report that the Tunisian campaign is over. All enemy resistance has ceased. We are masters of the North African shores.'[6]

The day before, John Randall had made his farewells in the Estaminée, the name given to various bars and cafes in French North Africa, and Fifi gave him other keepsakes: a pot of jam, a ribbon and a medal. They watched fireworks exploding over Algiers. The march east began at 5.30 the next morning, tramping south through the dust to Rouiba. It was a boiling hot day, and Randall had never seen such beautiful countryside – high hills, rocky gorges and cultivated fields everywhere. The Pioneer Corps did not impress him. 'My God, these pioneers cannot march whatever else they can do – terrible shambles.' But the Pioneer Corps did what they did best: built roads, repaired bridges, made it possible for an army to advance. Marching was the least of their worries. And John Randall saw his first Germans in wartime. They were behind the wire in a prison camp, broken, surly and beaten. 'Damn glad to see it,' Randall wrote. 'I hope I see many more.'

On Friday, 14 May, they reached Setif, halfway to the Tunisian border. There was a lot of waiting about here, eating tinned rations, while at every railway stop there were swarms of Arabs selling eggs at outrageous prices. As is usual in human nature, the keen officer anxious to be up and moving was now wishing he was back in the bar at Jean-Bart enjoying a drink with Fifi. He was suffering from hay fever again, perhaps because the land they rattled through now was flat, the golden corn awash with the scarlet of poppies. Randall wondered if this was what Flanders looked like, the graveyard of so many men of his father's generation. The men were in good spirits, although their faces and uniforms were caked in dust and it was not easy to tell them apart from the Arabs.

At El Khroub, they met more German prisoners, and this time Randall felt sorry for them: 'I am glad I am not in their position, although they are lucky to be alive at all.' There was frantic bartering going on as the Wehrmacht swapped cap badges with the men who had beaten them, the typical swapping ritual which had characterised war for generations.[7]

On Saturday, 15th, they woke up in Guelma, with its astonishing Roman theatre rebuilt by the French in 1905. They were now only 50 miles from the border. There were Italian prisoners of war here and they seemed far happier than the Germans. There was more badge-swapping, and Randall climbed to Souk Ahras, the old marketplace of the Barbary pirates, to call on Father Tuckerman at the 84th General Hospital. The man was in bed himself but pleased to see Randall. A Red Cross train was unloading, and for the first time the lieutenant saw battlefield casualties; men on crutches or on stretchers, patched with white bandages through which blood was seeping: 'Poor devils; they certainly have caught a packet.' When he got back to Guelma, his men were cooking their evening meal by the side of the track and French soldiers were walking about in their greatcoats despite the oppressive heat.

The locomotive broke down the next day, so, while the 1/4 Hampshires and the Royal Irish Fusiliers marched out on foot, Randall was in sole charge of the men. Keen to keep moving, he radioed the Royal Army Service Corps to get them to Medjez. The captain he spoke to could not guarantee a train. In any case, the journey would take twelve hours as opposed to two by road. 'Damn the authority!' Randall wrote. 'I expect I will get an awful raspberry from someone, but who cares – "C'est la guerre".'

The area around Souk Ahras was quite flat, all the more so because the crops had been trampled by so many soldiers' boots over the last weeks. There was a constant stream of vehicles, jeeps, lorries, armoured cars, rattling in both directions. Randall found himself chuckling as he was covered in dust and flies from head to foot and he was wondering what his mother would make of it all: 'how she would hate this filth'.

Eventually, three three-ton trucks turned up for Randall and his men. Two had got lost and one had broken down, but all was well now and just being on the road to Medjez was exhilarating. On the way, they saw the same sight General Alexander had seen – German and Italian prisoners driving themselves to their cages. 'A truly broken army,' as Randall wrote.

Medjez station looked like a battlefield. There were shell cases and empty ammunition boxes at the roadside, burnt-out trucks and the craters of artillery fire. Here and there were simple white wooden crosses: 'a sign,' Randall wrote, 'that one brave British soldier will not see home again. Brings it home to one a bit to actually see the graves, just a mound of earth and a rough wooden cross – not time for a more elaborate affair – heaven knows, they deserve it. I wonder what the thoughts of those at home are – missing presumed killed – no news and then killed on active service. That's the worst part of war – we only get a bit frightened at times, hungry and dirty. Those at home live through worse than this.'

Almost 2,000 men of the 1st Army died between 8 November 1942 and 19 February 1943. Those who died up to 13 May 1943 had, in many cases, no known graves. The fighting around Medjez had been very heavy, with appalling casualties, but a far worse battlefield was to come. Randall picked up his men and they were taken on to Tunis, the ancient Carthage. Just behind them was the already infamous Longstop Hill: 'not much "cricket" in this game', Randall noted ruefully. There were bodies still strewn over the hillside because there had not been time to bury them. Bloated and swarming with the black flies of summer, they were a horrible sight. The Germans had placed booby traps under them so that removing them for burial would cause more blood and death.

There was a rifle sticking nose-down into the soil with a Tommy's helmet on the butt. Oddly, some of the American tanks were facing the wrong way, in the direction of retreat. 'The Yanks have a lot to learn,' Randall noted, as many British soldiers did during these weeks. There was no doubt about the guts of the Americans or the quality of their equipment; what they did not have was experience.

In the hills around Tunis, every inch had been fought for. 'I suppose,' Randall wrote, 'that this is what it was like in the last war . . . The people at home don't know what our chaps have done and what a wonderful feat it is. Now it is all over no one cares.' The British had driven the enemy into the sea; Dunkirk was avenged: 'They can't swim home so the buggers had to surrender.'

Longstop had been a battlefield since December, and today there are a number of accounts written by the men who fought there who all attest to the grimness of the struggle. Randall and his men drove past ruins of a Roman aqueduct, the lads in the back of the truck relishing every moment of it. They were 'conquerors and how!' – all of them grinning from ear to ear. They stopped to scramble over the wrecked fuselage of a downed Luftwaffe fighter, its props mangled in the dust and its cockpit peppered with bullet holes.

History had repeated itself. Carthage had been destroyed again.

At the squadron headquarters at Sidi Bou Said, John Randall stood on the building's flat roof looking out on the moon over a tranquil sea. It was one of those days that would stay with him for ever. Tam Williams was there, and so was Julian Fane, who would soon receive the Croix de Guerre for his gallantry at Bizerta. Springett Demetriadi was also there. They talked over old times and new times, downing gin and sodas, 'with hair down their backs'. Tony Warre was as boorish as ever. 'Damn him,' wrote Randall the next day. 'He is a tactless man. The men hate him and the officers laugh at him.' Randall still felt like the tea-boy in the office. 'I *will* get a patrol and then I will show just what I can do.' The next day, the full extent of the battlefield became clear. Little white houses clustered on hillsides were empty shells. There were craters everywhere. 'Those lads certainly can bomb,' Randall wrote of the RAF. Tony Warre's old buddies from the 12th Lancers turned up, and Randall went swimming with Tam Williams. He was duty officer later in the week, directing traffic, and the heat was grim. Much of the time now was spent in vehicle checks.

Tunis was, in the end, a dirty old town and rather a disappointment. With an ancient past involving the Phoenicians, the three wars against Rome, the Ottoman influence and the current existence of the French, it had a long and exotic history. The medina, the old Arab city with its narrow, twisting alleyways, and people selling leather and filigree, became merely one section of an expanding city. Elsewhere, by 1943, there were broad boulevards in the Parisian style and modern factories and workshops. The city had fallen to the 1st Army at 15.30 hours on 7 May as the Afrika Korps 5th Panzer Division surrendered.

Phantom as a unit took stock of its performance in the campaign. Fifteen patrol officers wrote reports, which were collected by Hutton-Williams, and John Randall read them avidly, if only because it was likely to be his turn next. Officers, the reports decided, had brought too much kit,[8] transport would need to be overhauled and office arrangements improved. The reconnaissance car was too vulnerable in the line of fire and too prone to let in water. Radio sets, maps and message pads all needed to be kept dry. It was agreed that a patrol could function for 48 hours without rest. Moving with the infantry, where a battle could last for weeks, each Phantom man should have six hours' sleep in every twenty-four. With the faster-moving Armour, with patrols of seven to ten days, four hours' sleep was the allotted time. One insurmountable fact was that patrol officers were either lieutenants or captains; such men cut little ice when dealing with staff officers and crusty generals who regarded their advice as impertinent.

Randall does not mention the victory parade held in the city on 20 May, perhaps because he was directing traffic at the time, or perhaps because it was, rightly, reserved for those members of the patrols who had actually fought. The troops marched along the Avenue Maréchal Galliéni and the Avenue Jules Fermy to signal the end of war in North Africa. Five days later, he at last got a patrol – it was No. 6, Julian Fane's old unit and very smart. So smart, in fact, that it put Percy Pennant's in the shade and Randall was a little smug about that. He was less than smug the following day, however, when his driver, Trooper Bentley, crashed his jeep into an armoured car outside the prisoner of war camp. Randall does not record the jeers and howls of laughter from the prisoners, but he and Bentley had great problems with the wheel nuts. 'This is terrible,' he wrote later. There was no sign of a REME or RASC unit to help and, anyway, Phantom was supposedly self-sufficient. Mercifully, they found the missing nuts lying half buried in the sand and could continue on patrol. Driving later through a sandstorm that the Arabs called a *ghibli* was appalling. It stings and breathing is difficult. Everybody turned up their collars and wished they had *shemaghs*, the tasselled scarves the Arabs wore. At least Randall had managed to appropriate some Italian goggles so he could see approximately where they were going.

At night, they rigged up tents alongside their armoured cars and slung the essential mosquito nets across the front. There was little risk of enemy action now that the fighting was over but, that said, there *could* be pockets of the Afrika Korps who had not surrendered and who knew what the locals might be up to? For the civilians of North Africa had put up with somebody else's war being fought all over their territory for three long years. It may well have been the experiences of this time that led to the bitter fight for Algerian independence from France after the war.

At the combined RAF/USAAF headquarters, Randall went to a film, the first in English he had seen for well over a year. It was Deanna Durbin and Charles Laughton's *It Started With Eve*, a lighthearted comedy, which Randall thought 'quite good'. It was a little strange, however – his first taste of what the Americans had known for the last ten years – a drive-in theatre! Men were sitting on jeep bonnets, the tops of armoured cars and lounging in the branches of trees. On Thursday, 27 May, Randall went out in search of wire. For the first time in weeks, he was by himself, driving the jeep across the open plains of Tunisia. The only way that Tony Warre or Norman Reddaway could reach him was by radio and he felt strangely exhilarated by all this. The jeep went 'like the wind'. We take the vehicle and its descendants so much for granted today that we forget how new they were in 1943. Both Wally and Ford began to produce them from 1936 but it was the war that saw their widespread use among American and Allied troops. There were 145 of them issued to every American infantry unit and they could cope with almost every kind of terrain, even, with modifications, along railway tracks. Photographs of Phantom jeeps are very rare but they carried the 'P' emblazoned in white below the front windshield.

And so, John Randall spent a balmy night in the desert outside Tunis, under his mosquito net and inside his tent, alongside the jeep that was his lifeline to escape, freedom and safety. His men had rigged up a lamp that he could read by and he could just about get Forces Radio on his wireless set. He wondered if his mother or Betty at home were listening. 'The wireless is now playing Donkey Serenade. Good night.'

6

Omega and Alpha

'Mr Winston Churchill arrived,' Randall wrote in his diary. 'Good to see the great man.' Four thousand men had stood for hours in the burning sun of 1 June in the amphitheatre at Carthage, in its day the largest in the Roman Empire. Two Christian martyrs had died here in the 3rd century, and all that was left of the gladiatorial tradition were the gates of life and death, once dark passageways now open to the sun. Newspaper cuttings among John Randall's papers show Churchill in a white suit, holding his sun-hat aloft on a walking stick surrounded by scruffy, sweat-stained men in shorts and field caps.

Churchill's mind was already on the next push. Now that North Africa was safely in Allied hands, it would become a springboard for the invasion, first of Sicily, then of Italy. 'The sense of victory was in the air,' he wrote. 'A quarter of a million prisoners cooped up in our cages. Everyone was proud and delighted. There is no doubt that people like winning very much. I addressed many thousand soldiers at Carthage in the ruins of an immense amphitheatre. Certainly the hour and setting lent themselves to oratory. I have no idea what I said, but the whole audience clapped and cheered as doubtless their predecessors . . . had done as they watched gladiatorial combats.'[1] The newspapers remembered his words of course: 'Whatever campaigns follow they will not overshadow this one. Remember we had corporal Hitler all the time to help us. This self-made, self-unmade man has added sauce to the goose that you have caught, killed and eaten.'[2]

Because of the heat, Churchill's audience felt 'pretty limp' afterwards, but the sense of euphoria easily outweighed that. It was as though the headmaster had said 'Well done' after a victory by the First XV, but magnified a thousand times.

Randall and his Phantom colleague the Glaswegian Alistair Mackinlay, Royal Artillery, found an interesting bar in Tunis, but the officers far outnumbered the local girls so 'cherchez les femmes' was difficult. A parcel came from Randall's mother, containing everything he had asked for, along with a letter from his grandmother. He took it on the chin on 4 June when his patrol was taken over by Bill Adam of E Squadron. He knew it was no reflection on him; reshuffles like this happened all the time. The next day, he was scrounging spares for the Phantom vehicles and radio sets at Medjez, and he seems to have been pretty good at this. Water was in short supply so washing was difficult. Another paper cutting among Randall's ephemera shows an ingenious Heath Robinson contraption set up by the RAF involving oil tins and barrels to make a shower, all tastefully covered by canvas for the sake of modesty. It had been six weeks since Randall had had a hot bath – on board the *Maidstone* – and he was very aware of the fact.

He did swim in the sea, however, which in that heat was marvellous, admiring the girls with their 'remarkably fine figures'. He went to a peculiar party on Sunday 6th, dancing to French music played at a ridiculously high speed on a gramophone. He rode home on a motorbike in the dark and without lights. Shopping in the souk of the medina was an experience, with the stallholders trying to sell their trinkets in a cacophony of Arabic and French. He got a small boy to help him because the lad seemed a little more trustworthy than the adults. The flies were appalling as the temperatures climbed and Randall took to swimming naked in the sea to cool off: 'It is rather fun – what would my girlfriends say?' His men were doing better on the rifle range by now and there was an impromptu concert on the 11th. Trooper Reese, one of Randall's lads, played the piano. Tam Williams, as ever, was very funny as the star of the show, and a number of local girls joined in the singing. 'The men loved it,' Randall wrote. 'Their tongues were hanging out.'

The next day, the piano had to go back whence it had come, and Randall and Williams drove the 30 hundredweight truck with the instrument on the back and Trooper Reese playing it all the way.

These days in June were spent in a round of gaiety, with parties and concerts and listening to Frances Day singing on Forces Radio. But there was still a war on. On the 14th, Randall left Sidi Bou Said in an armoured car, stopping at 'Peter's Corner', the site of a major battle in the previous days. 'It seems strange,' he wrote, 'that so many should have lost their lives fighting for this damn place.' He slept in the open that night, accompanied by thousands of mosquitoes, lizards and caterpillars.

The next day, Randall was put in charge of squadron HQ, rushing around telling people to do this and that, and at last had a real job when given command of Motor Transport. It was vital that the jeeps and armoured cars were maintained or else the mobility factor in a highly mobile war would be lost. There was another VIP visit on 17 June when the king turned up. George VI was excellent at morale-boosting visits like this, but there is a sense that his arrival was a little upstaged by 'good old Winnie's' two weeks before. Again, there was the long wait under the torturing sun and Randall admits that the men 'get very browned off and talked an awful lot of cock'. Percy Pennant made a royal floral bouquet and was teased unmercifully about it. Randall thought it a rather fitting gesture.

Days later, an official notice appeared on K Squadron's board. It was the usual Order of the Day from Eisenhower as commander-in-chief, but this one was specifically from the king:

During the long years of the North Africa campaign – with its fluctuating fortunes – it was my constant hope that I might one day be able to come and see for myself the scenes of some of the famous and hard fought battles – and, still more, those who had taken part in them. My wish has now been granted and it has been my happy experience to be the bearer of the congratulations of all peoples of the Empire on a victory that will shine in military history. This victory I have decided to commemorate by the issue, in the near future, of a star to be known as the AFRICA STAR . . .

Randall's scrounging did not go so well the following Saturday, perhaps because the engineers of REME were wise to him by now. He and fellow Phantom Dennis Hart, of the Surreys, came across a house full of GIs and three very attractive French girls. One of them, Jacqueline Loiseau, invited Randall to play table tennis with her. He danced with her and spoke French. 'So at last I have met someone – it's only a question of time and patience. I could never wait.' He was visiting her again the next day, having made 'Jacquotte' a new ping-pong bat, only to discover that she had an even prettier sister, aged about 19, called Susie. By day, Randall was working with Corporal Reeves on two new Dodge trucks that had arrived. By night, he was at the Loiseaus'. His French was coming on in leaps and bounds: 'and so,' he wrote cryptically, 'are other things'. There was another soldier there on the Wednesday, but Randall was not afraid of a little competition. Susie was working hard for an exam, so Randall made small talk with her mother and brother, Jean-Pierre.

By the Friday of that week, the old boredom hit home again and Randall's diary becomes introspective. Edward Oliver remained a true friend but Randall was less than happy with some of the other officers. He was still waiting for a patrol and ruing the fact that his mother used to think *he* was lazy and idle! Norman Reddaway was particularly annoying: 'the silly twit'. Someone took a photograph around this time of the Phantom unit posing under a canopy of trees. Randall, in rolled shirt sleeves and army beret, is at the back, standing with others on chairs. He was now in Anchor Department, learning to load, and checking the messages coming in daily from various units. In the evening, he went out with Oliver and the Loiseau girls. He saw them home and Susie cried on his shoulder: 'poor little thing'.

Wednesday, 30 June was something of a red letter day. Randall had his first bath since leaving Algiers, at Rocher Hotel. Unfortunately, the water was cold. As July began, Randall was amused to find that the Loiseau radio was tuned to the BBC and Tommy Handley – the star of *ITMA* – was in fine voice. Three years earlier, it had jokingly been conceded that, if Hitler had wanted to invade Britain, his best time would have been between half past eight and nine o'clock on a Thursday, the half hour of *ITMA*; he would have met no resistance at all.

Sad news came from Jean-Bart, although the details were unclear, that several children Phantom knew there had been killed by a bomb. Since this town had not been in the front line for months, it was probably the result of an old, off-target bombing mission and the device had failed to go off until the children found it. Randall was working on the Austin utility vehicles and even slept in one from time to time. There was the daily routine of Arabs pestering everybody – 'Baksheesh! Baksheesh!' And the mosquitoes were appalling. Randall was decoding messages of all kinds and had an old-fashioned English breakfast of eggs, bacon and tomatoes, the first in a long time.

On 6 July, the sirocco arrived. This wind creates different conditions in various parts of the world, but in North Africa it can reach speeds of 100 miles an hour, whipping up sand and grit that stings and blinds. It is no respecter of buildings and snarls up engines, lasting for anything up to several days. Randall could not believe the heat: 'It is like the hot air in a tube station.' Perhaps it was that that made Randall snap and he had a blazing row with Oliver, telling him how lazy he was. Perhaps it was that too that made him down a few too many at a party with 'RN types' at the Officers' Club. He remembered singing and 'I am afraid I got absolutely stinking – my poor head.' Unsurprisingly, he got up the next morning 'feeling like death' and got a rocket for being late. It was particularly unfortunate that a new Physical Training course was beginning that day and Randall knew nothing about it: 'Christ, what a strain!'

Friday was a particularly pointless day. PT kicked off at 6 a.m. and then, just for fun, somebody decided it would be a good idea to take all the wheels off the vehicles. 'Oh, what fools they are,' Randall moaned in his diary. 'God help England.' But the next day, the world had turned and the diary reads, 'Heard the wonderful news that we have landed in Sicily. Hope Julian Fane's party have some fun.'

The 'fun' could have ended in disaster. Operation Husky, as the invasion of Sicily was known, had been in development for several months and Churchill had sailed to Washington for top-level talks with President Roosevelt long before he had been cheered by the troops in Tunis. The objective was to keep the enemy guessing where an invasion would strike, and to that end General Maitland-Wilson's troops in Egypt made a great pretence of gearing up for an invasion of the Balkans.[3] Stories coming through from the Russian Front spoke of a grim war of attrition, and it was by no means certain whether the Soviet Red Army could hold out. The plan was to invade Italy and knock Mussolini out of the war. This would expose the Wehrmacht's southern flank and force them to divert troops from the east.

The problem was the dreaded amphibious landing. The invasion of Sicily has become so overshadowed by D-Day in Normandy a year later that the risk factor in July 1943 has almost been forgotten. The British experience of such operations – at Walcheren against Napoleon in 1809 and Gallipoli against the Turks in 1915 – was that of huge casualties and ultimate failure. But it had been successful in North Africa itself in Operation Torch, so there was general optimism. The weather was crucial and the same winds that were playing havoc with John Randall's temper early in July threatened to destroy the Allied invasion force. So certain were the Italians that these winds would hamper operations they seem to have been off their guard when Admiral Andrew Cunningham's convoys hit the Sicilian beaches.

The airfields were bombed on 3 July, any Italian bomber that could get away flying to safety on the Italian mainland. Four of the five ferries that crossed the dangerous Straits of Messina were sunk. But the day of invasion was the 9th, a Friday, and while John Randall's unit were taking wheels off their armoured cars, the biggest armada in modern history was ploughing through rough seas to the north-east of him. On Sicily itself stood a quarter of a million men under General Alfredo Guzzoni. A quarter of these troops were German but all of them were demoralised after the pounding they had received in the last year all across North Africa.

The Allies' task was to land eight divisions (more than D-Day) with 2,000 landing craft, the amphibious vehicles known as 'Ducks', which could negotiate moderate seas and roll up onto the beaches themselves. Overall command was given to General Alexander, but under him there was a 50/50 command structure between the Americans and the British. Arthur Tedder led the aerial operations for the RAF; Andrew Cunningham for the US Navy.

A combination of winds and American inexperience led to the airborne glider units being widely scattered and, while all this was invaluable experience for D-Day, it did not cause quite the havoc that was intended in Sicily. Crews from some gliders were released too early and drowned in the Mediterranean trying to get ashore. Only 12 crews reached the crucial bridgehead that was their target and they lost 80 per cent of their number in hand-to-hand fighting before support arrived. By daylight on the 10th, however, George Patton's 7th Army made good their landings between Licata and Scoglitti and quickly took the nearest towns. Montgomery's 8th Army was equally successful to the east, taking Syracuse without a shot being fired.

Over the next few days, the British advance went well but the American sector was hit by the determined resistance of the Hermann Goering Panzer Division, and the Allied advance slowed in places to a crawl. As far as Phantom were concerned, the Sicilian invasion proved a mixed bag. H Squadron under Major George Grant was put through a gruelling training programme in Cairo and Suez and shipped west. Julian Fane's K Squadron was supposed to liaise with them and work as a team but that never happened. Grant felt the whole episode a waste of time. Radios did not work properly and the lack of Armour sent over meant that the fast communications for which Phantom were famous were not really necessary.

Fane's patrols fared better – and there, but for the grace of somebody's random choice, would have gone John Randall. Bill Adam from the Gordons had a patrol; so did Hugh Cuming and Lieutenant Laurie from the Artillery. They all slipped out from Sousse on 8 July.

John Randall got quite hooked on games of boules, although he realised that betting on the outcome was a 'mug's game, but I can easily see how it can get hold of you'. On the 12th, the actress Vivien Leigh turned up at the Rocher Hotel where the 6th Armoured Division were her hosts. Randall was entranced by her: 'Never forget the thing that caught my eye was the lovely way she walked – wonderfully slim and elegant.' She was 30 at the time, the Hollywood star of *Gone With the Wind*, and had been married to Laurence Olivier since 1940, acting with him in *That Hamilton Woman* a year later. She visited troops all over North Africa that summer before a persistent cough and recurrent fevers put an end to it.

Among Randall's papers in this period is a list of his girlfriends' phone numbers – the famous 'black book' that many eligible bachelors before and since were supposed to carry. 'Just another of those things which I miss so much . . . They are a comely lot, makes one's heart beat just a little quicker.' There is a letter too, written by Fifi from Jean-Bart. Nothing changes there, she says, and she hopes he is well and has fond memories of her. The letter, in fact, caused some consternation, because he was too busy reading it to dance with the Loiseau sisters, who took a pretty dim view of the fact. 'Oh, well!!' Randall commented. The ENSA concert that night consisted of its founder member, Leslie Henson, the singer/dancer Dorothy Dickson (who was a friend of the queen) and, of course, eclipsing them both, Vivien Leigh.

Randall was winning at boules, despite his misgivings about gambling, and won 3,000 francs on 16 July. Hugh Fraser was not so lucky and made rather a fool of himself, calling on the NAAFI money to put things right. The next day, all games of boules were outlawed.

Julian Fane's patrols were back by the 18th, by which time there were no airfields in Sicily still in enemy hands. No doubt the stories he told spurred Randall's diary entry for the next day. 'It is about time we did some fighting.' He met the 'definitely quite pretty' Sally Cunningham, a WREN, on the Thursday, and a number of dates ensued, with swimming and dinner. On the Saturday, a night out with Sally and the boys from the North Irish Horse[4] resulted in a knees-up. There were a number of the lads who were 'tiddly-pom' and American nurses were 'equally sozzled'. John Randall was duty officer that day and should not have been there at all. When his squadron leader, Tony Warre, turned up, Randall wanted the ground to swallow him. As luck would have it, Warre had no idea who was on duty, so all was well. Sally was less than happy, however, to have her new beau dancing cheek to cheek with American nurses. She got her own back a few days later when Dr Major from the local hospital began to notice her. 'Blast him,' Randall fumed. 'She loves it.'

A change in command of K Squadron on the 29th lifted Randall's mood. He was sorry to see Tony Warre go, although they rarely saw eye to eye, but was delighted that his replacement was Julian Fane. Randall was now Intelligence officer in squadron HQ and was far happier, especially when he received a letter from Bunny Steele back home: 'I am head over heels about her again.'

He went to a party with some RAF pilots and American nurses, despite the 'Provost people' making life difficult. The Provost's Department were the Military Police, responsible for discipline in the army. They no doubt turned a blind eye to various infringements in wartime, but links with the locals had to be watched carefully. Randall refers to 'unreliable French girls' at the party, as though their tipsy giggling might cause problems among the sharp-eared Redcaps.

Under Fane, Randall found a new lease of life, enjoying Intelligence work and still tinkering with Motor Transport. On Saturday, he went to Constantine, the city of bridges with its deep, rocky ravine. He slept that night in the officers' camp in Algiers and drank too much gin on board HMS *Maidstone*. It was a lightning nostalgia trip for him, driving across to Jean-Bart to see Fifi and the girls. In one of those strange coincidences that war throws up, Randall met Surgeon Lieutenant-Commander George Bradshaw, who had been the family doctor back home at Riverhead. Both men, it transpired, had been out with the same girl – Pam Beck – back home. It was a very convivial evening but Randall was less pleased the next day when somebody stole his ignition key and he staggered to bed later, appropriately 'tiddly-pom'. He had a sore throat and slept right through a cricket match played that afternoon.

The troops' concert was 'low and dirty' but very funny and he enjoyed a lecture on the Derbyshire Yeomanry,[5] a unit that had performed brilliantly in Tunisia. 'Well,' he wrote in his diary, 'this ends another book. My mood is a happy one nowadays. Julian Fane will make an excellent C.O. Mervyn Vernon is still trying to find me a job . . . Hugh Cuming is going back to his regiment [The Seaforths] and I hope I may get his patrol. The squadron now looks pretty good, the men are smart and efficient and everything runs well. There is still a little friction between E and K.' He was in love with Bunny Steele, but Jane Short and Doodles wrote to him regularly. He was convinced that the cork woods of Bugeaud where he was stationed was the best spot in North

Africa. 'Oh yes! I am growing a moustache. It looks shocking but one day it may be "so frightfully cavalry". I hope.'

'This starts,' Randall wrote in his new diary, 'as the last finished.' There was good news. The war in Sicily was won after 38 days of fighting and the RAF were giving the Germans hell. Phantom was buzzing with rumours of movement at last, Mervyn Vernon rushing to and fro, but most of them actually wanted to see England again. Randall was driving Dodges, scrounging parts for them and undergoing some intensive signals courses under John Hoskyns, the Royal Signals officer with Phantom: 'I ought to know something,' Randall wrote, 'by the end of the week.' The rest of that week was all about map-reading and vehicle painting, but still no orders to go on to Italy. The painted tents gave off a ghastly smell and there were lectures on 'Amps and Ohms and such things'. Looking forward to some dreamed-of future date, a war correspondent gave Phantom a lecture on the 'Ins-and-outs' of Berlin.

Lectures were one thing but Julian Fane promised some organised sport and that was much more up Randall's street. He was not well by the 25th, however – 'had the squitters' – and had to stay behind, taking the opportunity to write home. He was still ill when his diary entry – the only one in three books – reads 'can't remember'. Vernon was back from Cairo on Sunday, 29 August and, again, rumours flew. Home was a longed-for possibility, but Burma was also a possibility, and no one was longing for that. The fall of Singapore in February of the previous year was an unparalleled disaster in British history, resulting in the appalling torture of the defeated British, Australian and Dutch troops by the Japanese in the camps along the River Kwai. General Slim's 'forgotten' 14th Army had yet to be coordinated in the impenetrable jungles and, although it was ultimately successful, detailed plans for the campaign had yet to be drawn up.

Randall was still ill by early September, despite a visit to the Platoon's MO, and spent the 3rd and 4th in bed. The next day, however, there was an unexpected piece of news, which would, quite literally, shape his life from now on. He suddenly heard of a parachute course, and Julian Fane chose Randall to go on it. He immediately felt better and, on Sunday, 5 September, he and Peter Pike arrived at No. 2 Special Airborne Service at 5.30. The base was just outside Philippeville, and Randall was 'sure it will be fun'. The first day consisted of lectures, and they were an odd collection in the Mess, odder probably than Phantom. There was a mountain behind the buildings, which was used for fitness training, and Randall felt very unfit at that time. There was no 'sweat and toil' the next day either. He and two others went to a party that night but had to climb a wall to get in. It was worth it – the nurses were 'quite fun'.

Those first two days were clearly the lull before the storm because, on the Wednesday, Randall and Peter Pike found themselves scrabbling up the mountain and down again in less than 65 minutes: 'It almost killed us.' More was to follow, however, because parachute training hit them with a vengeance – dangling from swings and jumping from platforms, wearing oddly shaped helmets. They tumbled all over the place, and it was what today we would call a learning curve. Most of the officers in the Mess were Guardsmen so all was spick and span. Randall went to bed happier than he had been for weeks: 'We jump [for real] on the 20th . . . what a day!'

Peter Pike left the next day, as E Squadron were off to Italy, but he was back again on Friday in one of those incomprehensible 'snafus' that all armies are capable of. He and Randall were running up the mountain again, trying not to notice the agony in their feet. Randall had never known blisters so painful and took his mind off them by writing home to Bunny – 'I really think I am quite in love with her.' The days were unbearably hot and Randall was glad to soak his feet in a moonlight dip in the sea. He was forming an opinion of the others on the course – 'definitely not the Eton and Oxford type' – and after Phantom that must have come as quite a shock. He could not complete the mountain run on the Tuesday because of his feet, but the next day he was very much in action.

Typically, John Randall saved a man's life that day and, just as typically, he makes little of it. Details are sparse, but the sea was running strong and the man got into difficulties. He was terrified, floundering around and going under until Randall reached him and dragged him to safety, coughing and spluttering on the beach.

News was coming from home, and among Randall's papers is a newspaper clipping of the wedding of his old friend from the 83rd AA, Lieutenant 'Dickie' Pritchard-Jones to Margaret Woodburn. Dickie had wanted to join Phantom but Tony Warre had vetoed that for reasons of his own. News was coming in from Italy too. The country was 'in a bit of a mop-up – God knows which way they will go.' Randall presumed E Squadron was there 'and having quite a party'. The Italian government had effectively surrendered on 9 September, leaving the Germans in charge in Rome, and Hitler was paying the price for taking on a militarily weak partner in the so-called Pact of Steel. On that day, the battle of Salerno ended with the Wehrmacht outnumbered nearly two to one. Mussolini was hanging on by the skin of his teeth.

An aerogram arrived from Jane Short that same day:

My dear Hugh,[6]
You wrote to me from the mountains of North Africa so I feel I must do something pretty spectacular in return. This comes to you, as they say, from my office desk in Whitehall. That sounds terrific, doesn't it, rather as if I were the Under Secretary of State to the Under Secretary of State for something or other.

It's rather fun as I can watch the little tugs lowering their funnels to go under Westminster Bridge from my window. They look like this [in the original, a sketch follows]. I hope you will get the effect as you know that drawing is not my strong point.

The Wing Commander is out at a conference at the moment, but

all the same I feel this is not quite of national importance.
My nerve is going – Must stop – Love, Joan.

On Monday, everyone was keyed up for their first parachute jump
and the fact that Randall was unwell with a cold did not help.
The next day saw the group travelling to Talergma, 20 miles
beyond Constantine. There was an assortment of aircraft on the
runways and the jump would *definitely* be tomorrow. In the
Randall papers is a newspaper clipping of a paratrooper descending:
'This man,' Randall wrote alongside, 'must remember to "Keep
his feet and knees together"!! Very reminiscent of my jumps.'
Wednesday dawned: 'A day of disappointment. No plane. No
chutes.' Three men jumped on Thursday making good landings,
but the plane broke down, mercifully on the tarmac, before
Randall could get airborne. Four Albemarles, twin-engined
medium-range bombers made by Armstrong Whitworth, turned
up later along with Fane and Demetriadi, who were keen to join
the jump team. Randall checked his chute for one last time.

Came the day! The novice paratrooper got up, shaved badly
(had the cavalry moustache disappeared already?) and made a
mess of his diary entry too: 'All these scribbling out looks as
though I am jittery – am I Hell!' Julian Fane was No. 1 in the
stick and Randall No. 3. 'The big moment arrived. I hopped out
and down I sailed. Lovely and quiet, cool and comfortable. Landed
quite easily and had a good look round. It was definitely fun . . .
rolled up my chute and trundled back with it.' He rode back to
the Mess in a jeep, 'feeling like a million'; Julian Fane had broken
four bones in his foot.

Randall was soon back in the air to help Major Carey-Elwes
of the Norfolk Regiment to push the rest out. As the new boy
came to realise, there was always that split second when a man's
nerve might fail, when an aircraft is roaring over the desert at so
many thousand feet and the wind feels as if it will rip a man's
head off. In that split second, there has to be someone on hand
to give a gentle shove in the small of the back. Panic on a parachute

jump is the most unnerving experience of all. After another successful jump, Randall was greeted by a famous face – the flat, pugnacious features of Randolph Churchill, the son of the Prime Minister. He was due to take Fane's place as No. 1 in the stick that afternoon. In the event, Demetriadi led the jump and Churchill went in at No. 10.[7] 'Now you will push me, won't you,' he yelled at Randall above the Albemarle's roar, 'if I don't go?'

'Yes, sir.' Randall smiled. 'You can be absolutely certain of it.' And he did.

7

Glamorous Phantom

Having survived jumps with only a slightly 'ricked' ankle to show for it, Randall noted in his diary at the end of September 1943 that Julian Fane's spell in hospital meant that Springett Demetriadi took over as squadron leader: 'only acting, thank Heaven'. As an old hand by now at the parachute game, Randall 'talked frightful balls' giving a lecture on jumping. Half the squadron went to see Tam Williams in his latest film *The Day Will Dawn*, in which their old oppo was very young and good-looking. He had obviously found time in the previous year to make this piece of propaganda. He played a war correspondent caught up in the thick of things and falling in love with Deborah Kerr. No doubt there were lots of comments about camera angles and flattering lighting. After an inspection on 2 October, Randall rather overdid it in the Officers' Club that evening but was rescued by Phantom colleagues Dick Webster from the 10th Hussars and Stewart Davies, who were of 'invaluable assistance'.

Two days later, he was on a 'scheme' with No. 3 Patrol and was sent to Draham, where he met a French woman with whom he flirted outrageously. She was highly amusing and almost too encouraging. The town nestled on the slopes of the imposing Djebel Bir and the atmosphere was very humid. The ruins of Roman baths were still visible in the 1940s. Randall also got into conversation with Khaled, the son of the Bey of Tunis's Prime Minister, Slaheddine Baccouche, and stayed in a hotel with bed and sheets, which, after the privations of tents and barracks, was heaven. It rained so heavily on the 6th that everybody's tent was flooded, and not even that could alleviate the boredom. Everyone just wanted to go home.

The next day, Khaled took Randall on a tour of the Arab quarter in Tunis. He was not allowed very far, but met the man's father, the Prime Minister, who would go on to serve for a second term of office after the war. He got back from his unauthorised 'holiday' with only the ever-reliable Dickie Webster to notice. *Somebody* noticed, however, because Randall and fellow Phantom Pike were each given two extra duty days for not returning with their patrol. It was not worth arguing about and cheap at half the price. The Noceti family he had met in Bone took him under their wing. The town, occupied by the French in 1832, was dominated by the schizoid symbols of French Algeria – the Great Mosque and the Catholic Cathedral of St Augustine. Madame was charming; Pierre less so, but the daughters called him an 'enfant terrible'. 'What a thing!' Randall wrote in his diary.

By the 11th, rumours were flying thick and fast. E Squadron had sailed for Italy on the cruiser *Aurora* four weeks earlier but without enough vehicles for their liking. The ever-resourceful Norman Reddaway, now with E, was ready for this and had stashed two jeeps on a tank-landing craft. He had also got hold of three tons of extra equipment with the connivance of the navy. This was the start of Operation Avalanche, which saw Montgomery's army landing at Reggio and Patton's at Salerno. It was now that Hoppy Hopkinson, who had lovingly reared Phantom and appointed Randall in the first place, was fatally wounded with the Airborne Division. He was killed by machine-gun fire at a German road block near the town of Castellaneta, the only fatality among airborne officers of general rank.

Would K Squadron be sent north to join these outfits? Or was Egypt with H Squadron a possibility? There was a sense among them all that here was a job half done. One campaign was over but the Reich was still supreme on the mainland of Europe and there was a long way to go. Ennui was taking its toll; Demetriadi ended up in hospital, having fallen out of a jeep on his way back from Algiers. Randall was not impressed by him, man of action or not; he was lazy and a bad leader. Most people agreed with this. And life – 'the acme of boredom' – was beginning to get to them all. It made men tetchy, unreasonable. Edward Oliver, who had once been a friend, was now 'that lazy, indolent snob'.

The next day came news that two officers were to go to Italy, and names were drawn from a hat. One of them was John Randall: 'Christ, it is me.' For reasons of his own, Springett Demetriadi, out of hospital by this time, decided that this system of selection was not fair and he would choose the pair himself. In the event, the order was cancelled and nobody went. 'This,' wrote Randall, 'is certainly more trying on the nerves than parachuting.'

On Tuesday, 19 October, Randall's patrol used a trick the Japanese also carried out along the Kwai – catching fish in a river by dynamiting the water. Everybody dived in as the stunned creatures floated to the surface. One that Randall caught weighed 14 pounds.

The 21st and 22nd were given over to sports days, no doubt to try to alleviate the boredom. There was swimming and a hundred yards race between officers and NCOs; Randall won silver that day. He enjoyed the football in the afternoon but the seven-a-side rugger game nearly killed him, so out of condition did he feel. In the moments of enforced idleness, he wrote, 'I have started to read a few books,' as though it were the most unnatural thing in the world. He saw and enjoyed the Ben Travers farce *Rookery Nook* at the Garrison Theatre in Bone, and the next day various officers and men left to join H Squadron in Egypt. Pike, Webster, Oliver and Paul Barker of the 27th Lancers went; so did Troopers Bentley and Williams from Randall's own patrol. The Mess seemed strangely empty.

Dotted throughout Randall's diaries are various medical

inspections. For a week around this time, everyone was given inoculations against typhus and, on the 27th, Randall developed a septic lump on his cheek, which was very painful. The next day, it had swollen to horrendous proportions and looked like a balloon. The ulcer burst three days later but that put him in hospital: 'Bloody hell.' In the ward, Randall was bored to sobs. The Sisters were not up to much, and Stewart Davies brought him books to read. He did at least meet Dickie Carr of the Coldstream Guards in an adjacent bed and realised that he had once dated his sister Hilda while with G Squadron in Northern Ireland. By the 4th, 'this is too frightful'; he was still not allowed to get out of bed even though his swelling had gone down. Two days later, after a 'fight' with Sister, he was at last discharged and was picked up in a jeep by two officers from the Queen's Regiment. There was still no news of movement and he soothed his nerves by reading.

On Saturday 13th, Randall received a letter from Bunny Steele back home. She was engaged. 'I am damn sorry but she sent me a sweet letter – not much help however.' He had a late night at the Officers' Club and got back after hours, waking everybody up. It was the inevitable response to a literal 'Dear John' letter. There was firing on the ranges two days later, and Randall was flirting outrageously with French girls in Bone and making small talk with nurses. Sister Geordie was one of those; she was pretty and blonde with blue eyes, white teeth and a nice figure, but there would be no more of that; K Squadron were at last going home.

On the 19th, Randall's men returned a piano and chairs they had borrowed from the mayor of Bugeaud, who was a nasty piece of work, the sort of man who ran with the hare and hounds depending on who was occupying his country at the time. Bugeaud had had a bad start under the French. It was named after the general who occupied the area in 1830, allowing his men to rape and pillage at will. Arabs hovered around the camp, waiting for the unit to pull out so they could scrounge anything left behind. Randall was duty officer and had to put two of the men under close arrest for being too merry. 'Rather a pity,' he commented. 'Does not help the unit much.' The train journey was a nightmare, jolting along in a freezing compartment at night with no windows. Dennis Hart from the Surreys, Percy Pennant and Haymer Bagnall were 'all slightly pissed', and, as duty officer, Randall had missed out on the party; there is nothing more annoying than being the only sober one in this situation.

At the end of this diary, John Randall became introspective: 'So that ends yet another phase . . . Ambition and drive are fundamental to success and successful I must be. Those around me are lazy and rotten and I despise them.' He wondered what the future would be like with such people at the helm. Bunny Steele had gone, although he hoped that he could still count her a good friend. Betty was sweet and Doodles adorable, 'but still an unknown quantity'. Stewart Davies was generous and sincere, and Hugh Cuming was already back home, Randall eager to see him again. John Hoskyns from the Signals was a charming, progressive type; so was Chris Mayhew of the Intelligence Corps. They had obviously been talking over, as young men will with their boundless optimism, what their plans were after the war. Hoskyns wanted to go into teaching, as did Alan Laurie of the Royal Artillery.[1] Percy Pennant 'the future parson is very pleasant and harmless'. Others, however, Randall could not stand. Demetriadi was selfish, insincere and lazy; so were Mark Mainwaring from the Artillery, Haymer Bagnall and Ian 'Lightning' Mackrill of the Green Howards. Randall was not well because of desert sores that refused to heal, and if he let his hair down here it was probably a result of a long and frustrating campaign. 'Home,' he wrote, 'will correct all that.'

They had set out from Bone railway station in the early hours of Saturday morning, Randall wrapped in a blanket over his greatcoat and bunking with Stewart Davies. Progress was slow and it was well and truly daylight when they reached Mondovi, only 20 miles away. They passed Guelma where Randall had been on a scheme when he first got his patrol and stopped frequently to take on water. People were buying oranges at these halts, and by the time they reached Khroub south of Constantine, Randall was already wearing fur-lined boots, gloves and helmet. The compartment was partitioned with a gangway down one side, with benches for seating. This was uncomfortable but a positive luxury when compared with the *men* of Phantom, who were crammed 20 to a cattle truck. Because of the overcrowding, of course, they were probably warmer than their officers. Randall ended up trying to sleep on the hard boards of the floor at two in the morning to keep out of the draught.

The next day, again early in the morning, they rattled out of Khroub station, leaving their baggage wagon and the cooks behind. Randall had the remains of a hamper from the previous day but the men had no food until the afternoon. They crossed the flat plain dotted with Arab villages and passed the aerodrome at Talergma with its memories of parachute jumps. At Setif, the baggage wagon caught up and the men at last had hot food, improving morale enormously. Randall lived every schoolboy's dream and rode for a while in the locomotive cab with Percy Pennant. It was cold again that night.

They picked up speed on the next leg of the journey because they were in Maison Carée by six in the morning and saw the magnificent snow-capped Atlas mountains in the distance. Here they unloaded their gear and marched the six miles to No. 1 Transit Camp near the race course. They piled into tents, and Randall had his first hot shower in six months. Then he was back in Algiers 'wandering about in search of I don't know what'. The temporary membership card of the Officers' Club is among his papers. He ended up in the Atlantic Hotel 'to study form' with Bill Adams and Robert Harcourt, when who should turn up but Mimi, Randall's 'little friend' from his early days in the area. Harcourt became boorish, however, and the girl left soon afterwards. To fill time, Randall and Adams went to see Jimmy Cagney in *Yankee Doodle Dandy* at a cinema. Were they, as the film's tag line urged, 'Ready to laugh, to sing, to shout!'? Probably not; the exhaustion of the travelling hit them both now and they were glad to collapse into their tents.

The rain was torrential in the early hours, to the extent that one side of the tent collapsed completely, and Randall and his tentmates decamped to the Grandstand. It was hardly comfortable but at least it was dry. The food was good and hot water plentiful, so life was starting to look up. When the rain eventually stopped, the sun lit the bay with its waiting ships, and Randall watched the fine Arab horses being exercised each morning on the course. The *Maidstone* had gone by this time, so there was no chance of remaking the acquaintance of 'Bertie' Pizey. Randall 'did' Algiers the next day and was supposed to meet Mimi, but, after the incident with Harcourt, he did not really know how to face her. Included in the Randall papers here is a 5 cent note of the Bank of Algiers, with its curious blend of French and Arabic. Unlike British notes, it is dated – 16.11.1942. Then it was dinner at the Atlantic, and Randall and Davies chatted up the prettiest girl there before staggering off to the Sphinx, which impressed neither of them. This was not surprising and probably just as well. The Sphinx was, in fact, a brothel, built in a vaguely Moorish style in a side street. Girls lounged on an upstairs balcony, mostly naked, and the madam arranged 'peep shows', sex acts between them, before clients selected their girls and vanished with them into upstairs rooms. Randall and Davies were probably glad to get out.

Algiers may have been pleasant, but K Squadron just wanted to get home by now. On 25 November, it was Randall's father's birthday, and the measure of the young lieutenant's boredom is best summed up by a diary entry for the day – '. . . after a short conference on almost nothing at all . . .' he went into Jean-Bart. Here he met up with his old friends, the barmaids Fifi and Zezi, and Randall gave Fifi a present. He was struck by how much greener the place looked than when he had been there last. Most of the troops had gone too, and Jean-Bart had a seedy, rundown look about it.

The nightly ritual at the Atlantic followed, in the company of Stewart Davies and an old friend from St Lawrence College, Alan White, who was serving with an Ack-Ack battery in the area and must have had as little to do as Randall. The gorgeous girl of the previous night turned up but Randall realised that almost her sole topic of conversation was money.

That Friday, the news of embarkation finally came through and Randall had various goodbyes to say. He had a long chat with Pat O'Neill and other WRENs, and he promised to ring her mother in Ireland when he got back to let her know her girl was well. He had dinner with Jimmy of the Welsh Guards serving in the 6th Armoured Division and met Mimi at the Oasis later. He promised to see her tomorrow but knew there was little chance of that.

Algiers, as John Randall prepared to leave it for the last time, was a curious mix. As part of the colonial life that was soon to disappear for ever, its shops were lovely and very expensive, especially in the Rue Michelet. The clubs and cinemas were dives, however, and there was the sense that, once the British had gone, the desert would somehow take over. Among the Randall papers is a menu for the Officers' Club dated 9 December. It is a little reminder of the old England, the one J.B. Priestley wrote of in the '30s, of castles and cottages, thatch and old-fashioned values. It seems oddly out of place in a French colony in North Africa in what had recently been a war zone. Breakfast offered a compote of mixed fruit, oatmeal porridge and broiled grayling or 'pale' bacon and egg, with rolls, Bath buns, preserves, tea or coffee. Luncheon (the all-important 'eon' still survived) was potage garbure with braised sugar cured ham au jus, tomato, beans and jacket or boiled potatoes. A cold alternative was pressed beef, Leicester brawn, pepper and beetroot salad followed by apple pie or cheese. Dinner was Consommé brunoise with supreme of codling-duglere or fore and hind quarters of lamb, complete with mint sauce, garden peas and browned or boiled potatoes. Lemon pudding ended the night.

Having managed to get himself a new battledress, Randall was packing the next day and there was an 'end of term' feel about the place. He was proud to see that Phantom looked the smartest unit on the parade ground and off they marched. There was a delay at midday because 'the stupid idiot' [Demetriadi?] had not checked where the embarkation point was and everybody had to march back three miles because they had missed their objective – the Quay Falaise where the troopship SS *Samaria* was waiting to take them home. There was always a jockeying for position on board troopships, and Phantom should have gone on first. Because they were half an hour late, the Parachute Brigade got the best berths. The *Samaria* was a ship of Cunard's White Star Line, built in 1920, and was a regular crosser of the Atlantic in the heyday of the ocean liner in the '30s. In common with many other cruise ships, she had been commandeered as a troop carrier on the outbreak of war. Her sister ship the *Scythia* was sailing with her along with the *Frank* and the *Monarch of Bermuda*.

For all that opposition in North Africa was over, there was still a war on. Italy was a battleground by now, and of course the rest of Europe was still firmly occupied by the Germans. The only relative safety for ships at sea lay in the convoy system with a navy escort.

Randall was sharing a tiny cabin with Peter Vickery and four others, a tighter fit, in fact, than on the journey out. This hardly mattered; everyone was going home at last and the mood was buoyant. Randall had his first hot bath in months and he was delighted to see Julian Fane at dinner. The evening was all polished silver and glass, in the company of Hoskyns, Pennant and Laurie. The food was good, if in short supply, and Randall was asleep as his head touched the pillow.

Early next morning, after a bit of a scrum to get to the bathroom, Randall watched the bay, full of ships unloading mail. He wondered what Mimi was up to and realised that this part of his life was over. He could see Jean-Bart and Cap Matifou in the distance and he was able to drink in this marvellous view for another day and a half before the ship sailed. Then it was gang planks away and hawsers flying into the water. A little tug pulled the 20,000-tonne liner out through the harbour entrance, watched by the 'hands-in-trousers' men that every port has. It took a while for the convoy to position itself, and by this time Percy Pennant was in the sick bay with jaundice. He was lucky he recovered as quickly as he did. As they steamed away under a cloud of barrage balloons, Randall said goodbye finally to Jean-Bart and a Wellington of Coastal Command circled overhead.

The convoy swung east first of all, to pick up the escort ships of the navy, which made a wonderful sight. The destroyers, sleek and grey, sliced through the blue of the Mediterranean, crossing the bows and sterns of the sluggish troop carriers until the whole convoy was heading due west at a speed of 12 knots. The ship's steward estimated their time of arrival as the following Tuesday, and Randall sat writing his diary in his cabin as the conference room was too hot, with the fan going full pelt.

They were a mixed bag on board. The Paras were particularly scruffy, and Vickery, Laurie and Pennant were flaunting their Africa stars on their battledress. Randall was in no hurry to wear his. He wandered on deck that first night in a warm breeze, the stars bright overhead. '*Per ardua et astra*' or, as his mother would say, 'Hitch your wagon to a star.'

Off Oran the next day, they were joined by other ships making a large convoy of 20 vessels. There was boat drill in the morning and a smoke screen was carried out later. This was standard practice to confuse enemy warships; a sort of instant fog was created, behind which a vulnerable vessel could escape. Dirty black smoke belched forth from every ship and hung over the decks for a while before the wind dispersed it. Randall was on 'blackout' duty that evening. In wartime, ships did not travel with their usual lights because of the target they made for enemy aircraft. Although the use of cigarette lighters to signal to raiders 20,000 feet up has become one of the standard myth-jokes of the Second World War, smoking on board was dangerous in various parts of the ship and the blackout officer's job was to catch the culprits. As there weren't any, Randall chatted to the crew until bedtime. Then he had to fight his way through the cluttered chaos of his cabin.

That night, they passed the narrows of the Straits of Gibraltar and early in the morning Randall got his last glimpse of Africa, 'rather splendid in the pink light of dawn'. Nobody was that sad to see it go, however, because the Atlantic promised home and new challenges after that. Randall moved cabins, and the *Samaria* changed position to the end of the convoy. He was glad to be away from the rather boring Peter Vickery and noticed the different colour of the sea and the rising swell as they steamed west.

They were still going west on 2 December and the sea was becoming more choppy. The *Samaria* was a 'sturdy old tub' and took it all in her stride. The soldiers had no idea where they were and some of them were convinced they would hit America soon. Randall's bunk was comfortable enough, but he longed, as they all did, for his own bed again. He had a cold by now and was dosing himself with aspirin and Scotch. The rumour was that they were about 400 miles south of Newfoundland and at last were sailing north. It was Randall's mother's birthday in five days' time and she had no idea he was on his way home. He read, he walked on deck, he sang, both alone and in a duet with Stewart Davies. Ireland, they estimated, was about 600 miles away.

For men unused to the sea, having to travel the long way round and approach Britain from the west for safety, those days seemed interminable. The destination port was Liverpool, the weather good and the sea surprisingly calm for December. They all speculated and wondered how much longer it could last, John Hoskyns in his clear thinking, standing out in the crowd. On the Sunday, Randall had a shave and haircut and felt positively shorn afterwards: 'Damn the fellow; he cut most of it off.' He finished *Augustus* by John Bream, which he enjoyed enormously, and the talk now was of the Mersey as everyone's favourite river.

At mid-morning on 8 December, they finally sighted land. It

was far away and indistinct but it was 'home'. The weather worsened in the afternoon but no one noticed. There was a sense of euphoria that Randall could not describe. As dark fell, he was on 'blackout' duty for the last time and could see the lights on the distant shore winking in the darkness. This was the Isle of Man and the convoy expected to reach the Mersey by two in the morning. Randall was in charge of No. 1 Group for disembarkation purposes, and the noise reached a deafening crescendo as the moment neared, the Para boys playing cards and cracking old jokes, which everybody roared at, although they had heard them all a hundred times before.

On the last night on board, Randall was tucked up in his bed, hemmed in all round with kit. His trousers were creasing nicely under his mattress and his brass was polished.[2]

'Tomorrow,' he wrote as the last entry in this particular diary, 'I hope to see England and, more than that, I hope to set foot on its soil.'

John Randall does not record Christmas 1943, but he refers back to it as a sort of PS on the opening page of his new diary for 1944, this one, like his scrapbook, written in the ubiquitous buff-coloured exercise books with the royal monogram, the title S.O. Book 135 and 'Supplied for the Public Service'. Various display cases in London's Imperial War Museum show that a number of Commando and special forces units used them in the same way. This one has a black and white photograph of Randall with the ribbon of the North Africa Star beneath it and the letterhead of a unit he was to join before too long – the flaming/winged dagger and Who Dares Wins motto of the Special Air Service Regiment – the already legendary SAS.

Of course, in the January of 1944 all that still lay ahead. The Blitz as we understand it, of nightly raids that caused the sirens to wail and cities to collapse into rubble, was over. It would be six months before an altogether more terrifying sound would be heard in the skies over Britain, the spluttering and sudden silence of the V weapons called Doodlebugs. Britain was still a war zone. There were bomb craters everywhere, especially in John Randall's London. There were sandbags outside every major and minor public building. Windows were still cross hatched with tape designed to minimise the threat of flying glass. The blackout was still strictly observed, and ARP wardens still annoyed people by emulating Hitler and checking on lights that were unauthorised. Rationing was still in full swing, with family coupons not going nearly far enough and queues of housewives forming daily to whisper to the harassed grocer 'A U C?' (Anything Under the Counter?). The black market flourished, and on leave Randall must have walked past scores of spivs standing furtively on street corners, hoping to catch the unwary with goods made illicit by the paranoia of the time.

Randall had been away for ten months and, after the endless grime of North Africa, everything at home seemed new and clean and fresh. In common with most men returning home, he caught a cold in the freezing January temperatures. His mother, of course, was overjoyed to see him, and Grandy and Alfred Friend were still at Donnington Manor and all was right with the world. Because there was a war on, not everybody was still at Sevenoaks. The forces had moved several of Randall's age group to all parts of the world and there were some he would never see again. The Ashton boys and the Lott family's eldest were all killed on the same day in Tunisia. But at Donnington the food was good, and London, scarred and bombed though it was, was as bright and gay as ever, 'although one could not help noticing the very large number of Americans'.

Traditionally, the first 'Yank' to set foot on British soil was Private First Class Milburn H. Henke from Hutchison, Minnesota. In fact, 500 of his comrades of the 34th US Infantry were already in the camp at Belfast before the media arrived to take Henke's photograph. *The Times* could not help pointing out that Henke's father was a naturalised German. This does not take into account, of course, the number of Americans who had joined the Eagle

Squadron with the RAF even before the United States had come into the war. As the satirical magazine *Punch* put it:

> Dear Old England's not the same,
> The dread invasion, well it came.
> But no, it's not the beastly Hun,
> The goddamned Yankee army's come.

By the spring of 1944, there were one and a half million Americans in Britain. Convoys of trucks and jeeps rattled over winding English roads designed for horses and carts. B17 Flying Fortresses and even more massive B24 Liberators shook windows as they flew overhead from a dozen US airbases. More than 1,100 cities, towns and villages were home to the invasion, occupying 100,000 buildings from evacuated schools to country houses, aircraft hangars, Nissen and Quonset huts and bell tents.

London was inevitably a magnet for these men, whether they were city slickers from the ghettoes of New York or farm boys from Iowa. In 1942, a British private earned 14 shillings a week;[3] a GI[4] £3 8s 9d. The Americans also had seemingly limitless amounts of PX (Post Exchange) goods like candy, tinned meat and fruit and nylons. As a result, girls, both camp followers and the 'good-time' variety, were easily lured by the suaver cut of the Yank uniform. One contemporary joke ran: 'Did you hear about the new Utility knickers? One Yank and they're off!' The hub of American activity was the cafe-bar of Rainbow Corner at Piccadilly Circus. While the famous Eros statue was shrouded in protective boarding, thousands of GIs cruised the area, hooking up with 'Piccadilly Commandos' and 'Park Rangers', prostitutes who could earn a fortune in a single night.[5] Colonel Moroney, from Texas, was in charge of the Snowdrops, the US Army's Military Police, who hurtled round Soho in jeeps and who did not hesitate to draw their batons and pistols to keep or restore order in rowdy situations.

This was all part of the gay London to which John Randall

referred. And, of course, there were Poles, Australians, New Zealanders, Canadians and the Free French to add to the mix. It was good to see the familiar old regimental and divisional signs again – the HD of the 51st Highland Division, for example – and the large number of men wearing the Africa Star. Hugh Cuming was enjoying life once again with the 2nd Battalion the Seaforth Highlanders and James Ritchie, now with a Military Cross and bar, was back with the Gordons.

A New Year's party at High Wycombe gave Randall a chance to see Doodles Rayment again, and he met her brother and a lieutenant in the Tank Corps, John Rodney. One of the more colourful guests was 'Cobber', an RAF 'type' whom Randall described as a madman. He had been shot down in the Battle of Britain and evidently crash-landed or parachuted into France because he had only just returned, having escaped from a prisoner of war camp. There was plenty of music, plenty of food and drink and, about the witching hour, as the old year turned, Randall and Doodles' sister Moya put on fancy dress and made fools of themselves.

The plan, for that first day of 1944, was to attend Dugan Webb's wedding in London, but Dopey, the Rayments' dog, had been run over while most of the guests were still in their pyjamas and some of the men buried him. So they stayed put, drinking champagne and talking to Rodney and the Ellises who had made up numbers at the party. Randall's mother was a little upset that her boy seemed not to want to go home. Nobody could imagine that this leave would last for ever and who knew where Randall would be sent next.

Sunday in wartime was not perhaps the best time to travel but Randall had to get back to Phantom HQ in Richmond. He went with the Johns Rayment and Rodney but found he had missed the last train and had to walk from Turnham Green. To make matters worse, the wail of an air-raid siren sounded and the sky over London was bright with searchlights as the Ack-Ack batteries opened up. To cap it all, when he arrived in the early hours, he was told he was not required until the next day. Randall went to Donnington and kissed and made up with his mother. He knew how to bring her round and felt a little ashamed that he had put partying before her.

But, of course, there was a war on, and on 4 January an officers' course started at HQ. A lot of the old Phantom crowd were back: Roddy Pannell from Belfast; Michael Millar from the King's Own Yorkshire Light Infantry; and George Dully, who was to command Randall's own squadron, the RHQ. The course was run by John Wrightson from the Durham Light Infantry, who was now a major. The most frequent instructors were John Jackson of the Intelligence Corps, Maurice Macmillan from the Royal Artillery and Douglas Baker from the North Somerset Yeomanry. Wrightson had something of a gloomy reputation in Phantom. He had given regular lectures before on the general situation of the war a year earlier, when 'roll up the map of Europe' seemed to sum up his pessimistic predictions. Jackson had been with 'Hoppy' Hopkinson virtually from the beginning. Macmillan, of course, was the son of Harold, the future Prime Minister and heir to the publishing house of the same name. He had been commissioned in the Sussex Yeomanry on the outbreak of war. 'Swanny' Baker took his nickname from the 8th Army word 'swanning', which he used frequently, and was an excellent signals man.

The course was punctuated by visits at ten-thirty to Miss Marigold's cafe and a dash for the London trains at half past four. Lunchtime in the Mess was a great opportunity for leg-pulls, the leading 'puller' being 'Swanny' Baker. On Sunday 9th, Randall had a drink with the lads as usual at the Roebuck, a traditional pub run by 'Old Andrew', and he met Bunny Steele at Grosvenor House. He was delighted to find that, although engaged, she was still a great friend and very kind. Her father, a major, was almost fatherly to young Randall. The lieutenant did not let the grass grow under his feet in the female stakes either. He arranged to have dinner with a Russian girl, Sylvia Schweppe, and was told that the ravishing Kathleen de Villiers, the adopted daughter of

Field Marshal Smuts, would be there too. That was the day that Randall missed out on the Candle of Friendship ritual, a ceremony in which a candle of memory was lit on behalf of fellow officers killed or missing. He describes it as an 'ordeal' and, as a morale-booster among men who might soon be added to the list, it was perhaps not the best of ideas.

'Kay' de Villiers turned out to be a lot of fun at the dinner party the next day and totally unspoilt, despite the fact that she knew *everyone* in high places. Jan Christiaan Smuts was the Prime Minister of South Africa, and because of his long military experience (he had fought in the Boer War and the Great War) he was attached to Churchill's War Cabinet. He had been made a field marshal two years earlier and had known Churchill in the Great War. Typical of the man and his times, he supported segregation in his South African homeland five years before it became the established policy of apartheid. Untypical of a fighting man, he had also supported Chamberlain's appeasement in the '30s. He had six children of his own. Randall walked with Kay to Hyde Park Corner via Marble Arch and said goodnight at the Underground. He then faced an exhausting walk up Richmond Hill, which the guide books, then as now, describe as gentle, at half past midnight. Doodles was very fond of Randall but could not say so in words, only in writing. She was on duty at Amersham Hospital and Randall phoned her most evenings.

On the 12th, he should have gone to a cocktail party at Joan Street's parents' home – they were Admiral Sir Francis and Lady Tottenham – but, in the end, he decided to stay in Richmond and down a few pints of the more plebeian beer. Randall's diary is full of cuttings from various magazines and newspapers. On this date, there is a photograph of the wedding of Lt. Robert Maunsell, a Phantom officer from the Royal Signals, to Marie Cordasco of Welbeck Court. Marriages in wartime were always fraught because of the risk of grooms – and, indeed, brides – being whisked away on active service. Even material for wedding dresses was difficult to come by, and grooms in the service got away with wearing khaki with the Sam Browne belt.

Randall had moved by this time to 122 Hillbrow Flats, very much warmer than the vast and rather gloomy Pembroke Lodge. He met a nurse, Pamela Eastell, who was great fun and lived near RHQ. He played his first game of rugger for months for Rosslyn Park and had a few drinks at the Roebuck with Pam and Stewart Davies. Winston Churchill once told the story of a fellow officer in the 4th Hussars in the 1890s who was dumped in a water trough by his comrades because he did not sound his aitches. Nothing much had changed in half a century; although Randall found Davies a good natural chap and bright and counted him among his best friends, he was 'rather handicapped in the regiment by his social status which was rather given away by an unfortunate voice'. Randall had dinner at the Bagatelle and the Astor with a new girl, Eileen Mitchell. He was now burning the candle at both ends, socialising most nights, but with an exam hanging over him at the end of his course.

Saturday seems to have been one long party. Phantom officers Julian Fane and Geoffrey Lucas were at the Steeles' cocktail party, before going on somewhere else, and Randall took Kay de Villiers to Ciro's. After dancing until they dropped, the dashing lieutenant took the girl home, then got back to Bernard Baron's club in Kensington where he spent what was left of the night. He saw Doodles the next day. The following Tuesday, he took his mother and Alfred Friend to the Berkeley,[6] and ran into John Rayment and his girlfriend, with whom Randall flirted outrageously, rather to Rayment's disgust.

There was disappointment now. Instead of being posted to B Squadron, which in a few weeks' time would be incorporated into the plans for Operation Overlord, the Allied invasion of Europe, Randall, along with Davies and John Cooke from the Foresters, were assigned to train new arrivals to the regiment. 'Oh what a dreary game.'

Doodles provided distractions, however. They dined at the Bagatelle, and Randall stayed in town at the Park Lane Hotel before taking the girl to watch him play rugger at Richmond once the morning's Phantom session was over. Training went well; Randall had his own patrol with Sergeant Ridout as his NCO. The men had served together in Tunisia, but Randall realised he was not really cut out for this sort of work. Promotions were happening to his old G Squadron comrades – Dugan Webb, Michael Millar, Roger Brunsdon, Roddy Pannell and John Sadoine were all captains by now. On Saturday, 5 February, Randall played rugger against 21 Army Group, a unit that was to become famous in the months ahead.

There was another hectic social evening on the Tuesday when Randall went out on the town with Julian Fane, to the Berkeley (which was full), to the Lansdowne and to the 400 Club, with pretty girls on their arms, of course. The 400 in Leicester Square, which was to become a favourite haunt of Princess Margaret after the war, was described by one London newspaper as 'the night-time headquarters of society'. There was an 18-piece orchestra that never played too loudly to drown conversation and the dancing rarely ended before four in the morning. Anyone there after that was offered breakfast at a guinea a head. Blackout duty the next day with Sergeant Brett as orderly gave Randall a chance to write a few letters, and he had a drink with 'Old Andrew' at the Roebuck.

It was something of a red letter day on the 12th when Randall was selected to play rugger for London District against St Mary's Hospital. The programme is still among his papers. Kick-off was at 3 p.m., and his mother and Doodles were there to see him in action on the right wing. Just to remind everybody that there was a war on, the air-raid shelters could be found just behind the grandstand. This was the most serious and 'professional' game Randall had played. Rugby football was very much an amateur sport in those days, but certain clubs had a very high reputation and St Mary's was one of the best in the country. Randall's team lost but he felt he had played well.

A Home Guard dinner held at Richmond on the 19th was not as impressive as the Algiers Officers' Club and reflected the shortages of wartime Britain. There were hors d'oeuvres, soup, veal cutlets with peas, spaghetti and sauté potatoes, followed by apple tart and custard. The food situation during the war was very much a class thing. Food Control Committees operated under the Ministry of Food, which filled magazines and newspapers with health advice. Most foodstuffs were rationed and supplies limited, especially early in the war, because of the risk to the merchant ship convoys that actually imported the stuff. People were encouraged to grow their own vegetables and make Woolton pies, named after Lord Woolton – 'Uncle Fred' – of the Food Committee. These contained carrots and parsnips, which became regular fare among people who in some cases had never seen them before. Cranky alternatives were occasionally on offer – horsemeat (which the French had always eaten), sheep's heads, eels, cormorant eggs. Under the lend-lease programme by which America supplied food before Pearl Harbor, tins of purported meat arrived with unlikely names. Spam is the one that caught on, but there were also Tang, Mor and Prem, if you were particularly unlucky.

But if a man was in the know, it was almost business as usual. The leading pathologists of the day, Keith Simpson, Francis Camps and Donald Teare, would spend happy evenings at L'Etoile in Charlotte Street, Soho, where all sorts of goodies were obtainable at a price.

The Home Guard dinner was great fun, Randall and Davies being plied with beer and told tall tales of the Great War by the men of 'Dad's Army'. Randall was impressed. In the beginning, the Local Defence Volunteers were a 'Fred Karno'[7] outfit, and the idea of a local farmer standing ready with his shotgun against the panzers of the Wehrmacht was laughable. By 1943, however, now properly equipped and armed, the Home Guard, Randall believed, was 'on a par with the rest of the army'.

The following Sunday, a course began, which Randall describes as the best he had been on since he joined up. Brother officers Charles 'Scottie' McDevitt and Roy Burgess from the Signals joined him, along with Sergeant Tift, Lance Corporals Rumble and Fisher and riflemen Ralli and Reynolds. McDevitt had come up from the ranks and his 'particularly intricate form of Scots dialect'[8] would become particularly useful in France months later. The course was all about wireless, and when they arrived at Henley they were confronted with radio masts and aerials and a whole welter of wiring that Randall had never seen before. The unit was also confronted with a bevy of girls from FANY (First Aid Nursing Yeomanry), and Randall recorded in his diary: 'Evidently they do radio as well!' It was difficult to concentrate on Morse code work with distractions like that but he and McDevitt worked out 'the form' and he had a most enjoyable 24th birthday, despite having to get the 'cinderellas' back to their quarters by ten thirty. They played hockey against the girls the next day and Randall paired off with 'Ricky' Beard. McDevitt teamed up with Judy, but Roy Burgess was rather dull and his partner, Elizabeth, thought so too. The men paired off too and behaved well, 'no doubt,' as Randall wrote, 'inspired by their officers' good example'.

The example was not so good on Friday night because an officer named Beresford of the Signals smuggled one of the FANYs, Bridget Ross, into the Mess – strictly against the rules, of course. They all talked into the early hours, except Beresford who got annoyed with all the attention Bridget was getting from the others and went to bed.

There were French officers at Fawley Court on the wireless/ Morse course, and one of them, Didier Hoffmann, gave Randall his French Paratroop badge, white wings and parachute with the cross of Lorraine on a black field. It is still among his papers. The girls, most of whom were about 18, went on their leave the next weekend, and after that the news came through that they were to be sent to Dunbar in Scotland. Randall was 'spud bashing' and went to a Leap Year dance on the last day of February in Henley. He had a little too much to drink, but Bridget Ross surpassed the FANY reputation by providing aspirin and a hot water bottle. At the next – and farewell – dance, Ricky Beard was surrounded by Frenchmen making suggestive comments and the dashing lieutenant came to her rescue, hurtling her around the room in an eightsome reel. Farewells were hard the next day. Randall and Ricky kissed, 'Scottie' McDevitt was the life and soul, and the diary laments the fact that Randall was not born neuter!

Randall's next rugger game was against Cambridge University and this time two of the opposing team were internationals. He scored a try in the corner within the first five minutes, just managing to stay off the touch line. He was ready to drop by the end and went to the Berkeley with his mother, Alfred and Doodles afterwards in what had by now become something of a ritual. Among the Randall papers is a poem, written by the FANY girls who signed themselves D.M., W.T., A.M.H. It refers to a muddy game of hockey they had played against the men when they had washed his hockey jersey and sent it back to him wrapped in a mauve ribbon:

Dear G.P.
Herein returns a glorious shirt,
Scrubbed, washed and free from dirt
That now a glamorous Phantom may,
If he really cares to say,
That a shirt he wears at last
Freed from all its previous past!
To begin its life anew
On india rubber – pink or blue.
We hope the owner when he wears
The shirt, will think of copious tears
The washerwomen must have shed,
When they should have been in bed.
And so, I fear, our brains are worn,
We cannot do as we had sworn
To lighten so this bounteous day
And make it spotless, glad and gay.

However, by the time he received this, the 'glamorous Phantom' was going north. To join the SAS.

8

Out of Africa

While John Randall was still in Tunisia, two rather unconventional officers had turned up in the Phantom Mess one night. They were very 'get up and go', Randall remembers, and they were members of a unit calling themselves the SAS. They challenged the Phantom boys to take part in their training course. Out of this came the parachute training and Lieutenant John Randall, Royal Artillery, K Squadron GHQ Liaison Regiment, was now able to wear parachute wings on his battledress jacket. The next step, undertaken by very few, was to join the 1st Special Air Service itself.

The unit was even more shadowy and 'hush-hush' than Phantom and owed its inception to the seismic blow that was Dunkirk. The siege mentality, which saw John Randall cooling his heels in G Squadron in Northern Ireland and everybody bracing themselves for the Battle of Britain, got men thinking. There was a shortage of men and the notion was born of a small group of the elite, trained in night-fighting and sabotage work, that could deliver a disrupting blow to the enemy out of all proportion to their size. There were no units of this kind in either the Wehrmacht or the Italian army, but the British had seen examples of it firsthand. The Spanish guerrillas in the Peninsular War (1808–14), although unreliable because they fought independently of Wellington's forces, created havoc among the French communication systems. Armed civilians would ambush patrols and pick off stragglers from marching columns, cutting the throats of dawdlers, hacking off their penises and stuffing them in their mouths. Even though this kind of savage brutality had gone by 1940, the idea of hit and run tactics had an appeal to the more enlightened generals like Wavell and Montgomery,[1] and, perhaps just as importantly, to Winston Churchill.

The British had first come across the word 'commando' in the Boer War. Spelled with a 'k', it meant a militia unit used against the British Army. These men were highly mobile, mounted on sure-footed ponies and well armed, and they knew the country. It took the vast resources of the British Empire three years to beat them. T.E. Lawrence, a maverick officer if ever there was one, used the notion of armed 'civilian' raids when he took the Turkish-held port of Aqaba with Bedouin forces in 1917.

Out of this history came Special Services battalions raised in the Norway campaign. All too often they were wrongly used, merely thrown into conventional warfare to make up the numbers as shock assault troops. It did not help that such units were referred to as SS in official communications! One of these units was No. 8 Commando, which came to be known as Layforce, after its colonel, Robert Laycock of the Royal Horse Guards. Laycock was typical of the officers who made up John Randall's comrades during the war. He believed, as Michael Asher says, 'in going to war among friends'[2] and recruited many of his officers over gin-and-tonics in White's Bar in Cairo. In many ways, the whole commando set-up among the officers was an amateur 'gung-ho' spirit born of the public schools. It was still, in 1940, about 'playing up, playing up and playing the game'.[3]

Layforce was sent to the Middle East in February 1941 to invade Rhodes and generally carry out behind-the-scenes undercover operations on Italian positions, both in the Mediterranean islands and on the North African mainland. Two high-profile officers with Laycock were Randolph Churchill, son of the Prime Minister, whom John Randall would push out of a plane some months later, and Evelyn Waugh, perhaps the least likely Commando of all time, who was already a celebrated novelist and journalist. He wrote home to his wife about a third officer in the unit, David Stirling. He was, Waugh said, 'a gentleman obsessed by the pleasures of chance. He effectively wrecked Ludo as a game of skill[4] and honour. We now race clockwork motor-cars.'[5]

Although he was too modest to say it years later, David Stirling created the SAS. A keen sportsman and would-be mountaineer, the lanky Scot (he was 6 ft 5in.) had been to Ampleforth and Trinity College, Cambridge, where he read Architecture. He preferred attendance at the Newmarket races, however, to solid academe, and tried the Bohemian life of an artist in Paris. He was in the Rocky Mountains training for an assault on Everest when war broke out and he hurried home to join his brothers in the Scots Guards. Regimental life bored Stirling, rather as it had bored Randall in the Artillery, and so he joined No. 8 Commando.

As we have seen, the arrival of Rommel and the Afrika Korps reversed the military situation in the desert, and No. 8 ended up carrying out a series of ineffectual raids along the coast; ineffectual because the rough seas ruined them or the enemy spotted the assaults before they were ready. Stirling was 24 by this time and bored again by the lack of actual action. The image we have today of the SAS is of tough, rather thuggish young men in black camouflage gear, but Stirling, like Randall, was a gentleman, softly spoken and well liked by fellow officers and men. He gave off a languid air that earned him the nickname 'the giant sloth' and let his contempt for staff officers show, referring to them as 'fossilised shit'.

It was the longing for adventure that nearly killed Stirling. He and another officer of No. 8 Commando, John 'Jock' Lewes of the Welsh Guards, came across some parachutes that were on their way to India. Neither man had jumped before but they got permission from Laycock to have a go. They flew in a Vickers

Valentia, which was a transport biplane, with four other Guardsmen. This was the first time that a serving officer of the army had carried out a parachute drop and the whole thing was amateur in the extreme. Static lines were fitted to the seats in the Valentia's fuselage and it was they that opened the chutes on the way down. Stirling's lines got caught on the tail section and two panels of his chute were torn off as a result. Gravity did the rest and the giant sloth hurtled past all the others who were floating down gracefully. He lost the use of both legs in the landing and was blind for nearly an hour. He spent the next two months in the Scottish Military Hospital in Alexandria.

While Stirling was convalescing, Laycock wrote to the Chief of the General Staff, Major-General Arthur Smith, complaining about the inactivity of his Commandos: 'Unless we are actively employed soon I anticipate a serious falling off in morale which was at one time second to none.'[6] One of the most celebrated pastiches of the war was probably written by one of the Layforce on the mess deck of a transport in this context: 'Never in the history of human endeavour have so few been b-----d about by so many.'[7] The upshot was that Layforce was disbanded; there was simply no relevant Commando work to be done.

Stuck in bed with a germ of an idea, Stirling dashed off a memo to the newly appointed Claude Auchinleck as commander-in-chief Middle East. It is difficult to believe today that a second lieutenant, the lowest of the low among the commissioned ranks, should have the audacity to tell generals how to fight a war.[8] There were proper channels for such things, but all those would have taken Stirling through the various layers of 'fossilised shit' he despised, at any one of which his ideas would languish in somebody's in-tray and quietly disappear. And in 1941 there was no time for that. His *Case for the retention of a limited number of special service troops, for employment as parachutists* recommended the need for surprise and for raids to be carried out by highly trained groups of five men.[9] The larger forces – up to 200 – used up to this point by Layforce were simply too large and attracted too much enemy attention. A force of 200, subdivided in this way, could hit 30 different objectives, for example airfields, simultaneously, with highly damaging results to the enemy. Stirling also believed that such a force should operate independently of existing units, reporting directly to the commander-in-chief. Although he was undoubtedly right about this, it was the origin of the 'army within the army' concept that made the SAS unpopular in certain quarters.

Still limping from his parachute jump, Stirling went to GHQ but did not have the relevant pass for admission and had to nip in through some broken wire behind the building. He gave the memo to General Neil Ritchie, Auchinleck's Deputy Chief of Staff (it helped that his man shot grouse before the war with Stirling's father) and, three days later, 'the Auk' sent for Stirling and gave the new unit the green light.

All the sloth had to do now was to put the 'band of brothers' together and train them. They were recruited largely from Layforce and were given the title L Detachment of the Special Air Service Brigade. There was no such brigade in the British Army; the title had been devised by another Commando, Brigadier Dudley Clarke, to sow as much confusion as possible, should the enemy intercept the relevant orders relating to them. *So* confusing and *so* hush-hush was Stirling's outfit that, when Fraser McLuskey joined the SAS as padre on the same day that John Randall joined, he assumed it had something to do with a civilian airline company! The aim was to operate in conjunction with the Long Range Desert Group (LRDG) by jumping behind enemy lines two days before the November assault by the 8th Army. L Detachment was to hit airfields in the Gazala and Timimi area, reducing the air capability of the Italians when the ground offensive began.

The LRDG soon became indistinguishable from the SAS, although they had been in the Libyan desert since before the war. Under Major R.A. Bagnold, they had been organised as a reconnaissance unit in June 1940 to gather information from behind enemy lines. They drove 30 cwt Chevrolet trucks, wore shorts, beards and Arab *shemaghs*, which would no doubt have caused apoplexy among the 'fossilised shit', had they known.

Based at Kabrit on the edge of Great Bitter Lake, 98 miles east of Cairo, Stirling began to put L Detachment together. Jock Lewes was a given. The man was in bed with the same desert sores that John Randall suffered from two years later and he was under siege at Tobruk. Stirling reached him by sea and took him back to Kabrit. A great deal of mythology surrounds Stirling's next choice, the huge Irish rugby international Blair Mayne, known to all and sundry, but never to his face, as 'Paddy'. The man who would become a legend and John Randall's commanding officer had been recommended to Stirling by Laycock as a man of action like no other. He had impressed everybody with No. 11 Commando against Vichy French forces at the Litani River in Syria, but he had a reputation as a hot-head away from the battlefield too. He had threatened a nightclub owner in Cairo over a bar bill, pointing his revolver at him. He had even squared up to his commanding officer, Geoffrey Keyes, Director of Combined Operations.[10] Legend has it that Mayne was in the glasshouse as a result of this when Stirling found him, but that was just part of the Paddy myth. In fact, he was kicking his heels, waiting to see if his request to teach guerrilla warfare to the Chinese in their war against Japan would be accepted. Accounts differ as to how responsive Mayne was to Stirling's offer. Some say he leapt at the chance; others that he had to be persuaded because of Stirling's reputation for laziness.

Stirling now needed 60 Other Ranks to make up the force and he asked for volunteers from among the Scots Guards. These men became the 'Originals', and they would make their names in dangerous cover operations over the next four years. Stirling referred to them later as 'that bag of vagabonds', in a totally affectionate way. They were men who were unconventional and who became committed to the idea of L Detachment, and later the 1 SAS Regiment, perhaps because it offered something more than the endless drill of conventional warfare. Johnny Cooper, at

19, was the youngest, one of the few with a middle-class background. At the other end of the age range was Bob Lilley, married and nearly 40. Dave Kershaw had served as a volunteer with the International Brigades in the Spanish Civil War. Bob Bennett was a Cockney rebel, anxious to escape the monotony of life in the Grenadier Guards. Pat Riley, who was an American citizen, having moved to Wisconsin with his family as a child, became the first sergeant major. Reg Seekings was a boxer from East Anglia – John Randall would see him in action with his fists at Belsen concentration camp four years later. 'Gentleman Jim' Almonds had fought at Tobruk with Riley and Jock Lewes. Jeff du Vivier was a Londoner who had worked as a hotelier before the war.

However motley this crew may have been, Stirling insisted on a smart turnout. 'There had grown up in the Commandos a tradition that to be a tough regiment it was necessary to act tough all the time . . . and they were liable to be badly dressed, ill disciplined and noisy in the streets and restaurants of Cairo. We insisted with L Detachment that toughness should be reserved entirely for the benefit of the enemy.'[11]

That all-important wartime skill, scrounging, came into play next. John Randall was very effective at this with radio and vehicle parts with Phantom, and it was often the only way to get much-needed supplies in a hurry. Tents were a priority. Kabrit was in the middle of nowhere, without bars, clubs and brothels to provide light entertainment. Reg Seekings remembered it years later as 'a desolate bloody place'. Since the nearby New Zealanders' camp had been abandoned (the original inhabitants had been killed or captured in the battle for Crete), the Quartermaster Sergeant, Gregory Ward, organised everybody to drive there and help themselves to whatever was going. They built a canteen from RAF bricks left lying about, complete with beer and snacks. Somebody hung a sign 'Stirling's Rest Camp' over the door.

They had three months in which to shape up as a fighting unit. Anyone who did not reach the required standard was RTU'd

– returned to their original unit – and that was the ultimate mark of shame and disgrace for L Detachment. The detachment was split into One and Two troops, the first led by Jock Lewes, the second by Paddy Mayne. It was Lewes who took on the vital role of parachute training and set up scaffolding towers made by Jim Almonds from which men jumped, wearing fatigues and parachute helmets. The experiment of men jumping from the back of a truck moving at 30 miles an hour was less successful. Bill Fraser damaged his shoulder and Jeff du Vivier broke his wrist. A sled fitted to a track on an incline, off which the trainee rolled, caused fewer breakages!

The first actual jump took place from an old Bristol Bombay on loan from 216 Squadron of the RAF. The first stick dropped successfully but the second was a disaster. The first two men's parachutes failed to open and both were killed. It was the same problem that had caused Stirling's accident, and it shook the detachment's confidence badly. The next day, Stirling gave each man 50 cigarettes and made the first jump himself. There were no injuries.

There was, of course, far more to it than jumping. All that did, in essence, was to get a man from the air to the ground. In order to carry out a successful Commando raid, a lot more training was required. They had to learn to know the desert, to be able to read sketchy maps and to move noiselessly, especially in the dark. They had to be crack shots, with revolvers, automatic pistols and machine guns. They had to be able – and willing – to use a Fairbairn–Sykes commando knife at close quarters, the sort of killing that was highly unusual in the Second World War.

Then there were explosives. Jock Lewes set up a laboratory-cum-workshop in a hut at the edge of the camp and made the Lewes bomb, a new device made of plastic explosive and thermite. It was ingenious because it had a fuse delay mechanism and acted as an incendiary bomb, designed to blow up enemy aircraft on the ground. Since the bomb weighed less than one pound, a Commando could carry up to thirty of these at any one time.

The PT and route marches were intensive. They swam in the Suez Canal and worked nine- or ten-hour days. They marched in heavy kit and had to time their distances, avoiding the heat of the day and conserving water. On one march, 60 miles long, Douglas Keith's boots fell apart a third of the way through; he finished it in his stockinged feet while carrying a 75 lb pack.

All this gruelling training was tested in relative safety. A dummy attack was mounted on the RAF base at Heliopolis near Cairo. It was a hundred miles out into the desert, and each man carried four water bottles, glucose sweets and three pounds of dates. They carried packs of the same weight as the Lewes bomb, travelling by night and camouflaging themselves in the sand under piles of hessian sacks during the day. Large numbers of RAF planes were found at dawn two days later with the word 'Bomb' stuck to their fuselages. The station commander was livid. Not a single member of L Detachment had been caught and the RAF had been briefed in advance that the raid was going to happen!

As always, there was a huge ideological and emotional gap between war games and the real thing. L Detachment was given a few days' leave in Cairo before going into action. The unit's peculiarity was the rather outlandish white[12] beret, which was soon replaced with beige because of its unpopularity. Pat Riley remembered 'Wearing a white beret among Australians, New Zealanders and every type of nationality brought some great wolf whistles, which were naturally not received in the right manner.'[13]

Part of the all-important identity of L Detachment was the wearing of a pair of wings, looking distinctly Egyptian, which were based on a fresco design of an ibis in the foyer of Shepheard's Hotel. One interpretation of this design is that the central 'body' between the wings was originally a scarab beetle, replaced by a parachute in 1941. Anyone who had carried out three sorties behind enemy lines had the right to transfer the wings from his battledress sleeve to his left breast. Not since the 18th century when aristocratic colonels set up their own regiments had a colonel designed a badge for his men. There were those who thought that David Stirling was getting above himself.

Operation Crusader began, as far as Stirling's men were concerned, on the night of 16 November 1941. Cunningham's 8th Army were to drive the Afrika Korps out of Cyrenaica and relieve besieged Tobruk. L Detachment was divided into five groups flown in British Bombays from 216 Squadron. Stirling had 54 men ready for the drops under Mayne, Lewis, Eoin McGonigal, Charles Bonington[14] and, of course, Stirling himself. Their target was the airfield at Timimi, west of Tobruk, and they would follow to the letter the plan that Stirling had had in his head since the beginning; land at night, hide within five miles of the aerodrome during the day, and nip in and plant the Lewes bombs at one minute to midnight on the 17th. The group was split into two sections, one approaching from the east, the other from the west. At Bagoush, the RAF put on an excellent meal for L Detachment. Jeff du Vivier read this as an attempt to take their minds off the daunting task ahead; Reg Seekings believed that the RAF saw them as a suicide squad and this was the condemned men's last hearty meal.

Then Stirling dropped his own bombshell. The weather reports were bad and a storm was coming in with winds predicted of up to 30 knots. This would blow the 54 men all over the place, making rendezvous difficult, not to mention the actual act of landing. Stirling put it to the men of his command; what did they want to do? They wanted to go ahead. Each man travelled light, in shirts and shorts with overalls to prevent snagging on the rigging lines. They carried revolvers, compasses, entrenching tool, grenades and a pack of rations – raisins, dates, cheese, sweets and chocolate.

Mayne's aircraft took off late and reached the Drop Zone first. The wind speed was already up to 25 knots and the thorny acacia bushes on the ground made landing painful. Two of his men were hurt as they fell. The containers of gear had been thrown out first but not all of these could be found and the operation was already 40 minutes behind schedule. The injured men were ordered to stay put, while the rest pressed on in what remained of the desert night. At dawn, they were six miles from the airfield and could see through their binoculars seventeen planes. They waited that day in a *wadi* (a dry river bed) and then the rain started. The *wadi* was quickly awash, and the team had to move to higher ground, making them potentially ever more visible from the airfield. Mayne tried his detonators and found that the water had ruined them; they did not work. The whole mission had to be called off and, bitterly disappointed, the men made their way south to the Rendezvous Point with the LRDG, 34 miles away from Timimi. Here they met up with other sticks who had similar tales to tell.

Lewes' group had jumped well but both Cooper and du Vivier hurt themselves on landing, du Vivier having been dragged along the rough ground 150 yards by the force of the wind. They buried their chutes and met up, but soon realised, like Mayne's party, that their equipment canisters were nowhere to be seen. They could not even find the Gazala airstrip, which was their target, and the heavens opened. It was one of the worst storms in living memory and the compasses went haywire. So exhausted was Jock Lewes that he handed command to Pat Riley, the ex-policeman from Wisconsin, who seemed to be the only one unfazed by the weather. It was bitterly cold for men in desert gear of shorts and shirts and the freezing rain stung. Every hour, they marched for 40 minutes and rested for 20. It took them 36 hours to reach the Rendezvous Point, whistling the agreed code, 'Roll Out the Barrel', as they arrived.

Stirling's stick had hit trouble too. He landed badly and knocked himself out; virtually everybody had injuries. Sergeant John Cheyne was never seen again and he was presumed killed. With men and equipment scattered and the same damp detonator problem that Mayne had encountered, Stirling was forced to call off the mission and limped to the Rendezvous. By now, it was 21 November, with the 8th Army advance well under way and without the help of L Detachment. Bonington's and McGonigal's sections had disappeared into the combined maelstrom of the storm, Ack-Ack fire and the desert. It would be three years before anyone could confirm what happened to them. Bonington's plane was shot down by an ME109 and, although all the L Detachment men landed safely, they were caught by the Italian ground forces. McGonigal was so badly injured on landing that he died the next day, and his surviving unit missed the Rendezvous and were caught near Timimi airfield. McGonigal was a close friend of Paddy Mayne, who brooded over his loss, no doubt adding to his bouts of depression and drunken violence.

Of David Stirling's 54-man mission, only 20 had returned, most of them wounded in some way. Not a single plane had been blown up; not even a shot had been fired. That first disastrous raid could have been the end of L Detachment. Over the whole period, there are many memos and reports in the official record that criticise Stirling for his lack of communication and his tendency of going it alone in an amateur way, which was astonishingly arrogant in a mere captain. He was accepted as long as he got results, but, when he did not, there was the real risk that L Detachment would follow Layforce into oblivion.

Stirling's answer was to abandon the all-too-risky parachute jumps and to be driven to within a short distance of the target area by the LRDG instead – the Desert Taxi Service, as it came to be known. The love–hate relationship that existed between the two units can be summed up by the fact that L Detachment were known briefly as the 'Parashites'. There is very little official paperwork for the early raids by Stirling and Mayne, partly because of the initial failure and partly because Stirling did not want his hands tied by officialdom. Virtually all the details have been supplied by survivors of these raids, whose testimony has been collected by historians over the years.

The first raid took place in the middle of December using the LRDG's 30 cwt Chevrolet trucks, painted pale green and pink to provide the most effective desert camouflage and armed with

Lewis machine guns. They were operating in a desert area well away from the narrow North African theatre crawling with troops, so the only real danger came from the air. It was necessary to travel relatively slowly to avoid sending up too much dust, which would be visible to marauding Italian and German fighters.[15] This 8 December attack on airfields at Sirte was a brilliant success, not only proving that Stirling's concept had been right all along, but also vindicating his rather unorthodox methods. Mayne's patrol blew up ten aircraft, a bomb dump and petrol dump and destroyed several telegraph poles. Then they found a building full of German and Italian aircrew. 'I kicked open the door,' Mayne wrote later, 'and stood there with my Colt 45, the others at my side with a Tommy gun and another automatic. The Germans stared at us. We were a peculiar and frightening sight, bearded and unkempt . . . I said "Good evening". At that a young German arose . . . I shot him.'[16]

When all the patrols had returned by 23 December, they had blown up 61 aircraft, which, as Anthony Kemp points out,[17] was the same tally as the whole of Fighter Command at the height of the Battle of Britain. Large quantities of vehicles and supply dumps had gone up in flames too.

The third raid, launched on Christmas Day 1941, was to target the airfield around the Roman settlement of Arae Philaenorum, where Mussolini had had a huge triumphal arch built. This was known to the British as Marble Arch and was a monument to the Italian dictator's dreams of a new Roman empire.[18] Stirling and Mayne were often in competition in these night-time sorties, and on this occasion the score was: Mayne, 51 planes destroyed; Stirling, nil! The bad news for them both, however, was the death of Jock Lewes. He had been on his way to the Rendezvous with the LRDG when his vehicle was strafed from behind by an ME110. Two of the jeep's wheels were blown off and Lewes' body was riddled with bullets. Trooper Jimmy Storie riding alongside him remembered later, 'We just buried him, said a prayer, stuck a rifle in the ground with a steel helmet where his head was and scratched his name on the helmet, hoping that someone would go that way again.'[19] No one did; he is listed on the El Alamein memorial as 'grave unknown'.

With Lewes gone, Paddy Mayne was promoted to captain and left behind in Kabrit, much to his annoyance, to train new men and get vehicles up to scratch. The fact was that L Detachment was pitifully small with the loss of several men, and no one wanted to risk Stirling and Mayne dying in the same operation. It would become painfully obvious in the months ahead that Mayne was no staff officer; sitting in an office made him morose and introspective. As a lead-by-example field commander, of course, he was second to none.

New faces arrived – Ken Allott and David Sutherland from the Special Boat Service to help with a proposed attack on Benghazi harbour; Mike Sadler, who was a brilliant navigator from Rhodesia; and Bob Melot, a Belgian recruited by Stirling in Cairo, who spoke fluent Arabic. Stirling himself, a notoriously bad and reckless driver, had acquired the 'Blitz Buggy', a Ford V-8 shooting brake converted to an open-topped truck, complete with Vickers anti-aircraft machine guns, water condenser, sun compass and a coat of paint to make it look like a German staff car, at least from the air.

The Originals were promoted as the weeks went by: Pat Riley was now a sergeant major, and Reg Seekings, Johnny Cooper and Bob Bennett were sergeants. It was planned to create a second troop, as more key people, like General Ritchie with the 8th Army, realised the importance and potential of L Detachment raids. George Jellicoe of the Coldstreamers, the son of the famous Admiral of the Great War, was the most high profile here. Lieutenant Sandy Scratchley, of the 3rd County of London Yeomanry, had been an amateur jockey before the war. Then there was Carol Mather of the Welsh Guards and Stephen Hastings, still only 20, from the Scots Guards. One of the oddest officer recruits was Randolph Churchill, who, as we have seen, liked dicing with death jumping out of aircraft. He had been with

Layforce since the beginning, although his actual role was as press liaison officer.

Churchill was riding with Stirling in the Buggy one day, passing a truck convoy, when the vehicle slewed off the road, killing a journalist passenger and sending the Prime Minister's son home to convalesce with a serious back injury. Stirling himself survived with a sprained wrist, but, while temporarily out of action, it gave him a chance to bombard the Middle East Head Quarters with his plans for the expansion of his 'bunch of misfits'. The 'fossilised shits' were there, as always, to close him down or crowd him out. The Commando branch of the service in North Africa was complicated. There was the Special Boat Section, the LRDG, the Special Raiding Squadron and the Special Interrogation Group.[20] All these units overlapped to an extent, did or did not cooperate depending on circumstance and personalities, and were all in danger of being absorbed by the 8th Army, thereby losing their individuality, purpose and, as far as David Stirling was concerned, their whole raison d'être.

By July 1942, the reputation and status of L Detachment had risen to the point where the LRDG were no longer their taxi service and they became independently motorised. The patrols went out with a combination of Willy's bantams [jeeps] and three-ton trucks. Various photographs taken at the time show the jeeps converted for desert use. They had steel sand channels to help them move on soft ground (even two borrowed tanks of the 10th Hussars became immobile in some types of sand); drums of oil, fuel and ammunition; Vickers machine guns that fired 1,000 rounds a minute, camouflage nets as well as a three-man crew and all their personal equipment. Radiator grilles were removed to keep engines cool and to enable repairs to be carried out more quickly. Thirty-five of those set out from Kabrit on 3 July, and for the first time L Detachment had its own doctor with them – Malcolm Pleydell, who would later write his own book on the desert war.[21] It is from him that we learn of the casual bravery of the men, exactly the same as we have seen in John Randall's

Phantom. Very few people experienced a sense of foreboding and, if their idea of a raid as 'some fun'[22] was bravado, it was common to everybody. This mission saw the use of a radio truck, which was to be left at the rear, rather as Phantom used their Anchor vehicle. In fact, in the summer of 1942, there were enough communication breakdowns because L Detachment did not have radio trucks to make it necessary that, in later theatres of war, a Phantom unit would be assigned to them. This raid was another success, although the Blitz Buggy did not survive it.

It was now that L Detachment added a new 'blitz' tactic to its repertoire. To offset the softly-softly approach of Commandos creeping onto airfields and blowing up planes, they roared across airfields blasting away with machine-gun fire at aircraft, buildings, ammunition dumps and the shocked guards rushing out to stop them. So euphoric was Stirling with the success of this that he demanded 50 more jeeps, which was scaled down to a rather more realistic 25 when he had calmed down a little.

If Stirling intended to return to the parachute option for his raids, it was not to be. There are various references to it in the official record. Training continued under the jump expert Captain Peter Warr of the Ringway parachute training school in Manchester, but there was no opportunity to put it into practice. The end of July saw the replacement of Auchinleck by Alexander and the arrival of Bernard Montgomery to command the 8th Army. This reshuffle happened as a result of the sudden arrival of Winston Churchill; and Major Stirling, as he was by now, dined with the Prime Minister in Cairo, and had a chance to make his pitch for a bigger L Detachment to incorporate elements of the other disparate Commando units in the Middle East. Churchill asked him for a written memo the next day. Nothing happened immediately but the wheels were now in motion for the creation of the SAS.

In late September 1942, General McCreery, Alexander's Chief of Staff, urged the amalgamation of L Detachment, the SBS and the Special Service Regiment (who had now dropped the

Above: St Lawrence College, Ramsgate, where Randall excelled as a sportsman.

Right: The first known photograph of John Randall, in the first XV, St Lawrence College, 1937.

Below: The 83rd Anti-aircraft Battery, Royal Artillery, 1940. John Randall is second from the left, back row.

Always your devoted Son

John

Left: Lt Randall in battledress, with G Squadron, GHQ Liaison Regiment (Phantom) in Northern Ireland, 1942.

Right: Glamorous Phantom. John Randall in 1943 in the uniform of the Royal Artillery. The 'P' Phantom badge is partially visible on his right sleeve.

BRITISH TROOPS OF THE FIRST ARMY CHEERING MR. CHURCHILL IN THE ANCIENT AMPHITHEATRE AT CARTHAGE, AFTER HE HAD THANKED THEM FOR THE GREAT VICTORY IN TUNISIA.

a big day for us in Tunis but oh! it was so hot waiting for him — well worth waiting for'

1. Edward Oliver
2. myself.
3. Hugh Williams
4. Dennis Hart.
5. Norman Reddaway

Above: John Randall and 4,000 others wait under a burning sun for a visit from Winston Churchill, Carthage, 1 June 1943.

Left: A cloth warning sign from the Tunisian minefields, 1943.

Right: The Pegasus formation sleeve badge of Airborne troops, one of several that made John Randall's sleeve 'look like a Christmas tree'.

W.R.N.S. Officers at a Naval Air Station

...ow : 3rd/O. Williams, 3rd/O. Scott, 1st/O. Down, Capt. Walton, 2nd/O. E. Williams, ...Colyer, 3rd/O. O'Neil. Back row : 3rd/O. Kelham, 3rd/O. Titlow, 3rd/O. White, ...Talbot, 3rd/O. Bickford - Smith, 3rd/O. Drysdale, 3rd/O. Grenfell

Above: Girls in uniform – John Randall's friend Pat O'Neil is on the right, front row.

Below left: There were so many 'Johns' in Phantom and the SAS that Randall used his second name of Hugh. This postcard of a paratrooper is particularly apt.

Below right: The formation sleeve badge of 21 Army Group, 1944 (from John Randall's diaries).

NAME	REGIMENT	ADDRESS
MOORE, C. R.	Recce	30, Worthing Road, Heston, Middlesex.
MORGAN, J. A. T.	KRRC	Buxhill Vale, Nr. Stowmarket, Suffolk.
NEWALL, P. S.	RAC	Stoke Abbott, Beaminster, Dorset.
NEWMAN, W. A.	RASC	Donnington Manor, Dinton Green, Sevenoaks, Kent.
NIVEN, D. J.	RB	C/o Boodles Club, St. James, S.W.1.
OAKESHOTT, M. J.	RA	West End, Little Shelford, Cambs.

Above: The great and the famous – a page from the Phantom address book. W.A. Newman was John Randall's uncle Bill. Michael Oakeshott was a highly respected philosopher and David Niven, the quintessential British hero of dozens of Hollywood films.

Below: John Randall's entry in the address book of Phantom officers. Norman Reddaway swam to safety when the troop ship *Aboukir* was torpedoed.

NAME	REGIMENT	ADDRESS
RANDALL, J. A.	RA	Donnington Manor, Dunton Green, Sevenoaks, Kent.
REDDAWAY, N.	Recce	Impington Village College, Cambridge.
REDDAWAY, T. F.	RA	4, Adams Road, Cambridge.
REID, G. L.	RE	Yewtree, Pilgrims Way, Reigate, Surrey.
REID, M.	Gen List	Hoyle, Heyshott, Nr. Midhurst, Sussex.
RENDALL, H. A.	Int Corps	Manor Farm, Little Bookham, Surrey.

Lt. Col. "Paddy" Mayne D.S.O. (3 bars)
S.A.S. Desert Raider
North Africa 1941

Colonel David Stirling D.S.O., O.B.E.
Founder of the Special Air Service
North Africa 1941

Above left: The legendary Paddy Mayne, co-founder of the SAS and winner of four DSOs. From an original drawing, 1944.

Above right: Colonel David Stirling, co-founder of the SAS, who was a prisoner in Colditz Castle when John Randall joined the regiment. From an original drawing, 1944.

The High Street, Darvel, Scotland, training base for the SAS before D Day. As Signals Officer, John Randall had his own office and digs – the white building on the left.

Above: End of the road for the Beast of Belsen. Josef Kramer, the commandant of KL Bergen-Belsen, under arrest, 15 April 1945.

Below left: One of the gorgeous girls whom John Randall met during the liberation of Paris 1944.

Below right: 'Eddy' Blondeel: a 'John Buchan' hero and leader of the Belgian SAS, 1944. From an original drawing.

Lt. Colonel 'Ed. Blondeel D.S.O.
(code name : Capt. "Blunt")
C.O. Belgian S.A.S. Regiment
War time 1944-1945

Brigadier "Mike" Calvert D.S.O. and bar
American Silver Star
S.A.S. Operations Burma–Europe–Malaya

Above left: The rugby team of 1 SAS, spring 1944. John Randall is second from the left, front row, with Paddy Mayne just behind him.

Above right: 'Mad Mike' Calvert, the officer who took over the SAS Brigade shortly before the end of the war.

Above: Revisiting France in happier times – John Randall with his wife and daughter.

Right: 'Old Men Remember' – a reunion for SAS members at Loudon Kirk, near Darvel, 50 years on (1994). John Randall is third from the left. They are all wearing their Airborne/SAS berets.

Above: Randall is introduced to HM the Queen at a Holocaust Memorial Occasion at Kensington Palace.

Below left: David Stirling and Mike Blackman admiring the SAS Diary Book printed in a limited edition for members of the regiment. Blackman was John Randall's unit commander during Operation Haft, July–Sept 1944.

Below left: Saluting the legend – John Randall alongside the memorial to Colonel Paddy Mayne, Newtonards, Ireland.

unfortunate SS initials) as a single force to be known as 1 SAS. Its commander was to be a promoted Lt Colonel Stirling. The structure of the new regiment was as follows. There was to be an HQ Squadron; and A and B Squadrons. C Squadron was composed of the Free French and D Squadron the 'Folboat'[23] Section of the SBS. Not unlike Phantom, there was an Intelligence troop and a Signals troop, but it also had a parachute-training troop. At first there were 29 officers and 572 Other Ranks.

Sergeant Bob Tait's famous badge was now to be worn by all ranks. The original design was of a sword – Excalibur – with flames bursting from the hilt. His motto – 'Strike and Destroy' – was vetoed by Stirling, who preferred 'Who Dares Wins'. The design, especially when rendered on cloth as a cap badge, became distorted so that the flames actually look like wings. When 2 SAS Captain Roy Farran published his memoirs in 1948, he called the book *Winged Dagger*, and another myth was born.

New men were joining all the time. Harry Poat, Johnny Wiseman and Tony Marsh were attached to Mayne's A Squadron, while B Squadron stayed at Kabrit to run an intensive training programme to get newcomers up to the tough level of fitness and skill required for operations like this. Stirling won an ally in John 'Shan' Hackett, the colonel in charge of another new outfit called G (Raiding Forces). Together, the two went to see Bernard Montgomery with a view to selecting good men from his 8th Army. The general was not impressed, telling them he needed his best men and pointing to the SAS failure at Benghazi. Annoyed, Stirling and Hackett ran up a huge bar bill in Montgomery's Mess (the general himself was teetotal) and sent the bill to him![24]

From this point on, raids were carried out from a forward desert base, with A Squadron living in the wilderness for several weeks at a time, moving by night, striking from time to time at targets as directed by the 8th Army and hiding under camouflaged nets until orders came through. Patrols now had Phantom-style No. 11 radio sets mounted on their jeeps and could communicate with each other and HQ. In the event of breakdown, they had a cage lashed to the back containing two carrier pigeons. Phantom HQ in St James's Park would have been proud of them. By December, 1 SAS's total strength was 83 officers and 570 Other Ranks.

By early 1943, the desert war had swung west to Tunisia and 1 SAS found themselves operating along the Mareth Line, a pre-war French series of defences designed to keep the ambitious Italians out of French Tunisia. They were now within three hundred miles of the area where John Randall would be based three months later, when disaster struck.

On 23 January, David Stirling led a five-jeep raid in the direction of Grabes on the Tunisian coast. With astonishing bravado, they drove straight through a Wehrmacht armoured unit resting by the roadside and kept this going for five miles before coming to the conclusion that they had chanced their luck for long enough. This might seem unbelievable but they had the element of surprise on their side – what kind of idiot strolls casually past the enemy? And their jeeps and uniforms had no insignia whatsoever – just sand-caked vehicles and scruffy, sand-caked men. The Germans probably took them for Italians and ignored them. Tired after a long drive, they scattered in a *wadi* under the usual camouflage netting, and Stirling, uncharacteristically, did not post sentries. They woke up to find themselves surrounded by a Luftwaffe unit that had been alerted by a firefight with Captain Aspirant Jourdan's patrol hours earlier. While Cooper, Sadler and Sergeant Freddie Taxis all made a successful run for it, Stirling was caught. He escaped briefly the same evening, but was recaptured and the SAS had no idea what had happened to him.

The Germans had long been irritated by Stirling. Apart from other equipment and petrol supplies, he had cost them the loss of 327 aircraft over the past 18 months and was known to the German high command as the 'phantom major'. Just as Churchill had once acknowledged Erwin Rommel's skill as an enemy, the 'Desert Fox' now paid the same compliment to Stirling. In a letter to his wife, he wrote, 'the British lost the very able and adaptable commander of the desert group which has caused us more damage than any other British unit of equal size'.[25]

The command of 1 SAS passed to Paddy Mayne, but the man simply could not deal with the 'fossilised shit', whose measure Stirling had got long ago. Mayne was perfectly at home at the end of a Tommy gun, a pistol or a grenade, but making persuasive arguments with the 'scarlet majors at base' was not his forte. Not only that but the regiment was scattered with squadrons all over the place. Major Jellicoe was now in charge of training at Kabrit, but the confusion was such that, when Harry Poat turned up much later with his patrol from Tripoli, nobody knew who he was or where he had been or why!

Confusingly, while the second regiment, 2 SAS, went its own way (to combine briefly with 1 SAS in Italy), 1 SAS itself became SRS, the Special Raiding Squadron. They were transferred to Palestine to train for the forthcoming invasion of Sicily. It was obvious that the original purpose of the regiment was now ignored and all the training, including the use of mortars, was to be sent in as shock assault troops alongside conventional infantry. Paddy Mayne was furious about this. He had been denied compassionate leave on the death of his father in January and had developed an irrational hatred for war correspondents who hung around the bars in Cairo writing rubbish for the people at home. One in particular who had raised the major's ire (he was promoted to lieutenant colonel by June) was the BBC correspondent Richard Dimbleby, who would follow John Randall into Bergen-Belsen two years later. Unable to find him, Mayne picked a fight with six Redcaps (Military Policemen) and was slung into jail. There was, briefly, the serious risk that he would lose his commission for that.

We have already seen from the Phantom units sent to Sicily that the landings there were chaotic. On 10 July 1943, the sea was far rougher than expected, and the SRS got thoroughly soaked (and seasick) going ashore in their Landing Craft Assault vehicles.

There were already paratroopers there, some of them dead in the sea, others suffering from exposure on the cliffs. Mayne led the attack with only a .45 automatic and, altogether, by the next day, had captured nearly 500 Italian defenders. For this, he received a bar to his DSO; Harry Poat and Johnny Wiseman won the Military Cross.

But it all went horribly wrong at Termoli. By October, Sicily had been taken, and the British and Americans were landing on mainland Italy. All was going well until a German paratroop counter-attack on the 5th. A shell landed directly onto an SRS truck that Reg Seekings was loading up. His account is horrific but it is necessary to understand the mindset of survivors as part of the background of the regiment that John Randall was to join the following year:

> We were smothered in bits of flesh. It was hanging on the 'phone wires, on the roof, a helluva mess. There was a whole family that had been doing a bit of washing for us . . . They were dead, lying in a heap. The woman must have been split open. The man was blown apart, disembowelled and a young boy, about twelve years old. One of my men was burning . . . That was Skinner. He was dead . . . this young boy was lying on top. His guts were blown out like a huge balloon. He got up and ran around screaming. Terrible sight. I had to shoot him. There was absolutely no hope for him and you couldn't let anyone suffer like that.[26]

Eighteen men died in that truck, and in the SAS archive there is a photograph of the vehicle, a burnt-out shell in a quiet suburban street, the house walls pockmarked with shrapnel. Peter Davis remembered:

> The funeral was soon over. In a quiet voice the padre read the service and dismissed us. Somehow the occasion did not seem to warrant reminiscences of that empty and futile kind often vented upon the dead . . . perhaps our regrets were sufficiently sincere

and deep to make us realise how false and unavailing such sentiments are.[27]

In December came another order, one that was met with mixed feelings. The SRS were going home, not merely for much-needed leave but also to train in Scotland for what would become Operation Overlord, the Allied invasion of France.

John Randall's original regiment, the Royal Artillery, had been founded in 1716 when the world was a different place. Winston Churchill's ancestor the Duke of Marlborough had just won a series of dazzling victories over the French, and Britain was poised to become the dominant power of the 18th and 19th centuries, with a small, highly professional army and a navy second to none. Both regiments Randall joined later in the Second World War were brand new. They did not have time to build up a reputation and an *esprit de corps* over centuries. They had to make their mark quickly. Outside army circles, they remained virtually unknown. Yet each of them has passed into legend, and John Randall, having been part of one, was about to become part of another.

9

The Bunch of Misfits

On Monday, 13 March, John Randall heard that, once the wireless course was over, he was going to join Jakie Astor's unit in Scotland. He wrote to various people telling them that the leave he had hoped for was cancelled. In many ways, he was looking forward to Scotland, if only because he would have an opportunity to link up with Ricky Beard and the FANY girls at Dunbar. He carried out a night op on the Wednesday and played Cardinal Puff, a drinking game that requires a great deal of stamina, with Didier, the French officer. They played it with even more gusto the next night in the FANY Mess, with Randall and 'Scottie' McDevitt in fine form.

Friday, the 17th, was the day for the 'off'. Randall's team said farewell to the girls, and trained to Reading where there was the usual wartime hanging about, with luggage, greatcoats, the totally useless gas masks, whistles, steam and endless cups of tea. Tom Reddaway came in for some criticism as he was transportation officer and should have sorted the mess out. After dinner, Randall saw the colonel and John Morgan, who was now second-in-command, and the move to Jakie Astor was confirmed.

Bright and early the next morning, he and McDevitt dumped their luggage at Euston station and went to Kensington to see Kay de Villiers. They walked in Regent's Park on a gloriously sunny day and had dinner at the Berkeley. She saw him off at the station, and he was lucky enough to get a sleeper, so the long haul to Scotland passed in comfort. At 9.30 a.m. on Sunday, 19 March, he arrived at Kilmarnock. The town had a long history and was the home of Johnnie Walker whisky. The station with its tall clock tower is still there.

The SRS left Italy three weeks after John Randall left Tunisia. Johnny Cooper had gone on ahead to set up camp at Darvel, a small town nine miles to the east of Kilmarnock. Abandoned spinning mills there would be the regiment's home while they trained and recruited; the officers would be based in a manor house on the edge of the town. Darvel was sometimes referred to as 'the lang toon', essentially a ribbon development with a single main street. It was the centre of a lace-making area during the war and was part of the estate of the Earls of Loudon since the early 19th century.

At Kilmarnock station, Jakie Astor, sporting a maroon airborne beret, complete with wings, was waiting for Randall. Most accounts of this period contend that F Squadron of Phantom joined the SAS for signalling work in April, but clearly the major, at least, was already there in March. The radio communication system was complicated. The base signals unit of the SAS (SRS was dropped and the former title reinstated now) was at Moor Park, Kilbirnie, where the regiment had its tactical headquarters. Here, twelve BBC HP transmitters fed into five outstations with Jedburgh sets that could reach units in the field. Officers also had MCR 100 receivers that could receive instructions on broadcast channels using the codename SABU followed by an officer's unique number. Field units could not contact each other directly, but had to pass all information back to HQ who would relay messages out again as required. As was apparent from reports received after D-Day, many of these messages were too long or mangled in the ciphering process. This was why John Randall had been chosen to join the SAS in the first place. Not only did he already have his parachute wings – this was to be the mode of transport immediately after D-Day – but he was also a wireless expert who could teach his new regiment what to do. Two patrols of Phantom went with each of 1 SAS and 2 SAS. The French and Belgians had their own, different, signalling systems, but the operators were trained by Phantom.

Astor's squadron were on their way to the parachute training school at Ringway and Randall went on to Auchinleck House. The 18th-century house once belonged to James Boswell, the biographer of lexicographer Samuel Johnson. The laird in the 1940s had opened the place up to officers of the Polish, Canadian and Free French armies. Randall was apprehensive, of course, but found himself driving in a truck through the village of Galston, which sounded familiar. As soon as his OS map revealed the name of Loudon Castle, it all fell into place. The Countess of Loudon and her family were old friends of Hugh Cuming, and, on a whim, Randall decided to visit them. The castle had once been a magnificent baronial pile with a broad sweep up to the door in the west front and embattled turrets, square and strong. A serious fire had recently destroyed much of it, however, and the family were living in a bungalow in the grounds. Randall knew the Countess and her three daughters immediately by Cuming's vivid description of them. They gave him a drink and he promised to visit again. The 12th Countess's eldest daughter was Barbara, a few months older than Randall, but it was Jean and Edith who held his attention.

Randall's diary for that Sunday, 19 March 1944 is prosaic: 'Went to see the Colonel – Mayne DSO (and bar) and was introduced to all the rest. They seemed quite helpful and I felt it would not be hard to get along with them. The Mess was terribly crowded and I have never seen so many officers in so small a space.'

The Reverend Fraser McLuskey had obviously got there some hours earlier, because he arrived before breakfast. McLuskey was a university chaplain, five years older than John Randall, and he had a wife and daughter. Clergymen counted as a reserved occupation during the war, but he felt he should do his bit. Hoping the war would be over before he learned to fly, he rejected the RAF, and, because of seasickness, he mentally turned down the navy too. That left the army and, despite the influx of a whole bunch of padres in Tunisia, with whom Randall had played football, they were in short supply. McLuskey had attended the Chaplains' Training Centre at the vast army camp at Tidworth on Salisbury Plain, where he was given an excruciatingly uncomfortable uniform and taught how to march and salute.

One of the problems for the historian writing about a unit like the SAS is the security surrounding its organisation and training. McLuskey's book *Parachute Padre* was first published in 1951, so various place names have been changed for security reasons – as McLuskey says, 'the security being my own!'[1] So the training following Tidworth is shrouded in mystery until he chose to join a parachute unit. He was sent to Hardwick Camp in Chesterfield early in 1944 and was, for the first time, mixed in with Roman Catholic priests in the magnificent setting of the Elizabethan Hardwick Hall: 'And while one denomination or another might be held most efficacious for man's upward ascent, Church and Chapel, Protestant and Roman, bow all alike to gravity and fall with equal force.'

McLuskey underwent similar training for jumps to that undergone by John Randall, climbing cliff faces, jumping from heights, working out in the gym. He had to pass physical examinations and, unlike Randall, a psychiatric examination too to check whether he was psychologically suited to jumping. No doubt this was sensible – we have already commented on the panic that can ensue in a Stirling or an Albemarle rattling over enemy territory at dead of night – but the men trained in the desert had no such luxury; and, in the case of the first jumps made by Stirling and Lewes, no physical practice either. The real training happened at Ringway at the RAF Parachute Training

School, the institution that had eventually sent Captain Peter Warr out to help L Detachment in the desert. The padre was taught how to exit the plane, how to control the chute in flight and how to land (very little of which actually came into play when McLuskey first parachuted into France).

'We had to learn to fall. We fell from all angles and in all directions. We fell forwards and backwards and sideways . . . We fell until we felt as if we had nothing to fall on.' When it came to his first practice jump – from a balloon – the fear uppermost in McLuskey's mind was of letting himself and his teammates down rather than actually dying.

McLuskey had false teeth and, for safety reasons, took these out and tucked them into a pocket of his Denison smock. At first, men with false teeth were not allowed to jump at all, but the army and RAF had relented and special containers for them were provided. McLuskey never bothered to get one.

The padre's posting to the SAS was suitably shrouded in mystery. He expected to be sent to the 1st or 6th Airborne Division once he had got his wings but they had their quota of chaplains, so it was suggested he might like to try the Special Air Service. The interviewing officer had little information. It involved parachuting and was on the secret list. Since McLuskey was a Scot, the fact that the HQ was in Ayrshire was a plus.

While McLuskey was still at Tidworth and John Randall was still enjoying leave after Tunisia, the SAS Brigade had been reformed under Brigadier R.W. 'Roddy' McLeod with the quietly spoken Esmond Baring as his number two. The HQ was set up on 8 February at Sorn Castle in Ayrshire, a medieval tower house that had been extended considerably by its owners in 1909. By the end of that month, HQ had ten officers and thirty-one Other Ranks. The HQ French Demi-Brigade was commanded by Lt Colonel Durand; 20 Liaison HQ by Major Oswald Carey-Elwes. The 1 SAS, to which both Randall and McLuskey were assigned, was commanded by Paddy Mayne, who was delighted that the outfit was not only still in existence but was also being expanded.

2 SAS, which had been raised by David Stirling's brother William, did not join the Scottish centre until March, two days before Randall and McLuskey arrived. The 3 French Parachute Battalion was led by Captain Conan; 4 French Parachute Battalion by Commandant Bourgoin; and, finally, there was the Belgian Independent Parachute Company commanded by Captain Eddy Blondeel.

That was why there were so many officers crowded into the Mess when John Randall arrived. It was cold and grey as Fraser McLuskey was picked up at Kilmarnock station in a Utility with the winged dagger emblem painted on its side. The officers' Mess in Darvel was at the end of a long, bumpy drive and both the new men were jolted around mercilessly on their way to it. The house itself was splendid, set in wooded grounds. When McLuskey walked in, there were very young-looking officers lounging around, most of them wearing the Africa Star on their tunics, and an old gramophone record was grinding out 'Mush, Mush, sing Tooral-aye-ary'. A very large man wandered over to the padre. 'If he didn't actually ask who the devil I was and what the devil I was doing there, I gathered at least that that was at the back of his mind.' This was Paddy Mayne and he had had no idea that a padre was being sent to him. He invited McLuskey into breakfast.

One of the men there was Lieutenant Johnny Cooper, who remembered years later that Mayne had set up a beer barrel the evening before and had interviewed each new officer as they arrived. Cooper was told by the colonel to pull a pint for the padre and they all went into breakfast with tankards in their hands. Like Randall, McLuskey felt at home in this Mess very quickly. He noticed that some of his table companions wore their wings on their breasts rather than on their sleeves, but, because of their youth, he had no idea that this marked them out as veterans.

John Randall wrote a host of letters that night and confided in his diary that he felt 'very much like a new boy and hoped I did not show it'. It was daunting to be in a Mess with men of such experience. Randall at least had been in a war zone, heard and seen the effects of gunfire and had witnessed the results of the carnage on Longstop Hill. McLuskey had no idea of any of this; perhaps his ignorance was a kind of bliss. He was taken the next day to see Major Baring, who explained his duties. He was to be padre to 1 and 2 SAS as well as Brigade HQ. The French and Belgians had their own arrangements. A Morris Utility car was laid on to ferry the padre between the units. McLuskey asked Baring what the SAS was actually going to do in the weeks and months ahead. 'The answer was quite simple. The Special Air Service was about to drop small parties of men behind the German lines when the invasion began.' When McLuskey asked how a padre could fit into all this, Baring had to concede he had no idea.

Randall's job was more relevant but not without its complications. Although Fraser McLuskey waxes eloquently about the importance of Phantom in his book, devoting an entire chapter to it, wireless communication was not high on the list of essentials for the SAS. Primarily, they were not a parachute unit, whatever the officer who interviewed McLuskey may have thought, and the old hands must have been increasingly aware that, whatever big operation was clearly in the offing, the SAS would not be used in Stirling's intended capacity. Randall and his ex-comrades from Phantom would have their work cut out to prove their usefulness. His first scrounging sortie at Brigade HQ, to find radio equipment, was not a success, and he ran into Peter Miller-Munday, a Phantom from the old 12th Lancers crowd who was now a major.

The new boy made his name quickly, especially with Paddy Mayne, because on his second day there he played seven-a-side rugger and after fifteen minutes was 'shagged as a tiddly-wink'. The actual course with the SAS was not to start until the Wednesday, so Randall took the opportunity to drive the 50–60 miles to Dunbar, which took him 1¾ hours, dropping an officer and an NCO in Edinburgh first. He was ostensibly there to scrounge more gear from the local signals officer, but again had no luck. He met up with Ricky Beard and the FANY girls again, taking Ricky to the pictures and eating at a local pub. Trooper Newland drove back to Edinburgh, and Randall took over from there. It was midnight by now and the on-going blackout regulations meant that there were no street lights and that the vehicle was fitted with headlight shields that minimised the glare. Randall was sure it was only his good eyesight that got them back. All of this had of course been 'illegal', as he put it in his diary, but everyone, in the forces and out of them, took such opportunities when they could. There was something in the wind and who knew when it would be possible to meet up with old flames again?

The wireless course of the next day was short-lived, largely to the overwhelming lack of interest of most people on it. On Friday, Randall went over to Auchinleck House and called in at a dance in Darvel that evening. 'It was shocking,' and the new boy, used to the social life of London and its huge array of girls, could not understand how the other officers seemed to be enjoying themselves.

The next day, Randall played fly-half for 1 SAS and they won the final. His prize was a book token for 7/6d.[2] He then set off in a truck for Glasgow, where he was supposed to be meeting Kay de Villiers, but she failed to turn up so he caught a train to London. His first port of call was to be Phantom HQ at Richmond. He hoped to find the colonel but had to be content with Tom Reddaway. 'Having got that military nonsense off my chest', he went to see his mother, who was well and cheerful. Delighted though he was to be on leave again, the timing of this makes little sense. While Fraser McLuskey was getting to know his squadron comrades, Randall was already away from all that. At last, he met up with Hugh Cuming again, whom he had last seen in Tunisia. The pair went to a marvellous party in somebody's flat off Oxford Street, and Randall ended up sleeping on the floor. He had over-imbibed, however; not even coffee at Marshall's[3] and a hair of the dog at the Berkeley could put him right.

This leave was all about catching up with old friends from Sevenoaks and St Lawrence College. Six injections at a visit to Mr Southwood the dentist rather dampened the moment, but he managed dinner at the Bagatelle nonetheless. On Friday, 7 April, he caught a train from Euston back to Kilmarnock. His one regret was that he had not been able to see Doodles; she had chicken pox and was infectious and miserable. The journey was long, and at Kilmarnock he had to carry his baggage all the way to the Mess by himself.

Although no one at Darvel knew it yet, a week earlier, the high command had finally decided what to do with the SAS. Two years earlier, there was huge pressure on Churchill's government to open up a second front to relieve the pressure on the Russians in the east. An invasion of Italy was all very well, but the general consensus, both military and civilian, was that there would have to be a direct assault on France, partially because that, geographically, was the nearest point of Nazi-held territory and partially because the British ought to come back the way they had left. Dunkirk was not actually selected, but for some time planning had gone on to effect a landing somewhere along the French coast. The whole enterprise, which would culminate in D-Day, was vast and ran counter to the small, tightly knit fighting units of Stirling's concept. The Supreme Headquarters Allied Expeditionary Force (SHAEF) HQ alone comprised 15,000 men, the size of an average division. In overall command was the American Dwight Eisenhower and under him the British 21 Army Group led by Montgomery, about whom the SAS, like Phantom, had mixed feelings.

The build-up to Operation Overlord, which John Randall had witnessed in London with the vast number of Americans around, led to a polarisation of training. Broadly speaking, the Americans had the south-west of England; the British the south-east. One division trained in the Moray Firth in Scotland, but, largely, troop concentrations were confined to the south. Aerial reconnaissance was carried out along the coast, and the Normandy area between

Cherbourg and Le Havre was earmarked for the invasion point. To confuse the Wehrmacht manning the gun emplacements, the concrete and steel barrier that protected the west, information was leaked that suggested the Pas de Calais to the north-east was the likely target.

The SAS's role in all this was modest, and the situation was not helped by the fact that many of the staff officers operating out of Airborne HQ had no knowledge of the SAS, what they had done or how they had been trained. The on-going absence of David Stirling, of course, was central to this problem. In John Randall's papers is his Airborne badge, a pale-blue warrior riding Pegasus, the winged horse. He notes below it: 'Just another badge to add to the ever-growing Christmas tree effect on my arm.' The SAS were allowed to retain their mythical dagger cap badge, but the beret itself was the bog-standard maroon of all Airborne troops.

A certain amount of double-think was apparent from the first. 1 SAS was to be dropped on the night before D-Day (and not even Paddy Mayne, nipping down with increasing frequency to London, knew when that would be), and they were to hold up the German advance in the area from Lisieux to Nantes. 2 SAS and/or 3 French Para would hold the Dieppe–Paris line; and 4 French Para would operate from St Lo to Angers. This ran totally counter to the Operational Instruction No 2, which said that, 'For security reasons, no SAS troops to be landed before main landings start.' Not only that, but half the brigade was to be held in reserve at home. In other words, a unit that had been trained to operate covertly, carrying out deadly sabotage work behind enemy lines, were now to be sent in as some sort of 'forlorn hope' to stem the advance of an army that was likely to outnumber them dozens to one.

Randall was with the Headquarters Squadron at Darvel and the four other squadrons were headed by: Bill Fraser (A); Eric Lepine (B); Tony Marsh (C) and Ian Fenwick (D). The training was intensive and, as there was now actually six weeks to go until D-Day, it was stepped up. Men learned to fall on barbed wire as their comrades ran over them (the tactic learned in the trenches of the Great War). Live ammunition was used by machine-gunners to keep an advancing unit on the move, however exhausted they were by the weight of their packs. War games were carried out, whereby units would have to move across country, avoiding police and Home Guard units, stealing food and milk bottles, commandeering vehicles. Serge Vaculik, a Czech serving with 4 French Para, told later of tying up a policeman and driving off in his patrol car.

Yet there was time for relaxation. On Sunday, 4 April, Randall, John Sadoine and the Phantom boys had the chance to explore the country. They found 'Wallace's Grave' in a beautiful gorge where the Glen Water splashed over worn stones, one of the many sites supposedly the last resting place of the 13th-century Scottish hero.[4] Morale rose considerably among the laughter and the prospect of doing something at last lifted everybody.

Unlike Fraser McLuskey, who had no experience of any other outfit, Randall had some reservations about his new SAS comrades. 'They strike me as being just too "happy go lucky".' A regiment with the experiences that the SAS had took some getting used to. Randall took Sadoine to Loudon Castle on the 18th and everybody had a good time. The old animosities of Tunisia were clearly forgotten, and Randall took one of the Countess's daughters, Edith, to the pictures.

It was now that he moved out of the hopelessly crowded Mess and was billeted above his office in Darvel High Street. His landlord and landlady were Peter and Aggie Tarbet and, according to Randall, Tarbet had been in bed for 43 years! Despite that, he remained ever cheerful.

After duty on the 19th, he, Sadoine and Tom Moore went to Loudon again to find the place full of Belgians from the Independent Para Company. After a few whiskies, Randall became annoyed at the flirting that Edith Loudon was doing with Freddie Wimbosch and wrote, 'My God, I nearly hit that man!' Since, thanks to Paddy Mayne, there was something of a tradition of this in Randall's new unit, it was not too out of place. It soon became a duel of stamina – who would outstay the other in vying for Edith's favours? Sadoine insisted they should hang on, although Randall was all for calling it a night, and the Belgians finally blinked first. Edith was furious with Randall for being 'stupid', and he felt totally ashamed of himself: 'What a nasty, jealous person I must be.'

Saturday, 22 April was literally a Field Day. The whole brigade paraded on a field near Loudon Castle for an inspection by General Montgomery who by now, of course, was commander-in-chief of 21 Army Group. As close to D-Day as this, he must have been hurtling all over the place on morale-boosting exercises. There must have been those who had not forgotten his indifferent attitude to David Stirling and Shan Hackett; on the other hand, he had an easy manner with him and was good with crowds and the media.[5] Randall was not impressed with the turnout of 1 SAS, but 2 SAS looked like guardsmen with their white belts and gaiters. The Belgians were undramatic, but the French looked extraordinary – bearded and with 'their hats at the most incredible angles'. They wore their berets slung the opposite way from the British. Three ATS girls were on parade too, although no one could quite work out why. The inspection over, Monty stood in a jeep and gave an impromptu speech: 'Typical Monty, but very good.'

After that, it was a rugger game, combined Forces against local Ayrshire clubs, and a pipe band played on what was a gorgeously sunny day. The dance in Kilmarnock was excellent that evening; Sadoine 'did well' with Edith, and Randall gravitated to her sister Jean. There is no mention of how Tom Moore got on, but Fraser McLuskey described the man as 'a pleasanter and imperturbable companion it would be hard to find . . . his slow, lazy smile never absent for long and whether the news was good or bad . . . he puffed away placidly at the pipe which was his inseparable companion.' Perhaps it was that that put the Loudon ladies off!

Daily route marches were increasing now to get the men up to fitness, and Randall led a three-man section out in true SAS style at ten thirty on the night of Saturday, 29 April. They covered seven miles by 2 a.m. and holed up in a hut on the edge of an airfield. When the place came to life the following morning, they decamped to a railway station cottage to wash and shave, then walked up the line to find somewhere to stay for the day. The other section had not reached the Rendezvous at Gailes station, but Randall bumped into 'Henri' Wickham, a girl he knew from Ireland who was stationed nearby with the WAAFs. Her father had been Inspector-General of Police in Belfast. They 'romped around for a bit' and went for a ride in a Sherman tank. If all this sounds unprofessional and unsoldierly, it was not out of keeping with the SAS tradition. Following the capture of Augusta in Sicily, the SRS, as they then were, held an impromptu street party, complete with plenty of alcohol and a pianola. On another occasion, Paddy Mayne, echoing Francis Drake at the sighting of the Armada in 1588, insisted on finishing a game of snooker before launching a counter-offensive against the enemy.

Back with his men again, Randall resumed the march at 11 p.m., crossing hills and fields until they found a welcome barn with lovely thick hay and they all fell asleep. The next morning, in keeping with the need to split up and operate independently, even in small units, only Randall and Signalman David Danger went on to Kilmarnock. The aptly named Danger was a veteran of Sicily. At Augusta, the unit had been offered Benzedrine tablets to stay awake. He had declined, having a horror of any medicines. He had faced enemy fire before, having been pinned down in a ruined house near Termoli. Shells were screaming overhead but what really terrified Danger was the sudden arrival of a donkey that stuck its head through the door and brayed at him. At the Hurlford crossroads, near Kilmarnock, Randall decided that enough was enough and got transport the rest of the way. He had taken his men over rough terrain without food for four days and had proved to himself that it could be done. All that was necessary now was to do it in enemy territory.

On Tuesday, 2nd, there was a signals conference at Auchinleck House, and Randall went to a dance with Henri Wickham at the WAAF base. He learned the hard way that the walk he had been on did not mix with the hectic social life he had been used to further south. Somebody else who learned this was the anonymous officer with A Squadron who described a local brew called 'Suki'. It was a mixture of rum and red wine and was drunk in pint and half-pint glasses at 'shindigs'. 'It had a kick like a mule and people passed out right and left. We put many men and officers to bed. We took advantage of one of the latter and cut off half his moustache. He was not awfully pleased the following morning.'[6]

There was a certain animosity from time to time in the regiment, probably because the old Phantom boys were a little cliquey. John Sadoine was described as unhelpful at one point in France, and Randall was trying, unsuccessfully, to get a new signaller sergeant as his was clearly not up to scratch. It did not help that he was now living away from the Mess where Fraser McLuskey found such camaraderie, and, of course, he had Loudon Castle as a bolt-hole too. The countryside was beautiful and the spring sunshine warm and inviting, even if the rabbits were a little small for shooting purposes.

Tony Marsh's C Squadron held a party on Tuesday, 9 May. Fraser McLuskey was disturbed to find so young a man in charge of an entire squadron and remembers him being ragged for his good looks. He had a marvellous sense of humour combined with a tough resilience that made him a natural SAS leader. He had already had his baptism of fire at Bagnara in southern Italy and, despite being outnumbered at Torrente Sinarca, had driven back a determined attack by the 16th Panzer Division in October of the previous year. True, he had once accidentally burned down an officers' Mess, but all was forgiven by his being awarded the DSO at Termoli for his 'high standard of courage and complete disregard for personal safety'.[7] The party was an evening of drinking, singing and story-telling and, when Randall left by 11 o'clock, he was a 'little muzzy . . .'

The SAS had a reputation as a singing outfit. The piano-playing padre Fraser McLuskey was struck by this and quickly earned the nickname 'Fingers' for his dexterity on the keys. The song most closely associated with Paddy Mayne's men was 'Lili Marlene', to which they wrote their own words. The 8th Army had picked this up in North Africa where it had been transmitted from the German-held Belgrade Radio, and the translation and arrangement by songwriter Tommy Connor, as sung by the 17-year-old Anne Shelton, became the smash hit of 1943. It cannot have been often that the same song was equally popular with both sides in a war.

This was the period when 'invasion mania' gripped the country. The huge troop movements in the south could hardly be concealed. Southampton, which had been all but flattened in the Blitz of 1941, was choked with convoys of trucks, jeeps, tanks and armoured personnel carriers. Ships were berthed seven or eight abreast. Dummy landing craft floated in the harbour and rivers of the east coast to give the rare reconnaissance raiders of the Luftwaffe the impression that an invasion would be mounted from much further north. Engineers were building mysterious concrete caissons 200 feet long that would later be bolted together to make the Mulberry floating harbours that would be towed across the Channel in June. The WVS who brought these men tea and sandwiches were sworn to the utmost secrecy. Careless talk could still cost lives. The Darvel camp was buttoned down so that mail was coming and going with less frequency. On 5 May, Randall received a cable from Kay de Villiers from Air Force headquarters in Pretoria, South Africa. She had no idea, of course, of his address, but wrote hopefully to 'Lieutenant Hugh Randall, 1st SAS Regiment, Home Force, Great Britain'. She had just received his airmail letter of 1 April. They had had a marvellous trip out but she wished he could have been there too. She was about to embark on a month's leave, spending a fortnight in the

Transkei[8] with one of her half-section colleagues. 'God bless,' she wrote, 'and look after yourself.'

Saturday, 20 May was one of the sports days that Paddy Mayne arranged both to test the men's fitness and to lighten the increasing tension of the moment. None of the men who ran and jumped that day had any notion that the greatest armada in history was to set sail in 18 days' time. Randall was not pleased with his performance; he came third in the long jump and his team lost the tug-of-war, despite their coaching. His high jump and shot-put did not work out, although he finished second in the hop, skip and jump. Most of Darvel had turned out to watch, including Aggie, Randall's landlady, and Ian Fenwick, D Squadron's leader, who gave a running commentary over a loudhailer from a police car. Fenwick was a brilliant cartoonist who had an unusual background. He had recently been recruited by Mayne from an auxiliary unit raised in 1940 to launch guerrilla attacks against a possible German invasion.[9]

Randall had a plan to invite his mother up to Darvel 'in a day or two' but the whole town was full of soldiers and he could not find a billet for her. He and John Sadoine took a picnic that Sunday: 'how remote the war seems in spite of its really alarming proximity'.

Men were being sent south in small units now. The conferences went on for longer and the amount of 'bumf' the officers were supposed to absorb was almost overwhelming. The normally unflappable Tom Moore was becoming more and more keyed up as his time to go came nearer. More information was being passed down the line, and it was obvious that Randall's mother's visit was not going to happen; the timing was all wrong. On the 18th, General Sir Frederick 'Boy' Browning visited 2 SAS. He was commander of the 1st Airborne Corps and had insisted that the SAS come under his wing for the invasion that was about to happen. Clearly, by this time, Browning knew exactly what the D-Day plan was, and Bill Stirling (the brother of David), commanding 2 SAS, was far from happy about it. Bizarrely, he resigned his commission and left command of his unit to Lt Colonel Brian Franks, who had been brigade major at Termoli. This was an extraordinary situation and not one that was guaranteed to inspire confidence at so crucial a juncture. The fact was, however, that Stirling had been critical of SHAEF's intended deployment of the SAS from the start and, even though there was talk – from Browning – of dropping them deeper into France to operate with the Maquis (the underground) to Stirling, it was too little, too late. Captain Anthony Greville-Bell of 2 SAS said later, 'We were in absolute agreement with [Stirling's] decision because of that thick-headed idiot Boy Browning.'[10]

On Thursday, 25th, Tom Moore left, and Randall organised his section during the day and laid on a party at night. With him were the Auxiliary recruit Peter Weaver; Tim Iredale, who had a bit of a chip on his shoulder about Auxiliary 'types', calling them 'wizards'; the Medical Officer Michael McCreedy; and Ian Stewart, himself due to leave in three days' time. They all met up at the Kilmarnock cinema and went on to the house of Janet Paul. After several drinks here, it was off to Loudon Castle, and Randall made a concerted play for Jean. As things turned out, he ended up with Edith and staggered off to bed at 4 a.m. 'A good-night kiss was just about my last conscious memory and I had been "quite a good boy". Yes. "Quite".'

The morning after the night before was a test of endurance. The Loudon toddlers were crawling over Randall as he lay groaning in bed, and Lady Loudon offered the lieutenant a double-yolked egg for breakfast when he was not even up to a single-yolked one. He was put back to bed and rather enjoyed the fuss that Edith made of him. He found the clothes that had been hidden from him and made his way back to Darvel via the stony causeway. Ian Stewart was keen to get back to Darvel that night, and a hectic round of dancing, drinking and flirting got under way again. Randall spent precious time with Jean at last, and, when the officers got back to Darvel, Stewart gave his drinking buddy two Benzedrine tablets, which kept him going for another six hours.

'So far as security allows I have gone,' Randall wrote in the last entry in his diary, 'and this rather unintelligible book must be drawn to a close, not perhaps before its time. It may help to recall to me at some later date some happy memories and some amusing incidents, also to answer the old, old question "What did you do in the last war, Daddy?"'

Ian Stewart, Ian Wellstead and Norman Poole went with their sections to Fairford Aerodrome in Gloucestershire, which John Randall knew well. They were joined by John Tonkin and Richard Crisp, both of B Squadron, and driven to London for briefings. These involved map work and close cooperation with the Special Operations Executive (SOE), which had been created by Churchill years before to 'set Europe ablaze'. Their agents in the field were astonishingly brave men and women whose exploits remained highly classified until many years after the war. Because of this and the fact that those agents worked hand-in-glove with the French Resistance movement, the Maquis, SOE saw themselves as the arbiters in all things related to covert operations. At first, this was not a problem, but by the time John Randall was parachuted into France it was.

Stewart and the others plunged themselves into London's social life. They had a slap-up lunch in Regent Street and went to a show, but the proposed takeoff from Sandy, Bedfordshire, was delayed because of bad weather. Wellstead remembered listening to the king's speech on the radio and he chatted up the FANYs: 'How we blessed those girls whose pleasant chatter kept our minds off what was in store.'[11]

Every man who took part in Operation Overlord received two official letters. The first, still among John Randall's papers, was a personal message from the commander-in-chief 21 Army Group and was signed by B.L. Montgomery, General. It is lofty stuff, it is propaganda, but it is worth quoting in full because it summarises the hopes and ambitions in the British Army in the summer of 1944:

1. The time has come to deal the enemy a terrific blow in Western Europe.

The blow will be struck by the combined sea, land and air forces of the Allies – together constituting one great Allied team, under the supreme command of General Eisenhower.

2. On the eve of this great adventure I send my best wishes to every soldier in the Allied team.

To us is given the honour of striking a blow for freedom which will live in history; and in the better days that lie ahead men will speak with pride of our doings. We have a great and righteous cause.

Let us pray that 'The Lord Mighty in Battle' will go forth with our armies and that His special providence will aid us in the struggle.

3. I want every soldier to know that I have complete confidence in the successful outcome of the operations that we are now about to begin.

With stout hearts, and with enthusiasm for the contest, let us go forward to victory.

4. And, as we enter the battle, let us recall the words of a famous soldier, spoken many years ago:

'He either fears his fate too much,
Or his deserts are small,
Who dare not put it to the touch,
To win or lose it all.'[12]

5. Good luck to each one of you. And good hunting on the mainland of Europe.

Eisenhower's letter from SHAEF (whose badge was, incidentally, a flaming sword) said much the same thing. It was a little shorter, more prosaic and perhaps more realistic: 'Your task will not be an easy one. Your enemy is well trained, well-equipped and battle-hardened. He will fight savagely.' But, of course, Eisenhower shared Montgomery's faith in the Allied fighting man and in divine providence: 'Good luck! And let us all beseech the blessing of Almighty God upon this great and noble undertaking.'

It all depended on the moon. And on the tides. Between Carentan in the west and Ouistreham in the east, there was an 85-minute discrepancy in terms of tide. Go in too soon and the landing craft would hit the German defences submerged by high water; go in too late and troops would have hundreds of yards of open sand to cross in the teeth of murderous machine-gun fire.

The idea that became Operation Overlord was deceptively simple and the basics had been worked out as early as 1943. A joint force of British, American and Free French troops would land along the beaches of Normandy, 21 Army Group divided into the British Second Army and the American First. They would go in at first light, three hours before high tide, on beaches with the now legendary codenames of Utah, Omaha, Juno, Gold and Sword. The Allies would be setting foot on the soil of Nazi-occupied France for the first time in four years. Everything that could be done to minimise casualties was done. Commandos of the Airborne Forces dropped silently from gliders in the darkness of 5 June, knocking out bridgeheads and reconnoitring roads.

The prospects were daunting. No one had ever mounted an amphibious operation on this scale before.[13] The weather was vital. For centuries, men had gone to war in the spring and stopped fighting in the autumn. The nature of warfare by the middle of the 20th century had changed all that. The Second World War was total war, waged every day and all day. Darkness and the seasons were neither here nor there. Even so, the tide and the moon conditions were perfect, according to predictions, on 5 June. If the Allies missed that, they might have to wait for a month before the chance to try again.

Then there was the scale of the invasion. In two days, it was planned to land 176,000 men, 20,000 vehicles and thousands of tons of military and medical equipment. Churchill, Eisenhower and their various chiefs of staff and experts paced the corridors of power, watching the weather on an hourly basis. The Meteorological Office, for those brief hours in the long days of June 1944, became the most important and talked-about institution in the entire war. The forecast for the agreed day was bad – a strong, south-westerly wind, rain and a moderate sea. The cloud ceiling was low with its attendant problems for aircraft. Eisenhower postponed. Men in the waiting ships at Portsmouth were filling latrines and their own helmets with vomit. One convoy, already under way across the churning Channel, had to be recalled.

On the morning of 5 June, a little after 4.15 a.m., Eisenhower made his irrevocable decision. The wintry weather would last for up to two weeks, but there was a break in it forecast for the next day, the 6th. The convoys met south of the Isle of Wight, the mine-sweepers ahead. It was the largest armada ever to leave the shores of England and it was on its way to deliver Europe from the tyranny of the Nazis.

D-Day, despite all the things that could have gone wrong, was an astonishing success. Churchill sent a telegram to Joseph Stalin, whose own Red Army was achieving increasing success against the Germans in the east: 'Everything has started well. The mines, obstacles and land batteries have been largely overcome. The air landings were very successful and on a large scale. Infantry landings are proceeding rapidly and many tanks and self-propelled guns are already ashore. Weather outlook moderate to good.'

Of course, there were losses. Two thousand Americans died on the beach at 'bloody Omaha' in twenty minutes. The German lines of steel and concrete defended by heavy artillery and machine guns were formidable, and the Wehrmacht commander in the west, Feldmarschal Karl von Runstedt, was one of the most impressive commanders of the war. In military terms, the Germans were fighting on interior lines of communication. The Allies would have to be equipped by sea, at least until they could break out of the Normandy beach-heads, and that would take time and cost lives. Waiting to go in at a moment's notice, the men of 1 SAS checked their chutes and gear. They packed their weapons and food rations. It was time for the 'bunch of misfits' to win their wings all over again.

10

In the Belly of the Beast

From now on all enemies on so-called Commando missions in Europe or Africa, challenged by German troops, even if they are to all appearances soldiers in uniform or demolition troops, whether armed or unarmed, in battle or in flight, are to be slaughtered to the last man.

So ran a Reich order issued by Adolf Hitler on 18 October 1942. The Allies did not know of its existence until the Nuremberg Trials of 1946, by which time the war was over and the threat had gone. What it meant was that the members of L Detachment in the desert and the men, like John Randall, about to be catapulted into the 'belly of the beast' in Nazi-occupied France would not be captured and interned but would be shot. In that context, David Stirling had got off lightly. Very soon after his capture, Malcolm Pleydell, SRS's Medical Officer, wrote to his wife:

I arrived back yesterday to hear that David Stirling is missing, believed Prisoner of War. I suppose that doesn't convey much to you, but he is our commanding officer and there is no one with his flair and gift for projecting schemes . . . the ship is without a rudder.[1]

While this was a little unkind to Paddy Mayne, everyone would have understood what Pleydell meant. From day one, then, it was widely accepted that Stirling was a prisoner. He spent the next three years trying to escape from the officers' prison camp at Colditz Castle and became part of that legend too.[2]

The Stirling and Albemarle aircraft that took off from Fairford and Tempsford in the summer and autumn of 1944 carried stores in cylindrical drums. They contained clothing, weapons, ammunition, medical supplies, tents and sleeping bags. They also contained cigarettes and rum and – in the case of Padre McLuskey – a portable 'church' complete with altar cross, prayer books and hymnals. Soft items were dropped in panniers, but they tended to explode on impact on the ground, and the worst possible scenario for the SAS was that they should leave a tell-tale trail of equipment for the Wehrmacht and SS to find. Because the target area was firmly in enemy hands and D-Day had not yet actually arrived, the initial missions were called 'heavy drops', involving parachuting in of serious equipment like jeeps. Many years later, the comedian Tony Hancock, in one of the half-hour programmes that made his name on radio and television, recounted his war memoirs in which he parachutes down in a jeep and drives straight off for Berlin, shouting to his men 'last one in the Reichstag is a cissy!' The Germans threw down their rifles and applauded. Of course, it was not quite like that. There is a photograph in the SAS archive showing a jeep of A Squadron that had landed in Operation Houndsworth. The parachute had not opened properly and the vehicle, mangled in woodland, was a write-off. It was more extraordinary that some of these vehicles, dropped in easily reassembled units, *did* survive such landings and were used for reconnaissance later.

The first operation carried out by 1 SAS was codenamed Titanic 4 and was more in keeping with SHAEF's idea for the unit to act as a front-line holding force until the main body of the Allied army could catch up. The specific purpose was to drop men inland from the Normandy beaches to give the impression of a full-scale airborne landing. The six men would carry several dummy parachutes to spread confusion among the enemy. At this distance in time, it is not easy to see very much sense in Titanic. Some books on the SAS do not mention it at all, partly because it achieved nothing and partly because it was completely illogical. The idea of disguising a seaborne invasion with an airborne one only a few miles away made no difference to the actual *act* of invasion. Had Titanic made a similar feint in the Pas de Calais or elsewhere along the French coast, it might have had some merit. As it was, brave men were risking their lives for nothing.

Freddie Poole from A Squadron and Harry 'Chick' Fowles from B Squadron set off with two troopers each. Their target was a Drop Zone a few miles south of Carentan, covering a crucial area that would have enabled the Americans from Utah and Omaha beaches to link up. The mock parachutes were attached to dummies made from sandbags and carried detonators, which would explode to simulate the rattle of rifle-fire. But it all went pear-shaped. Freddie Poole 'rang the bell', in SAS terminology: he caught his head on the Albemarle's narrow jump hole and knocked himself out. Fowles landed a couple of miles away in the darkness, and the troopers could not find their containers. They set off a few Lewes bombs and hid in hedgerows the next day (D-Day), while the beach-landings were going ahead. Four days later, Fowles joined them holed up in a ruined abbey, thanks to the local Maquis.

Staying in hiding was what the SAS had been trained for, and they did it brilliantly for three weeks, being fed by the Maquis and warned of any approaching trouble. There is no mention in the account of all this by Trooper Hurst of a radio, which would, of course, have been of vital use to them. On 28 June, the Germans nearly caught up with them and they had to move on. Having bumped into three GI parachutists, the unit kept going until 10 July, when a firefight broke out and three of the SAS men were wounded. In Operation Haft, John Randall's first drop into enemy territory, it was instilled into the team that it was vitally important to avoid clashes such as these, not only because of loss of personnel but also because reporting back enemy positions would be impossible. Titanic was vaguer on this score and, as the intended purpose had been carried out five weeks earlier, the unit's only objective now was to get back to their own lines. That was not to be. Despite Hitler's draconian order of October 1942, none of them was executed on capture; in fact, the wounded men were well cared for in a hospital in Rennes. Brave men had been lost for nothing, although Private Hurst, whose account is the only record of events, was liberated by the Americans at the end of August. One of the more callous staff officers back at base might just as well have stamped 'Pointless' on Titanic's paperwork.

Houndsworth was altogether different. The objective for A Squadron under Major Bill Fraser was to drop into the hilly region west of Dijon, an area called the Morvan, link up with the local Maquis and blow up railway lines and *anything* that would prevent the Wehrmacht from moving reinforcements up quickly to hold the Front together. Many of the men of Houndsworth were desert veterans, Originals like Reg Seekings, now a sergeant major, and Johnny Cooper, now a lieutenant. They went in on the eve of D-Day, 5 June, in the teeth of the weather that would lift temporarily the next day. In the driving rain and buffeting winds, the pilots could not find the Drop Zone, and A Squadron had to somersault through the air, hoping for the best in what paratroopers call 'dropping blind'. Cooper hit a stone wall on landing and knocked himself out, but they all managed to find one another, released two pigeons to tell base they had landed and, since there were, after all, standards, made a cup of tea! This was interrupted by Seekings, who noticed that the pigeons had already landed in the next field. He scared the traitorous birds away and hoped they were flying homewards.

The Morvan was a backward region, with a sparse population that made its living from timber-felling in the thick forests between the lakes. Settlements – and, hopefully, Germans – were few, and it was not until the next night Houndsworth could meet up with the Maquis. A Squadron were determined that a better Drop Zone should be found for the rest of the unit. Regulations were perfectly clear on this, but they were, by definition, theoretical. No amount of Ordinance Survey map work, or even aerial photography, could replace the actual appearance of the ground from the point of view of Bill Fraser's stick. There should be no tall trees, no power lines and no marshes, and the Zone should be reasonably flat. No doubt Johnny Cooper would add, it should have no stone walls.

The next night saw the second drop of equipment. Three small bonfires were lit, a hundred yards apart, and a torch operated by the Maquis signalled the relevant Morse code recognition letter. Various gadgets intended to improve on this system, such as the S-Phone (a direct link between pilot and the Maquis) and the Eureka device (a radar beacon), were unreliable. Twenty-four canisters were dropped successfully and were spirited away by local farmers who doubled as the Maquis.

The rest of the squadron did not land until 17 June. Fraser, Seekings and Ian Wellstead drove to the Drop Zone in a Maquis car to prepare the ground. Nothing illustrates more clearly the problems of communication for Commandos in the Second World War. The three had no idea that one of the aircraft had been spotted by German anti-aircraft guns and had had to turn back, unable, in torrential rain, to see the lights. Another plane, carrying Lieutenant Les Cairns' stick of 15 men, disappeared into the night and has never been found. More men landed successfully on the 19th, but Captain Roy Bradford's stick did not make it until two nights later.

One man who remembered (some!) of that drop well was John Randall's friend Fraser McLuskey, the padre. The medical officer was going and McLuskey volunteered too. He drew 14 days' rations and stuffed them somehow into his kitbag. Officers carried a map, compass and binoculars, as well as firearms. McLuskey was concerned about this. His calling meant that he could not kill anyone, but what would happen if he had to, to save his own or a comrade's life? Reg Seekings taught him how to fire a pistol but he was never a good shot and never actually carried a gun. To offset the missing firearm, the padre carried an Airborne communion set, complete with maroon silk altar cloth. He also carried, in a pannier, copies of the New Testament, copies of the Book of Common Prayer and as many hymn books as he could manage. The only weapon on him was his army jack-knife; it would arguably save his life on the night of the drop.

McLuskey was Number 9, jumping first in the second stick out of the draughty, rattling roar of the Stirling. They saw the fires burning in bombed Cherbourg far below and passed mugs of tea around to alleviate the numbing cold. They strapped their kitbags to their left legs, and, in the cramped confusion, the padre lost his gloves and helmet. After a moment of panic, all was well; not quite all – one of the gloves never did turn up. The red light inside the fuselage flashed green and Roy Bradford led them out, tumbling and twisting in the blast of air somewhere over France. The blackness below McLuskey resolved itself into a forest. He was heading for a tree and there was nothing he could do about it. The weight of his kitbag carried him down through the branches, crashing and snapping as he fell. When he came to a halt, he was hanging upside down by a leg that 'hurt like blazes'. Hacking at his tangled harness with his knife, he cut himself free, only to crash further into oblivion.

When he woke up, he was on the ground, vomiting noisily over the grass. It was about three o'clock and he fell asleep. 'Chalky' White had not been so lucky three days earlier and spent a month in hospital, having fallen on his back onto a corrugated roof. Regimental Sergeant Major Rose had written a letter, which was posted to the families of all the men who had jumped that day:

He [the named soldier] will not be able to write to you for some time but will be able to receive your letters, so please keep writing. Cheerio, keep smiling and don't worry.[3]

By the time the Houndsworth team had got together, they were 126 strong with 18 officers and 9 jeeps. They also scored a first for the SAS: two 6-pounder anti-tank guns were dropped to them. The various accounts of the Maquis involved in those missions differ widely. Anthony Kemp has them 'itching for a fight to try out their new weapons';[4] Ian Wellstead, who was there, found them undisciplined and easily discouraged. It was all about the quality of the men who led them and their incomparable knowledge of the area.

The size of Houndsworth meant that their presence could not remain a secret for long. In that sense, the operation was not typical of SAS missions. The hated French paramilitary organisation the Milice[5] operated with Germans and 'White Russians' (Soviet soldiers who fought for the Reich) combing the Morvan in search of Maquis. Ian Wellstead's unit ambushed these men on 24 June near the village of Montsauche with devastating success. The Germans and Russians, taken by surprise, went down in a hail of bullets and their vehicles were destroyed, except a motorcycle that the SAS commandeered. This was tit-for-tat warfare, guerrilla fighting that had been going on all over Europe for centuries. It had nothing to do with the sweeping grand strategy of Churchill, Roosevelt and Stalin. It did not even have much to do with the large-scale troop movements of Eisenhower and Montgomery. It was small scale, but no less terrible for that. The Germans murdered three Maquis in the village of Ouroux; the Maquis killed fourteen Germans. And so it went on, with villages burning far into the night and anyone on the road becoming a target.

When Bill Fraser's men went into action again, four-fifths of the men they were firing at became casualties. Reg Seekings was crawling through mud and rain to reach the German positions on the road. Many of his men had never seen action before, and he was trying to organise them when a machine gun opened fire right in front of him. A bullet ripped into his neck but the gun jammed and he was dragged to safety. Still conscious and with his battledress blouse saturated in blood, he dropped his pipe and went back for it before he let a Maquis doctor examine him. Padre McLuskey was there, helping the doctor work by torchlight under a tarpaulin. The bullet had lodged at the base of Seekings' skull and the doctor could not find it. Back in England later, a surgeon described the man's survival as a miracle.

More reprisals followed – six civilians were murdered by the Germans in the village of Vermot and a fourteen-year-old girl was raped. At Duns-les-Plas, 19 men were executed in the village square and their women raped. A local priest who tried to intervene was hanged from his own belfry.

David Danger, who features in John Randall's diaries, was signals officer for Johnny Wiseman, one of the three officers leading Houndsworth. He was caught sending radio messages towards the end of July by a member of the Milice, but he got away before the man had time to open fire. The bad weather that dogged most of the month meant that the men of Houndsworth could not move far or fast, but the arrival of more jeeps meant that they could range further. John Noble was shot while grappling with a German officer in a staff car they had bumped into in Ouroux, but the wound was slight. More serious was the incident that led to the death of Roy Bradford. On 20 July, his unit ran into a nine-lorry convoy of Wehrmacht troops. In the firefight, Bradford was killed, as was the jeep's rear gunner, Bill Devine. Chalky White, still in pain from his injured back, had three fingers blown off his left hand. Lying in pain in a Maquis camp that night, he said, 'Maudie will give me hell for losing her ring.'[6] He had killed 62 Germans on that fatal road.

By the end of August, Operation Houndsworth came to an end. As the Allies advanced through France, the need for such dangerous missions disappeared. As far as these things can be measured, A Squadron had taken light casualties – two men dead and seven wounded. By comparison, the Germans had lost two hundred and twenty men, twenty-three vehicles, six trains and an oil refinery.

The forest of Fontainebleau lies to the south of Paris, in an area between the River Loire and the Orleans Gap. And it was here, on 13 June 1944, that Ian Fenwick's D Squadron landed their advance party led by Captain Jock Riding. The main party arrived five days later and one of them, Lieutenant Watson, was not impressed by the Maquis here. They were badly organised, full of dubious characters and they quarrelled among themselves.

This was Operation Gain; the objective was a number of railway lines in the area crucial to German troop movements. Initial attacks, using men on foot with explosives in their backpacks, were successful but things fell apart on 4 July. On that night, 12 men under Captain Patrick Garstin saw the flashed B for Bertie signal from their Stirling and leapt out over the Drop Zone. As the first men hit the ground, the rattle of machine-gun fire opened up and those still coming down had no choice but to drop into the centre of a murderous field of fire. Garstin and Lieutenant Jean Wiehe, a French officer from Mauritius, were hit, as was Lance Corporal Howard Lutton. Troopers Leslie Norman and R. Morrison landed last and obeyed the wounded Wiehe's orders to get away and make for the beaches to the north west. After several days hiding in a cave and getting food and clothes from local civilians, they reached safety. Trooper Castelow was not so careful. He reached a village called Vet-le-Petit and somebody gave him a bicycle. When he stopped for a rest, however, in civilian clothes in the middle of a retreating German unit, someone stole the bike. Furious, Castelow swore in English and was immediately arrested. He was interrogated by the Gestapo but gave nothing away. On 9 September, alone with one guard, he saw his chance to escape. He killed the guard and ran for it. With the cool bravado for which the SAS have become famous, he wrote later, 'I swam the Moselle and started walking back towards the Americans.'[7]

Back on 5 July, Garstin, Serge Vaculik, Thomas Jones and Thomas Varey were captured at the Drop Zone where someone had betrayed them. For four weeks, they were interrogated in Paris by the Gestapo. Those men were masters at obtaining information, using a variety of vicious techniques out of the Dark Ages, and Garstin was already at a serious disadvantage with a bullet in his neck and a broken arm and leg. On 8 August, they were told to change into civilian clothes and driven to woods near the capital. When it was obvious that they were to be shot, all but Garstin dashed off through the trees. A Gestapo officer put a bullet through Garstin's head, and Varey was caught later and killed. The others got away. When other members of the SAS reached the area in September, there were fresh flowers on Garstin's grave.

The betrayals and losses of the SAS in these operations pale into insignificance alongside Bulbasket. Like Houndsworth, Captain John Tonkin's role would be to drop ahead of the main unit, liaise with the Maquis and estimate whether a sizeable SAS force could be dropped in the Vienne, east of Poitiers. As we have seen, Tonkin and Richard Crisp, both from B Squadron, went to London to be briefed by SOE, who still felt that all covert operations behind enemy lines belonged to them. The SOE told Tonkin to land in France with a gun in one hand and a bar of chocolate in the other. The weather was causing delays and the pair were taken to Hassells Hall, not far from Tempsford Aerodrome, where Tonkin did jigsaw puzzles with a girl whose name among SOE and a much wider public would become legend – Violette Szabo.[8]

The drop took place without a hitch at 1.37 a.m. on the morning of D-Day, and Tonkin and Crisp came down, as planned, 20 miles south-west of Chateauroux. Here, they were met by 'Samuel', actually Amadée Maingard, the local Maquis leader. Two nights later, an eight-man stick led by Lieutenant Thomo Stephens landed followed by the rest a few days after that. The area, Tonkin had discovered, was crawling with Germans, and changed orders had sent nearly half his men on sabotage missions nearby. Tonkin had not been informed, let alone consulted, and he now had half the force he had expected. Undeterred, he attended a secret meeting at the nearby Chateau Manès, headquarters of the Armée Secrête.

The same problem that Lieutenant Watson had noted became apparent now. Whereas Padre McLuskey and John Randall have fond memories of the Maquis and admired their dogged heroism in an unsung war, Tonkin realised that there were too many chiefs here. Colonel 'Bernard' ran the show, but the Communist Resistance, the Forces Françoises de l'Interieur, seemed at least likely to go their own way. Tonkin's closest go-between on the ground was Captain Dieudonné, codenamed Maurice.

There were too many Germans in the area, including the notorious 2nd SS Panzer Division, Das Reich,[9] for foot attacks to be successful, so a Phantom patrol was sent to radio back exact positions for RAF bombing raids instead. This was exactly the work that Phantom had been set up for, and, in Operation Haft in July, Randall was essentially carrying out Phantom work as a fully fledged member of the SAS. The Drop was nearly a disaster. A German division – perhaps Das Reich – was thundering along the road between Limoges and Poitiers, but the die was already cast, and the risk was taken to set up the landing lights. The first stick of 12 men bailed out, then a second plane dropped their equipment. Presumably, the noise of the division on the road drowned out the drone of the Stirlings, and their bright headlights disguised the fact that the tumbling containers' lights had come on prematurely. These were supposed to illuminate as the canisters hit the ground, yet here they were, advertising their position in the sky like fairy lights. Nobody in the ground forces noticed.

The wailing sirens of an air raid rang out over the countryside as the railway sidings at Poitiers took direct hits by the RAF, and John Sadoine's Phantom boys dropped 30 miles from the Zone, the pilot thoroughly rattled by the lights of the convoy.

Despite this nervy beginning, and the fact that Bulbasket's commander had been left totally in the dark in respect of last-minute changes, the fragmented units inflicted some damage. Lieutenant Morris, who had once ridden the sand-coloured jeeps with the LRDG, blew the main Poitiers–Tours line with his three men. Lieutenant Peter Weaver's team destroyed a train on the

Bordeaux to Saur track. Corporal Kinnevane's outfit, however, blew off course and one of them was captured in the town of Airvault. They all lost their kit.

Either SOE had got it wrong or the Reich was moving faster than expected, because, by 12 June, Tonkin reported via his radio that the area was 'lousy with enemy'. The Maquis told him that his presence was known and that 400 soldiers had been handpicked to find and eliminate the SAS. He needed jeeps and firepower. He had neither. Nor did he have John Randall's friend Captain Sadoine. In his subsequent report, Tonkin is scathing of Sadoine, claiming that he was being difficult and had no intention of joining up with him. It is an odd situation, but Sadoine was known to be difficult in Phantom; perhaps this was a manifestation of the same problem.

The much-needed jeeps were dropped on the night of 17 June, but that incident too caused problems. Thomo Stephens would go with La Chouette, the Communist Spanish Civil War veteran Camille Olivet, to reconnoitre the Drop Zone in civilian clothing. This was not SAS procedure. Men in uniform should be captured as prisoners of war; men hiding in civvies could be shot as spies. No one knew about Hitler's directive that made such distinctions irrelevant. Olivet quietly saved Stephens' life by removing from his coat pocket a packet of English cigarettes and an army-issue roll of toilet paper. Peasants in that area, Olivet explained, wiped their bums with grass, soaked in chlorophyll. Stephens' French was not very good and, as they paused at a café, people took him for a German. The Drop Zone had been planted with saplings, so it had to be altered, and a Vichy-sympathising vet helping to deliver a calf nearby was held under house arrest until after the jeeps came down.

Four of them landed close together, one sliding off a barn roof and crashing into a vineyard. This was Tonkin's and he hauled the steering wheel from under a seat cover and a Vickers machine gun from the back. He assembled both and sat in the vehicle. Olivet remembered later that the gun's magazine looked like a box of Camembert, but he was quietly proud when the captain said, 'La Chouette, your place is beside me, at the machine gun.'[10]

Tonkin's next comment in his subsequent report again mentions John Sadoine. He was trying to contact him, but 'Maquis jealousy and distrust' made this impossible. This may be due to the fact that Sadoine was himself a Belgian, speaking the language fluently. Did he have some personal agenda about which Tonkin knew nothing and which still eludes us after all these years? The SAS man could only claim that Sadoine made excuses for not joining the others and seemed to relish his independence. Tonkin had no Eureka device, and umpteen supply drops failed because of bad weather. There is a sense that the captain was losing it. John Tonkin was only 23 and, although a veteran, he seemed bowed down with responsibility. Peter Weaver thought so, in an unpublished memoir years later, and Olivet, who owed him nothing, pointed out some basic lapses of judgement.

On 3 July, disaster struck. Four days before John Randall took to the air in Operation Haft, Tonkin's camp near Verrières was hit by an ambush. The jury is still out on whether this was an act of betrayal by locals or lax security on Tonkin's part; it may have been a combination of both. Two of the most experienced SAS men, Ken Bateman and Dougie Eccles, had not come back from a sabotage raid the day before. Some of the boys may have wandered into town; some of the local girls may have wandered into the camp. Olivet, in a letter to the historian Max Hastings years later, explained the situation. There were no sentries on duty on 3 July. Hastings had postulated that the SAS were outgunned that morning, but Olivet is adamant that they were well armed, with machine guns, carbines and bazookas. 'Why didn't they reply?' he asked in the context of the SAS returning fire. 'And why, on the German side, were there no wounded or killed? Mystery.'[11]

Peter Weaver was so deeply asleep that he could not make out the noise at first. It was the crash and thump of mortars that had shaken him awake. There was chaos and panic, most men dashing for the woods where the Wehrmacht were in position. Tonkin tried to organise people into small units and planted bombs on the three jeeps parked nearby. Maurice and two of the Maquis lay flat in a field of cabbages and prayed. The captain stayed put, destroying the code book, and then hid behind a rock. Incredibly, the Germans did not see him. Lieutenant Thomo Stephens, wounded, was half dragged to Verrières where they tied him to a tree. The locals, already aware of gunfire early in the morning, were hauled out to witness the punishment like a British regiment in a hollow square or a ship's company in Nelson's day. Stephens was beaten to death with rifle butts.

A similar, if quicker, end faced the 30 prisoners taken by truck to Poitiers. Three nights after the ambush, they were marched into the darkness of the forest of Saint Sauvant. An American airman, Lincoln Bundy, was with them, as was an anonymous member of the Maquis. They were shot by firing squad, bullets from the Maschinengewehr 42s thumping into bodies that jerked and writhed, then lay still. Later that day, Tonkin reported that he had eleven men left, as well as Sadoine's five-man Phantom unit. Bulbasket had ground to a halt. Too many men with too few vehicles had dwindled to not enough with only one jeep. The survivors were air-lifted along with a French SAS unit and brought home.

While the various SAS operations got under way soon after D-Day, John Randall was with Paddy Mayne in Gloucestershire. As a Phantom, he had waited for long months in Algeria and Tunisia while other men were sent to the Front. While his fellow officers landed on the beaches of Sicily and then Italy, Randall had been sent home on leave. Now, it was happening all over again. He had trained with the SAS, played rugby with them, sang 'Lili Marlene' with the best. He already had his parachute wings and was arguably the best radio operator in the regiment. 'Sir,' he said to Mayne when the waiting got to him, 'when are you sending me?'

The twice-winner of the DSO, the man of action, the Lion, looked at him and said in his soft Irish accent, 'You're not going. You're signals officer; I need you here.'

John Randall fixed his commanding officer with those ice-blue eyes. 'Colonel,' he said, gravel-voiced, 'I didn't join the regiment to stay at home.'

Two days later, he was floating down into enemy territory, his pistol on his hip, his kitbag strapped to his leg. And his heart in his mouth.

11

Seven Brave Men

Titanic had been a waste of time; Bulbasket a disaster. Houndsworth had worked, but only just. All three operations are illustrations of what can go wrong in a war. In France the SAS were fighting a war that was unique. Front-line troops had gone ashore at dawn along the Normandy beaches, bringing immortality to a stretch of coast. They faced their own kind of hell as they jumped out of their 'Ducks' to land waist-deep in surging water and began to fight their way inland. Machine guns rattled in the morning and men dropped in the shallows where the tide would carry their bodies in later.

At least the men of D-Day faced an enemy from the front only. The SAS faced an enemy that was all around them. Theirs was a silent war, a war in which John Randall's radio communication was absolutely crucial. On paper, the various operations set up by SHAEF looked simple. Drops behind enemy lines by parachute from Stirlings or Halifaxes, liaison with the local Resistance, the Maquis, and then 'cry havoc' and unleash as much mayhem as possible in terms of blowing up railway track, bridges and roads. The broad strategy was to delay the heavy armour that was being sent to stop the Allied advance. The German high command had to accept that the Tommies and Amis had got off the beaches, but Normandy – and indeed much of France – was criss-crossed with hedges and ditches, murderous country for infantry. There were rivers and other obstacles where the invasion would be stopped in its tracks.

The object of Titanic was one of subterfuge and misinformation. Just as the Allies had kept the Wehrmacht guessing about the location of the invasion itself, so they would continue to confuse. It was all about delay. It was all about catching the enemy on the back foot. But luck had not been with Titanic.

Bulbasket had been altogether more ambitious and, consequently, more prone to failure. The political truth was such that the welcome the SAS were likely to receive was open to question. France had been occupied for four years, but, for every Frenchman (and woman) who despised the Nazis, there could be half a dozen with a Vichy mindset, prepared to inform on night-arriving Commandos at the drop of a hat. And the Resistance itself was riven with rivalries, local, feudal, political. The Communists were not likely to share much information with anybody else and that cut two ways.

The men of Bulbasket were shot by firing squad in the forest of Saint Sauvant. We have no information about the last moments of these men. The Geneva Convention demanded that they be interned as prisoners of war, but the Nazi regime had long ago abandoned any pretence along those lines and it followed Hitler's deadly extermination of Commandos order of October 1942. The most they could have hoped for was the proverbial cigarette and blindfold. Their bodies were kicked into ditches.

It is not likely that John Randall knew anything of this as he climbed aboard the Halifax at RAF Tempsford on the night of Friday, 7 July. The detailed information we now take for granted has been pieced together by researchers over many years. Much of it was classified until recently, and all of it was top secret at the time. We know that John Tonkin had been able to get a radio message off to base on the previous afternoon, to the effect that, despite the stark horror of Bulbasket, he still had eleven SAS men with him and a five-man Phantom unit under Randall's old friend

John Sadoine. Even if base could have got information to Randall's unit in time, it was perhaps thought to be unwise. No one wanted to send men on suicide missions, but Randall's Operation Haft Drop Zone was only 20 miles from Bulbasket, and base was already wondering whether Tonkin's main problem was the sheer size of his unit. David Stirling, no doubt champing at the bit in Colditz, had he known of it, would have said 'Precisely!'

Haft had just seven men, commanded by Mike Blackman, who, at twenty-eight, was three years older than Randall, and the Intelligence officer for HQ Squadron of 1 SAS. With them was Lieutenant John Kidner, who had joined the regiment from the Wiltshires. Corporal Brown, who would become Randall's jeep driver in the months ahead, was also there, along with Troopers Baker and Harrison. The seventh man was Lance Corporal De Maison of 4 SAS, who was there, essentially, as an interpreter. Randall's French was good, but, in the highly charged area of covert operations behind enemy lines, there could be no room for misunderstanding.

Randall had been waiting for this moment for months. After all the arduous training on the bleak Ayrshire terrain around Darvel, hauling kitbags and carbines and sliding on the frozen grass, this was it. Actually getting Operation Haft and Blackman's team to France lay in the hands of Flight Lieutenant Kidd of 138 Squadron, one of two squadrons based at Tempsford, whose losses throughout the entire war were extremely high. Tempsford itself, two and a half miles from Sandy in Bedfordshire, was typical of wartime airfields – flat, level ground, small, flat-roofed control towers and miles of barbed wire. It was possibly the most top-secret airfield in the country because it was from here that a number of secret missions were flown, taking agents of the Special Operations Executive to cause havoc in France.

The Halifax was a four-engine heavy bomber made by Handley Page that somehow failed to reach the same legendary status as the similar iconic Lancaster. Blackman's unit almost certainly flew in a B.11 Series I model, specially adapted for SOE work. The usual nose armament of twin-machine guns was removed and so was the dorsal turret. This gave more space in the cramped fuselage for its 'special' passengers. Now that Allied bombing had destroyed so much of the Luftwaffe, it was less likely, at least in theory, that the Halifax would encounter enemy flights.

Kidd's job was to drop Blackman's men in the Baroche-Gondouin area five kilometres north-west of a small town called Lassay. Its position was 48° 25' North; – 00° 25' W of Mayenne. In the daylight, the place could be found easily enough. Second World War pilots relied on visibility as well as their instruments, and Lassay had no fewer than three medieval castles! But Kidd was not flying in daylight. He was flying in the dark. Into the unknown.

We can have little idea of what those seven men were feeling that night. John Randall had been practising parachute jumps at Prestwick Aerodrome, first of all with no equipment and then with a kitbag strapped to his leg. Timing was of the essence. The cords had to be released so that the bag fell away and gravity took it to the ground first. If that didn't work, a man could veer badly off course or break his ankle under the weight. We have already seen what happened to Randall's friend the padre Fraser McLuskey.

Randall, like the others, was dressed for the occasion. Long gone were the carefree days of the desert for the SAS, when men wore shorts and Arab *shemaghs* and sported beards. As an ex-'glamorous Phantom', Randall had always been very much smarter than that. He wore his green and khaki camouflaged Denison smock over his battledress and the tight-fitting circular jump cap strapped under his chin. His boots were rubber-soled so that, God forbid, should he land on tarmac, he could scuttle away without waking up any dozing sentry. The old Halifax was a 'total war machine', according to Blackman's later report, which best translates as appallingly uncomfortable. The men of Operation Haft sat opposite one another in two rows on either side of the rattling, clanking fuselage. Conversation was almost impossible because of the roar of the engines that vibrated every metal plate and rivet on board. The noise got into Randall's head, and all of them were probably looking forward to the utter silence of the drop. It got colder by the minute as the Halifax crossed the coast and the Channel. Best not to think that it was several thousand feet below.

By the time they crossed the French coast, the bumping and buffeting of plane and air pockets combined to tangle up kitbags and webbing. Randall was grateful for the RAF tea and the rum that kindly old George White, the quartermaster, had provided for each man.

Only once did Flight Lieutenant Kidd have to take evasive action, banking his plane so that the occupants tumbled about all the more. Who said the Luftwaffe were finished?

The cold was all the more intense because the floor of the Halifax had the odd hole. After three hours, Randall looked down to see the ground below. You can do this yourself today. Look up Google Earth for the area around Lassay and you will see a patchwork of fields, bright in summer green. John Randall saw a patchwork of grey, black lines marking the hedgerows and roads. There were no lights. After all, this was Occupied France and there *was* a war on. Blackman remembered hoping that the ground was actually 800 feet below, not the 500 he feared was the case. If Kidd brought the bus in too low, the chutes would not open properly and what had happened to McLuskey would look like a Sunday school outing. The men of Haft seemed poised over that hole for years before the shout came from the despatcher Tommy Thompson: 'Go!'

Adrenalin kicked in. Randall had done this before, many times. God, he had even pushed Randolph Churchill, the Prime Minister's son, out of an aircraft once. But this was different. This was real. This was war. What had Benjamin Disraeli called the Second Reform Bill? A leap in the dark? The man had no idea.

Out over the Loire, the seven parachutes opened one by one, like petals bursting silently with the help of time-lapse photography today. Above him, Randall felt the tug of his chute and the roar of silk as it opened. Men of the SAS had not always been that lucky. No one dwelled on the Roman candle – of the chute that failed to open; but it had happened. It could always happen.

Randall released the kitbag from his leg, and felt his boots hit the ground seconds later. He rolled, hauling in the chute's ropes before it carried him too far. In the darkness, he saw the others come down, spread over an area, but an acceptably small one, and heard the Halifax's engines die away in the distance. The first job was to get rid of the chute. Kidd's flying had been so accurate that Mike Blackman actually landed on the Maquis member flashing the recognition letter from the shrubbery, so they were definitely in the right place. Even so, it was impossible to know how many Boche were about, and parachutes in the night were so very *white*. They all had their compass bearings and blew their bird-call whistles to find the others.

The process took about half an hour, while each man scrabbled his way through the hedgerows, anxious to make as little noise as possible. And what, cramped and tired and cold, had the men of 1 SAS landed into? Although none of them could have known it, the previous day – 6 July 1944 – George Mandel was shot by the Milice in the woods at Fontainebleau. Churchill had called him 'the first resister' and would have liked to have had the man leading the Free French in Britain rather than the impossibly prickly Charles de Gaulle. As a Jew and an outspoken journalist and politician, Mandel had been arrested back in August 1941 and shunted to the camps of Oranienburg, then Buchenwald. Three days before Randall landed in France, Mandel was transferred to Paris to be executed in reprisal for the Maquis killing of Philippe Henriot, Minister of Propaganda under the Vichy government. Before the bullets of the Milice thumped into his body, he said, 'To die is nothing. What is sad is to die without seeing the liberation of the country and the restoration of the Republic.' In their own quiet way, John Randall and the men of Haft were going to do something about that.

Intelligence reports suggested that the locals around Lassay were 100 per cent reliable, but no one could be sure, and the longer a unit like the SAS stayed in an area, the greater their chances of betrayal and discovery. This was what had happened to Bulbasket and no one wanted a repetition of that. The greatest problem were the Milice Française, the militia, who were a fanatical Fascist organisation bent on smashing the Maquis in any and every way possible. Blackman had nothing but contempt for them. They were 'the most hated men in France. Traitors, cowards and bullies'.[1] In military operations, they dressed like Italian Fascisti with floppy berets, brown shirts and blue tunics, and even wore pre-First World War-style Adrian helmets in combat situations. No one in the SAS regarded them as soldiers; they used assassination and torture and rounded up Jews and Communists for deportation – the infamous 'resettlement in the East'. By the time Haft landed, there were perhaps 30,000 of them across France, infinitely more dangerous than the Gestapo or the SS because they were Frenchmen, able to pick up every nuance of local dialects and knowing everyone in a given area.

Blackman's problem over the coming days was the sort of reception his men would receive and, if it was good, whether it would last. Intelligence suggested that the greatest obstacle among the French was apathy. Like hunger, the long period of Nazi occupation had driven men in on themselves. They became listless, uninterested and unable to believe that the Allies had really landed; and, if they believed that, it could only be a matter of days before they were beaten back to their ships. Everybody remembered Dunkirk. They had no idea that, as the Halifax took off from Tempsford on that July night, Hitler was making another of his many errors of judgement. He replaced the brilliant Feldmarschal Gerd von Runstedt with the ineffectual Günther von Kluge; it would be weeks before he realised his mistake.

As dawn came up on that 7 July, the American VII, VIII and XIX Corps were about to resume their attack against formidable opposition along a line from La Haye du Puits to the Vire. The

British battleship *Rodney* opened up that morning on German positions around Caen. Out of the half-light in the fields of the Drop Zone, a little group approached, men and women of extraordinary bravery who had made these clandestine early-morning rendezvous before. In his report, Mike Blackman refers to the leader of the group of Resistance fighters as '"Scientist", the British agent in the area'. In fact, 'Scientist' was not an individual but a 'circuit', a cell of 12 agents who specialised in dangerous liaisons like this.

The 'Scientist' leader was Claude de Baissac, a lugubrious-looking Frenchman with a pencil moustache. With him was his sister, Lisé, typical of the fearless young women who acted as couriers for the circuit. She had joined SOE in England, while her brother stayed behind in France, and had joined the First Aid Nursing Yeomanry (FANY) in July 1942. When the liberation came, she would dig out this uniform from its hiding place and wear it proudly. Her codenames were Odile, Irene, Marguerite and Adele, and she had been interrogated by the Gestapo more than once, telling them nothing. She had been the first female SOE agent to be flown out of Tempsford months earlier. Blackman's report mentions another woman with 'Scientist'. It is possible that this was Mary Herbert, codename Claudine, who was tall and blonde and Claude de Baissac's mistress, but, because she had given birth to his daughter the previous December and was in hiding with the baby in July, the 'other woman' who met John Randall that night was probably Phyllis 'Pippa' Latour. Her codename was Genevieve and she had been born in South Africa to a French father. Like Randall, she was a wireless expert, and during her time with 'Scientist' sent over 135 coded radio messages to London.

There was a hurried, whispered conversation, headed no doubt by De Maison, although both the women spoke fluent English. The unit then followed routine and split into two, the Maquis carrying the paratroopers' kit, to two little farms two and a half kilometres away. The object of Haft was to carry out reconnaissance of the Mayenne-Laval-Le Mans area. In particular, they were looking for troop concentrations and areas suitable for later parachute drops. Their brief was also to identify strategic targets such as roads, railways and bridges, petrol dumps and ammunition stores, so that the RAF bombing raids could be accurately pinpointed. No heroics were expected. One of the things that Blackman impressed upon his team was that they were never to attempt a pitched battle. They were seven against thousands and odds like that were not even worth considering.

John Randall's brief was crucial. In fact, in many ways, he was the most important member of the team. As radio operator, with the code signal SABU 6, it was his job to feed all the information back to base and, if need be, London. 'Scientist' had four radio signallers of their own, but they did not know the SAS codes and lacked Randall's military expertise. These men and women were recklessly brave, but they fought a war in the shadows and had little grasp of the coordination of large military units. John Randall was going to call in the RAF to bomb hell out of the Wehrmacht. He stuck to his radio like glue.

The 'Scientist' people told the Haft men that the Germans had seen them land, but, oddly, the alarm was not raised until it was well and truly daylight, by which time they were hidden in the farmhouses. The Maquis went about their usual business, cycling past troop formations and gun installations, sitting in cafés in the long summer days and picking up what gossip they could. There was a large German garrison at Lassay – John Randall radioed to say there were '150 Boche' there and this included the Gestapo. But the Gestapo had got it into their heads that the night visitors would be in civilian clothes by now, perhaps they had even been dropped in them, and they checked everybody's papers carefully. Even men they knew were stopped, challenged, searched and interrogated. In fact, at no time did John Randall change out of his battledress uniform, a fact of which he became all too aware as the campaign wore on and he attended liberation parties in Paris dressed to kill and smelling like a battlefield.

He set up the radio in a disused farmhouse, one of those oddly elegant pieces of architecture that France is renowned for. Everybody was naturally jumpy that first day, expecting a knock at the door any minute, but the Maquis kept them well informed and kept the meals coming three times a day. Denison smocks, lifejackets and kitbags, which they still had with them, were buried piecemeal in the yard outside, hidden under brushwood. All they kept with them were their compasses, their weapons and John Randall's precious radio.

Randall's reports were meticulously logged at base. Between 7 July and the middle of August, he made no fewer than 103 transmissions, all of them coded. The unit's own position and any information they could see for themselves or had gleaned from the Maquis concerning the enemy had to be relayed. Reading these messages and Blackman's reports side by side, we can construct the most detailed description of a wartime SAS operation ever written. The third of Randall's messages spoke of the low morale of the Wehrmacht. The SS remained fanatically committed to the end, but the ordinary army units knew what they were facing. The extraordinary scale of the Allied landings had shaken them badly, and some of them would never recover from that psychologically. They were terrified of the bombing, Randall reported, and moved, when they had to, by night, keeping to secondary roads where they hoped the canopies of overhanging trees would give them cover. Vehicle markings had been removed and insignia ripped from uniforms. The SAS were impressed by the German use of camouflage and cover, and got used to seeing bushes hurtle past them at 40 miles an hour. Birnam Wood had indeed come to Dunsinane.

'Blackman starts recce tonight,' Randall radioed. On that third evening, the captain set out with Lieutenant John Kidner and a Maquis guide called André. This cannot have been the 'Scientist' agent André Grandclément because later events would reveal him as a double agent; Blackman's unit would have gone the way of Bulbasket had that been the case. Before the war, André had been a teacher. He knew the area like the back of his hand, all the 'planks' or hiding places. He could hear the Germans before Blackman could, smell them before that. And he moved like a cat. But then, André had been doing this for four years. The three men flattened themselves into the undergrowth by the roadside as cars and motorcycles passed, all of them carrying Wehrmacht or SS. There was a sneaky temptation to open up with their guns, but Blackman knew such cowboy tactics were dangerous and pointless; a handful of dead Germans weighed against an entire operation. He let them pass.

The three reached a village, Le Ham, ten kilometres from Lassay. Like all villages in the area, it was quiet and calm. There was always a church (this one dedicated to St Pierre), a pub (or two), perhaps a mill. In one of those strange situations that war throws up (but no film script writer would contemplate), André took his lads to a house in the main street, and the owners, Bernard and his wife, provided the SAS men with an excellent meal at four o'clock in the morning. They slept in comfortable beds that night and awoke in the late morning to the rattle of German truck convoys snarling below their windows. Blackman and Kidner watched it all from their beds; Blackman called it 'observation deluxe'.

Moving at night in British uniform was one thing, but, of course, it would have been suicidal in the day. So leaving Kidner at Bernard's, Blackman borrowed a scruffy jacket, trousers and cap and sauntered through the village. He must have been confident that his French was up to it because he makes no mention of De Maison. He climbed the impressive Mont du Saule, a peak over a thousand feet above sea level. From here, he had a clear view of the German troop dispositions but he was well aware that his men had been in their abandoned farmhouses now for four days. It was time to move on and find a new 'plank'. Back at Bernard's, he and Kidner were able to pick up Paddy Mayne's broadcast over the radio, although how he could do this without Randall he doesn't say. This must have been the RoMo system, by which personal messages could be transmitted. In general terms, both Blackman and Randall knew that the BBC news could be useful too, but it was often misleading and inaccurate. The British public were no doubt cheered by Churchillian propaganda, but men in the field needed something more.

Back at the farm by four o'clock the next morning, John Randall had some news. The Germans had found a Maquis container in the area. Time to move on. Under cover of darkness that night, the unit crept out, this time to end up under one roof. The Maquis went ahead to lay provisions into the 'plank' that Blackman had found the day before. Once again, the genial Bernard and his wife provided a meal, at 3.30 a.m., and Randall set up his radio in a disused barn near Le Ham. It was 11 July by now, and the reconnaissance carried out from the heights of Mont du Saule was proving useful. There were booby traps everywhere, especially on the roads that led through the Forêt de Pail, and convoys were moving on Caen with heavy guns, ammunition and ambulances coming from Alençon. On that day, too, there were troops from the Russian Front. This was part of a policy that the Reich adopted from time to time. Germany's problem had always been its geographical position in the heart of Europe. In two conflicts in twenty years, it had faced a war on two fronts and had to split its armed response accordingly. Depending on what was happening on the fronts, troops could be transferred to the area of most need. There was no doubt that the Wehrmacht *should* have stopped the Allies at the Normandy beaches. Now, they were having to play catch up.

The comeback from base was that these reports were much appreciated. The RAF would be along shortly to bomb the targets. 'Complaint re coding,' reads the message. 'Randall uses too much vocab.' Randall left no written response to this rebuke; presumably because he was using too much vocab already!

A few days later, Blackman and Kidner were off again, walking due east to Courcite and beyond to the hamlets of St Thomas, St Aubin and St Mars. There was a curious schizophrenia about this area. It was openly anti-German, with many locals walking about in various French uniforms. On the other hand, the SAS men's 'host' was much more rattled by their presence than Bernard had been. Blackman did not sleep well as a result. In the pre-dawn light, he peered through his blackout curtains to see German ambulances heading north. If the Wehrmacht line was holding, it could only be by the skin of its collective teeth. Evacuees from Caen began drifting through Courcite. It had been the story all over Europe for five years – columns of terrified, exhausted people, trying to carry the kitchen sink with them, moving from one bomb site to another. Blackman and Kidner held their breath. In their doorway that evening, local girls were laughing and canoodling with drunken German soldiers only feet from them. 'Collaboration?' a number of French women asked after the war. 'Not us.'

Under darkness, the pair moved on again, this time to a Maquis HQ near St Mars. Here they met commissioned officers, a doctor and 150 hard-boiled eggs prepared for a Maquis team who would now not be arriving. Blackman doesn't record how many he and Kidner polished off. Back at the 'plank' that night, it was Randall's job to relay all the information Blackman had discovered, as well as Maquis reports that had come directly to him.

It was time for Randall to stretch his legs. One of the problems of being a radio operator is that you cannot walk around with your equipment in the open and you cannot stray too far from it or it defeats the whole point of an operation like Haft. That night, he went with Blackman to look at another 'plank'. This one was in the village of Hardanges with the heights of Mont du Saule to their back – ideal observation ground. The Maquis were covering 40 to 50 kilometres a day on their bicycles, and Randall was impressed with them. Today, he has nothing but respect and fond memories. Blackman agreed: 'They are hardworking, thorough and with a large reserve of stamina . . . They are in general cool, clear-thinking and untemperamental.'[2] Even children as young as 12 could read maps and draw diagrams, and the SAS employed them too.

The new 'plank' was another disused farmhouse with two rooms on the ground floor they used for living and dining. Every day, the troopers swept out old straw and laid more as a carpet. The latrine was outside, but that was a small price to pay for security. Randall sent through a vital report to the RAF – their targets for the next day were the bridges west of Javron. All convoys passed this way and destroying them would cause huge delays.

It was days later that Maquis reports came in with the news that Erwin Rommel was in the area, but locating the 'Desert Fox' was difficult. Although he had been beaten back by Montgomery and his 8th Army in North Africa, he had a brilliance that inspired his own troops and rattled his enemies. The officers of Haft considered asking for an SAS unit to be sent in to take him out. Was it coincidence that the Feldmarschal was badly wounded as he returned in his car from a troop inspection? Or had the Maquis reports, as relayed by Randall, been accurate after all? Rommel had been returning from a visit to Sepp Dietrich's 1st SS Panzer Division, and his car was strafed by a Spitfire of 602 Squadron flown by a South African pilot, Chris de Roux. Rommel was thrown from his car, his skull fractured in three places. He would never again pose a serious threat to the Allies.

Blackman was preparing for the possibilities of joining up with additional reinforcements, and Randall's radio messages refer to an SOE agent named Dennis. The man was asking for supplies to be provided via Blackman's unit, particularly wireless transmitter sets and Michelin maps. Although Blackman's report makes no mention of the fact, it is clear that someone back at base doubted Dennis's authenticity. The problem with tracking SOE agents in the war was that their work was shrouded – and still is – in secrecy. To take two high-profile examples, the actors Anthony Quayle and Christopher Lee were both working for the organisation. Quayle, who died in 1989, was disturbed by his experiences with SOE and declined to talk about it. Lee, still with us, has made one or two enigmatic statements, but has provided no details. Exactly who Dennis was is a mystery. A message from base asked Randall to ask him where he lunched (presumably, he had a regular haunt in London) and the day on which he was given his DSO. The only Dennis in the SOE lists is Denis John Barrett, who was killed in action some time in 1944 and no information is available. Because agents routinely used aliases, however, Dennis could be anyone. Since Blackman's unit continued to liaise with the man and no harm came to them, we must assume he was genuine.

In wartime, no one trusted anybody. They did not trust equipment either. Randall's transmissions were, of course, sent in code and that sometimes mystified base. For example, in August FORENDERS MSNBOCH BIKE was presumed to refer to a German motorcycle that Lieutenant Anderson (with whom the unit had teamed up by this time) had acquired – he needed petrol for it. At some point, too, a courier pigeon was used. These birds had a long history of service, having winged their way with vital messages over the trenches of the First World War; and, of course, Phantom had their huge aviary in St James's Park. On 16 July, Randall reported that a pigeon had been found one kilometre away without a daily paper. Could this be right? he asked. All pigeons dropped by the RAF were accompanied by a newspaper and a questionnaire![3] The pigeon was OK, said base, and demanded a full report of progress in cipher via said pigeon. The pigeon was released with relevant information on the 21st, but base reported it had not arrived by the 25th and there is no further mention of the bird.

For three days, the unit stayed in the open, the most dangerous and exposed position they had held. They realised that a retreating army might occupy any abandoned building, to rest or to dump wounded men. Randall set up his transmitter in some bushes on the edge of a wood next to a cornfield and hoped for the best. Every day at eleven o'clock, the unit listened to messages from base. These were always in code and delivered to individual officers via their codenames. Randall, as we know, was SABU 6;

Blackman was SABU 52; Kidner SABU 54. One particular message came to Blackman by name and it was a personal greeting from his wife. It was a huge morale boost – and the others never let him forget it!

On 26 July, the Maquis told Randall that the Das Reich, Adolf Hitler and Gross Deutschland Divisions had been seen on the road. The Das Reich had already become notorious in the annals of SS atrocities. Six weeks earlier, the unit – the 2 SS Panzer Division – had been told that an SS officer was being held at a village nearby. Das Reich went in with all guns blazing. In a scene that was a horrific action replay of the work of the *Einsatzgruppen* in Eastern Europe in 1940 and '41, all the women and children were locked in the village church. The men were then forced into six barns and systematically shot. The six survivors told a disbelieving world months later that the deaths had been slow – bullets to the kneecaps first. When the shooting stopped and the dead or dying lay in piles, Das Reich poured petrol over them and threw in matches: 190 men died.

Then it was the turn of the women and children. The SS blew the church up with an incendiary device and machine-gunned the survivors as they ran out screaming from the rubble: 247 women and 205 children died. The oldest was ninety, the youngest just over one week. There was the deepest of ironies about these killings; Das Reich had gone into Oradour-Sur-Glane by mistake – they had hit the wrong village.

Only three days before the division was sighted, recognisable by the Wolf's Hook emblem on its vehicles, base had told Randall that cases were being prepared against war criminals and any information relating to atrocities and the names of officers involved would be much appreciated. It took years for this sort of detail to emerge, leading, in some cases, to trials; in others, to nothing. Unknown numbers of SS men merely slipped off their armbands at the end of the war and wandered away, relying on victims' bad memories and burnt paperwork. Base's information from elsewhere was that Das Reich was still on the Eastern Front. On the last day of July, the RAF attacked near Villains. For 15 minutes, the ground shook and black smoke filled the sky. 'Splendid show,' radioed Randall.

By early August, the campaign was hotting up. Messages between Randall and base talk of Belgian SAS being dropped nearby to undertake a similar reconnaissance to the one Haft was carrying out. Randall reported that the Germans were continually on the move and that morale among the various units was very low. Some of them had no boots.

Blackman had been arranging for the rest of his men from B Squadron to join the unit. The Drop Zone had been chosen and the Maquis were standing by to assist when the war intervened. A sudden German retreat spread alarm among the men of Haft. The Americans reached the outskirts of Lassay by 15 July, but the advance halted there to give units time to regroup and the thrust of the local attack was directed against St Lo. Only a few hundred yards from the farm, where seven faces peered out cautiously over window sills, Wehrmacht units, panzers, guns and even female agents were streaming east. Time to move again.

The last 'plank' that Blackman's team occupied was in an open meadow surrounded by cornfields near the village of Loupfougères. The SAS men were snug in a warm haystack with a corrugated roof over their heads, and a pump nearby provided fresh water. Here Lieutenant Anderson caught up with them, having been trying to find them for some days. With the battle of Mayenne exploding across the fields, Blackman and Randall crept out one night to take delivery of supplies at an agreed Drop Zone. All went well and the pair dragged the bags back to the haystack. It was a surreal experience to watch a battle bursting nearby and not to be part of it. The artillery barrage rarely stopped and the sky was streaked with the vapour trails of aircraft. There cannot have been many of the Luftwaffe machines left, but Randall saw more of them go down during these days, hurtling to the fields of France in a column of black smoke and bursting flame.

By 6 August, it was clear from base information that the

Americans had virtually outflanked Haft. Randall was in communication with them by radio. This was George Patton's newly constituted Third Army, making for Le Mans, and Blackman decided to contact them. Randall's last messages – his *very* last was sent at 2100 hours on 9 August – talk of total confusion. To their north, Mortain had been retaken by the Americans after fierce fighting and an out-of-his-depth Feldmarschal von Kluge begged Hitler to let him pull back. Hitler refused. Events were now spiralling so rapidly that radio information could not keep up with them, and, now that Patton's Third had arrived, the work of Haft was virtually over.

So, on the afternoon of 10 August, the SAS set off, bristling with side arms in the company of two Maquis guides and two German prisoners who had stumbled on them as they were getting the hell out of the area and possibly the entire war. There were still Wehrmacht units in place, hidden in woods with 88 mm guns at the ready. There were German Military Police everywhere, and that night the seven were out in No Man's Land, with the Americans in front and the Germans behind. Everybody knew about friendly fire, and an armed unit, moving on rubber-soled boots in the darkness, to a jumpy GI, could be just about anybody.

In the event, the unit's meeting with the Americans was anti-climactic. At lunchtime the next day, the first three Yanks Blackman and Randall saw were lounging about as though on a picnic. One was sunbathing and two were asleep. This was XX Corps, protecting the Third Army's right flank, and these three must have missed Patton's famously profane speech in which he declared his intention to get to Berlin quickly so that he could personally shoot 'that paper-hanging son of a bitch Hitler'.

Blackman reported to the XX's commanding officer, and Haft climbed aboard a half track, bouncing along the Laval–Le Mans road on their way back to base at 21st Army Group. Montgomery himself wanted to see the men who had successfully guided his support aircraft to bomb so many targets into oblivion. As it turned out, an urgent staff meeting was called, and Blackman,

Randall and Kidner reported to the Intelligence officer instead.

Haft won the Military Cross for Mike Blackman, and John Randall was Mentioned in Despatches. The citation reads:

Normandy, France, July 7–August 12 1944. During the operations in France in which Lieutenant Randall took part, it was necessary to transmit by wireless much vital and important information which not only affected the tactical situation but also the main battle situation. It was of utmost importance to transmit this information immediately it was received, often irrespective of personal safety and the close proximity of enemy concentrations. Lieutenant Randall, who was the signals officer on these operations, did invaluable work in organising and transmitting this information. At all times, he managed to bring the wireless sets into operation when required, not only at the normal scheduled times but also on the emergency schedule. Often it was extremely difficult to transmit owing to the nearness of the enemy, exact local position and the possibility of RDF[4] but nevertheless during the whole operation, no signalled scheduled timing was missed. Further, the maintenance and repair of the wireless sets themselves was continuously carried out successfully under difficult conditions and at times when urgent information had to be sent. Lieutenant Randall at all times maintained the sets in perfect working order, thus ensuring that all information requiring transmission was up to date. As commander of the operational party, I therefore recommend that Lieutenant Randall be mentioned in despatches for his invaluable assistance and devotion to duty.

It was time, after five weeks behind enemy lines, for John Randall to go home.

12

'Is Paris Burning?'[1]

John Randall kept no diary for the early autumn of 1944. After Haft, a small but perfectly executed SAS operation, the seven brave men went home. He touched base with his mother, Alfred Friend and the people at Sevenoaks, and spent time renewing friendships in London. Like a number of the returning soldiers, he could not talk in detail about Haft or even the training at Darvel. Undercover work like this was beginning to be hinted at in the Press, but actual details were not forthcoming for years. In the case of Haft, this book is the first time it has been covered in such detail, 70 years after it happened.

London was no longer the 'gay' city that Randall remembered, although the 'business as usual' spirit of the Blitz had returned now that a second wave of bombing terror had arrived. Rumours of rocket attacks from long range had been in circulation since 1943, but now the V1s, known as Doodlebugs, arrived for real. With hindsight, Hitler stood no more chance of subduing the civilian population now than he had in 1940; in fact, less so, because the Hun was on the run, as the tabloids put it, and, surely, the Reich could not last much longer. On 15 July, while John Randall was still radioing his vital messages from the hedgerows of France, the air-raid sirens wailed at eleven thirty. The all clear did not sound for another 11 hours. For the next two weeks, about a hundred V1s fell every day, mostly on the capital. Fighter planes could bring some down, anti-aircraft batteries a few more, because, once launched, there was no pilot on board the flying bombs to take evasive action. At night, the tails of the Doodlebugs looked like shooting stars, and at first watchers on the ground took them for blazing enemy aircraft on their way down. Their noise was so indescribable that we have hundreds of different versions – 'a grating, sinister growl'; 'a disagreeable splutter'; 'an express train with a curious hidden undertone'.[2]

When that noise stopped and the engine cut out, the bomb dropped like a stone, with civilians flinging themselves flat, hoping to God that that particular Doodlebug did not have their name on it. June and July were cloudy, with the same bad weather that had hampered D-Day lasting for most of the summer, and the V1s were not visible above the low cloud until it was too late. Evelyn Waugh, that most unlikely of Commandos, wrote, 'It was as impersonal as a plague, as though the city were infested with enormous, venomous insects.'[3]

John Randall realised, along with many others, that London 'was becoming once more the city of the brave and the few'.[4] In his diary for 1943, he had already sympathised with those at home, waiting anxiously for news of loved ones. Now, the front line had again come to London and it was all so much worse. But the SAS were still in France and there was a war going on there too, so, after a fortnight, Randall was back.

By the middle of August, the Wehrmacht were in full retreat, the scenes of hurried departure that Randall had seen for himself in Haft being replayed all over France. On the 17th, the Canadian 2nd Division captured Falaise, and, the next day, the 'gap' between the Americans and the Poles was closed at Chambois. Three days later, the US XV Corps established a bridgehead on the Seine. Feldmarschal von Kluge, the wrong man placed in the job of commanding the Axis forces in the west by Hitler, was dismissed by the Führer. Time and again, as men failed him, Hitler smelled treachery rather than incompetence. On the 18th, von Kluge killed himself rather than face a trial for treason and a desperate-looking Feldmarschal Walther Model took his place.

If anything, the retreat made life *more* hazardous for the SAS units scattered beyond what had been enemy lines, because the structure of the Wehrmacht was crumbling. What is euphemistically described as mopping-up operations, clearing the enemy out of villages and camps, was highly dangerous. Behind any door, in any barn, crouching under any hedge, there could be a pocket of German resistance that had far more firepower than the SAS. Paddy Mayne had parachuted into the Houndsworth area on 7 August, after his plane almost crashed on takeoff. John Randall was on his way home on leave then, but Ian Fenwick's D Squadron in Gain had been overrun by the Germans in the Forêt d'Orléans. The brilliant cartoonist was killed as he fought his way past a machine-gun nest in his jeep. Two Originals who were nearby, Vic Long and 'Gentleman Jim' Almonds, were horrified that the man had been so reckless, breaking the SAS protocol of common sense by taking on an enemy too powerful to beat. Mayne got to the Morvan instead, liaising with Bill Fraser's A Squadron.

On the 15th, Operation Haggard was set up under the command of Major Eric Lepine. Six officers and forty-six men of B Squadron linked up with 3 French Para Battalion to sow discord and chaos between the towns of Nevers and Gien. Although they remained in the area with the usual Maquis support, the war was virtually outstripping them. Most of the Wehrmacht had gone as Model regrouped. The man had a fearsome reputation as an Eastern Front specialist, and was not impressed by what he saw as the flabbiness in the west. When the Panzer Lehr Division, exhausted after trying to stem the tide of the Allied advance, asked to be allowed time for recuperation, Model said, 'On the Eastern Front we rest and recuperate IN the front line. In future it will be like that here.'[5] The order from Hitler was unequivocal; Paris must be held at all costs.

Haggard quickly merged with Operation Kipling, because, with an estimated 233 Germans killed, 2 bridges destroyed and 37 motorised vehicles put out of action, its work was done. Kipling, led by C Squadron under Tony Marsh, began on 14 August with an advance party led by Captain Derrick Harrison. By now, there was more likelihood that SAS men would come under fire from Americans or trigger-happy Maquis, so Marsh gave orders for the Union Jack to be flown from radio aerials. All went well until 22 August when Harrison ran into a large SS unit in the village of Les Ormes. In the firefight that followed, Lance Corporal Jimmy 'Curly' Hall was killed and Harrison had his hand smashed by a bullet. James McDiarmid, an Original famous for his 'Puddle Dance' at SAS parties, took revenge, not just for the popular Hall, but also for the civilians the SS were shooting at random. He found a crowd of Germans two days later, put them up against a wall and let rip with his machine gun. It was not Geneva Convention, but it was retaliation and, many would say, a kind of justice.

John Randall was part of the mopping-up operations. He was not exactly a free agent, because he was technically in Paddy Mayne's Headquarters Squadron and came later under the command of John Tonkin. The very nature of SAS work lay in high mobility and flexibility, small groups of men operating semi-independently of large units. So, armed with pistols, machine guns and a jeep-mounted Vickers, Randall and Corporal Brown roamed the roads of the Loire, searching for the enemy. With the possible exception of Tonkin in Bulbasket, no one was ready to relax yet. As the Reich withdrew, every river, every forest, every ridge could serve as a point where Model would make a stand. No one imagined that Paris would fall without a fight and, should that be taken, there was still a long way to go before the Rhine. The two SAS men found themselves rattling through the largely deserted countryside around Brière and Pouilly sur Loire, looking for a billet, and came upon a trout farm run by a lady whose husband had been German ambassador to Austria before the *Anschluss*. At more or less the same time, the Inns of Court

Yeomanry turned up. The Yeomanry were all for blasting the fish out of the water with grenades, which Randall saw as both pointless and an act of sheer vandalism. He talked them out of it, but clearly he had made his point more forcefully than he thought. When he and Brown got back to base, Randall had to report to the CO. The Inns of Court boys had accused him of collaborating with the Germans!

Collaboration was a dirty word in France as the Reich pulled back. The whole area of Vichy had collaborated by definition, but there were unknown thousands of men and women in the rest of the country who had aided and abetted the Nazis. Anti-Semitic policies were adopted along the lines of the 1935 Nuremberg Laws. Jews were no longer allowed to be citizens of France in the full sense, and lists were drawn up by a police inspector, André Tulard, which resulted in the genocide masterminded by Theodor Dannecker. In a country that had already shown its anti-Semitism in the Dreyfus Affair[6] 40 years earlier, this stance was not too surprising. A total of 90,000 Jews were deported for 'resettlement in the East' by 1944. On an official level, the Gendarmerie Nationale was responsible for the arrest of 80 per cent of the 'undesirables' in the war years, including homosexuals and Communists. What is interesting is that not a single German was involved in these operations; the persecution was entirely French. Such people were described by Charles de Gaulle, leader of the Free French in London, as people 'who had forgotten honour and handed [France] over to servitude'.[7] De Gaulle was sentenced to death, in absentia, for high treason. While the Nazis were the dominant force, this made perfect sense and was often a matter of survival. Whereas the Milice made a conscious and free choice to rally to the swastika, many civilians collaborated just to stay alive. Once the Wehrmacht were in full retreat, of course, the tables were turned and bitterness, old feuds and ancient grudges were played out with increasing brutality. In some cases, merely saying 'Hello' to a German was a sign of collaboration and 'Sieg Heil' open treason.

Women in particular were targets of this, if only because they were perceived as the weaker sex and offered sexual favours to soldiers far from home. In the Nazi-occupied Channel Islands, they were called Jerrybags. Even before the war was over, women guilty of sleeping with the enemy were paraded through the streets, their heads shaved. They were treated as Aryan girls who had had sex with Jewish men had been in the Germany of the 1930s, spat at, kicked, punched and, at the very least, thrown into prison. That was the fate, briefly, of Madame Couleau at Nevers. John Randall never did get to the bottom of the accusations against her; they may have been part of the old animosity referred to above. As far as he and Corporal Brown knew, Madame Couleau could not have been more helpful. Just as the two lovely daughters of the lady who owned the trout farm had cleaned Randall's kit for him, the lady from Nevers gave them meals and found them beds. Then, one day, they heard that she had been arrested and thrown into Nevers jail on charges of collaboration.

Nevers' glory days were well and truly over by 1944. It had once been the home of the dukes who had ridden against the English at Poitiers and Agincourt, but their castle was the Palais de Justice by this time, and the factories on the city's outskirts, in common with much of industrial France, had been taken over for the war effort. John Randall told Brown to wait outside the jail with the jeep, the engine ticking over, while he straightened his Airborne beret, put on his best French and demanded that the prisoner Couleau be released. The desk clerk, no doubt by now a model of patriotic rectitude, asked on whose authority that should happen. Randall sighed with impatience and told him that General de Gaulle was on his way and would probably be here by nightfall. The leader of the Free French had heard of Madame Couleau's wrongful imprisonment and had sent the SAS on ahead to right that wrong.

A bewildered Madame Couleau was brought from the cells, recognised Randall at once and played along. Even as they walked down the corridor, Randall could hear rising voices and the tap-tap of telegraph communications. Phones were ringing and the edgy gendarmes were fingering their pistols. By the time they reached the courtyard, the young lieutenant and the astonished Frenchwoman were running flat out. Randall screamed at Brown to get into the back. He would drive and he could not expect Madame Couleau to clamber into the back of a two-seater jeep. Randall hit the accelerator so hard that Brown was thrown out, somersaulting over the vehicle's back onto the concrete. He shook himself, scrambled up and just managed to grab hold again as Randall roared out of the gates.

A few days later, the SAS men were driving through Epernay when they passed a school. It was in this town around this time that John Randall cleaned his teeth with champagne – a messy job, but someone had to do it! There were no children visible in the playground, but public buildings like that were obvious places for retreating soldiers to hole up, and Randall went in through the front door, while Brown covered his back with a machine gun. There were two middle-aged ladies inside who turned out to be German, and Randall, ever the public schoolboy, asked them politely if there were any soldiers or ammunition in the building. They scowled at him defiantly and said, 'Nein.' Then they slammed the door in his face. They were lucky; James McDiarmid might have shot them, but John Randall was made of finer stuff. He kicked the door open and pointed his machine gun at them, sending the now terrified ladies scurrying backwards, clutching convulsively at their throats. He remained chillingly, terrifyingly polite, and searched the entire premises with his gun aimed at them. He fought down the temptation to deliver a lecture on the inhumanity of their race and left, careful to slam the door behind him.

John Randall cannot remember the name of the village where he and Brown came upon a firing squad. The events of that early morning somewhere in France are probably seared on his brain, but he makes little of it. Men of Randall's generation and his upbringing were not given to shows of emotion. It was all about a stiff upper lip and clichés about seeing things through and playing the game. The events themselves are written nowhere in the SAS archive, because the hectic pace of the days around the fall of Paris made accurate reporting back to base impossible. The little patrol reached the village in the early morning, where a firing squad of SS were standing to attention 30 feet away, alongside their officer, facing the wall of a church. Against the wall stood six men, civilians in scruffy clothes with their hands tied behind their backs and blindfolds over their eyes. There was no time to intervene with anything other than bullets, and Randall stood up in the jeep, blasting the SS to pieces with the Vickers. Brown opened fire too, and, in seconds, as the smoke cleared, the firing squad was just bodies, twitching on the ground. I needed clarification from Randall on this. He said, in an interview with me, 'We had the satisfaction of eliminating the German patrol.' 'You shot them?' I asked him. 'Yes,' he said. It was the way of the SAS, of the men who fought the Second World War – no false heroics or sentimentality that was the legacy of the Victorians; no over-the-top gung-ho purple prose of today's writers on the regiment's exploits. Just a simple statement of fact.

The reaction of the village was ecstatic. People came hurrying out of houses, cutting their men free, kicking the dead Germans and clamouring around Randall and Brown. They were the heroes of the hour and a great deal of drink flowed. There were speeches and toasts, laughter and tears. For that particular village, the war was over. They had been liberated by two young soldiers of the SAS. That evening, after one long street party that had lasted all day, there was a service held at the village's war memorial commemorating the dead of the Great War that had taken the lives of more than a million Frenchmen. Randall and Brown were given the honour of laying a wreath, but the toll of the celebrations was too much for Brown and he passed out during the ceremony. All, however, was forgiven. The man had collapsed because of French wine imbibed after saving French lives; that was good enough.

216

By definition, Paris was the objective *par excellence*. Hitler had had himself photographed under the Eiffel Tower in June 1940, as his panzers swept to the sea and carried all before them. There was something iconic about capturing an enemy's capital and it was usually a sign that the country would follow in short order. Take Paris in 1940 and the will of the French to fight on will be gone. Flatten London that same year and the British will surrender. As the last example proved, of course, it did not always follow. But in the summer of 1944, if Paris fell, there was surely nothing to keep the Germans in France at all.

As supreme commander in the west, Dwight Eisenhower was anxious not to have to take Paris in a full-frontal assault. Similar actions at Stalingrad and Warsaw, coupled with a civilian underground rising, had resulted in hideous casualties. Later historians have criticised Eisenhower for advancing too slowly, for wanting to avoid unnecessary loss of life when victory was so near. He intended to surround Paris and give the garrison of General von Choltitz time to evacuate the city. The Americans had crossed the Seine near Nantes by 20 August and had reached Fontainebleau. The police of Paris had effectively gone on strike and the Maquis were dodging from street to street, blowing up cars and sniping at anybody in a German uniform. Feldmarschal Model found to his horror that the divisions he thought he had were fragmented, shell-shocked and exhausted. Hitler ordered that Paris was to be burned to the ground rather than fall into Allied hands. Model, like Eisenhower, did not think Paris was worth dying for. He relayed the Führer's orders to von Choltitz and prepared to dig in along defensive lines along the rivers Maas and Mosel.

It was now that Charles de Gaulle turned up, a little late perhaps to 'spring' Madame Couleau, demanding from Eisenhower that General Leclerc's 2nd Armoured Division should enter Paris first. There is still considerable controversy over this. Most Frenchmen believe that Leclerc's troops led the assault on the city with the zeal of men who were liberating their capital. Most Englishmen and Americans believe this was merely a piece of propaganda on the part of Eisenhower with the connivance of Churchill. Either way, German Paris was doomed. The French 1st Army moved up from Orleans, and, on the night of 24 August, reached the Hotel de Ville. Colonel Billotte's tanks straddled the Seine opposite the Isle de la Cité, and the German high command, von Choltitz and his staff, were surrounded in the Hotel Maurice. Fighting broke out in various sectors with bullets biting into masonry and the Maquis fighting on street corners. While they still had the capability, the Germans set fire to the Grand Palais, the Ministry of Marine and the Hotel Crillon, in an attempt at least to follow the Führer's orders. But these defences were ragged and uncoordinated. Von Choltitz was taken to Leclerc, who said, '*Maintenant, ca y est*,' and the German garrison surrendered.

The biggest street party Paris had seen since the Revolution of 1789 now gripped the capital. There was euphoria everywhere, and John Randall found himself marching down the Champs-Élysées as part of Leclerc's bodyguard, wave after wave of men in khaki and camouflage, surrounded by an ecstatic people brandishing tricolours, Union Jacks and the Stars and Stripes. The swastikas that had decorated the city, the long scarlet, white and black banners of the Reich, were torn down and burned. Collaborating women had their heads shaved, collaborating men were clubbed and kicked. Anybody, in or out of uniform, who had shown German or Vichy sympathies was spat at and beaten. Among John Randall's papers is a series of studio portraits of gorgeous girls. In the days of the liberation of Paris, he knew them all, wining and dining in restaurants and cafés where the food and the wine were free for the Tommies who had brought freedom after so long. 'I, of course,' he told me in the context of these girls, 'behaved like a true English gentleman . . .' There was a pause, 'Or was I a bloody fool?'

At one point, he found himself out on the town of towns with a very pretty girl and a general who was trying his luck perhaps with a girl who might be impressed by the man's scrambled egg[8] rather than the stained battledress of a mere lieutenant. Although the general insisted on sitting very close to the girl in a taxi, he was gentleman enough to know when he had become a gooseberry. He got out of the cab, told the driver to take the young people wherever they wanted to go and said goodnight.

It is not likely that Randall knew it at the time, but the SAS were already in the capital before he arrived, in an incident that is as murky as it is mysterious. The operations of 2 SAS in France are beyond the scope of this book, but Operation Wallace under Major Roy Farran had just come to an end, and a small unit led by a French captain, Michel Courand, known as William Lee, made for Paris. There were perhaps a dozen of them, but not all the names are known. In looking up an old girlfriend, he found a German, 'Freddy', hiding in the girl's apartment and decided, against all procedure and reason, to take him back to England. When the regular British troops arrived the next day, 2 SAS were ordered back to base. 'Freddy' in a borrowed SAS uniform went with them, first to Arromanches, then by ship to Southampton. All this inevitably came out and Lee found himself facing a court martial at the Duke of York's barracks in Chelsea in November. He was dismissed from the service, and we are no nearer understanding why he brought an enemy alien into the country in the first place.

On the afternoon of 26 August, de Gaulle made his formal entry to the Place de la Concorde and then in a motorcade to the cathedral of Notre Dame. Shots were fired both inside the cathedral and outside by Vichy snipers taking collaboration to the wire. It would not be the last time that disgruntled Frenchmen tried to kill Charles de Gaulle.

The SAS rolled on, sometimes ahead of the army, sometimes alongside. The opportunity for 'dirty work', as Michael Asher puts it, became less. 'Behind enemy lines' from now on would be in Germany itself and the race was on for the Rhine. On 7 September, General Frederick Browning broadcast a message to all SAS troops in France: 'To say that you have done your job well is to put it mildly. You have done magnificently.'[9] Paddy Mayne was awarded his third DSO and the French award of the Croix de Guerre with palm.

Some of 1 SAS went home in the early months of 1945, but the Allied attack now swung north-east into Belgium, making for the heartland of industrial Germany, the Ruhr. Feldmarschal von Runstedt, the most formidable of all Hitler's panzer officers, was reinstated as commander of the Reich forces in the west early in September. Operation Market Garden later in the month was a near disaster, as the British XXX Corps and the American 82nd Airborne came to grief over the bridges across the canals of Holland and the rivers Maas and Waal.

Intensive bombing by both the RAF and the USAAF now hammered Germany night and day. In October, 57,000 tons of bombs were dropped on Kassel, Koln, Ham and Munster, while the RAF delivered 50,000 tons on Duisberg and Essen. Aachen surrendered to the Americans that month too. Inside the Reich, panic began to take hold. Albert Speer, as Armaments Minister, cranked up production of weapons to impossible levels. Every male aged between 16 and 60 was forced into the *Volkssturm*, the Home Guard that would defend their homes and hearths against the invaders and save the Reich.[10] The railway system was now a shambles, with tons of bombs destroying locomotives, freight and lines. The once-dreaded Luftwaffe was reduced to a relative handful of planes.

However, the Germans still had fight in them and, in December, launched a desperate counter-attack in the snow-laden forest of the Ardennes. It was through this timber that Heinz Guderian's panzers had crashed in the spring of 1940, driving Blitzkrieg home and France to its knees. The attack now caught the Allies off their guard, and the aim was to split the British and American components in two. Bad weather kept Allied aircraft grounded, and the so-called Battle of the Bulge threatened briefly to upset the apple cart. Even so, the sheer numbers of the Allies, as well as their materiel, proved too strong – Model, Guderian and von Runstedt all counselled Hitler to pull back. He refused. On Christmas Eve, the German offensive ground to a halt and the Allies spent a merry Christmas launching their own counter-attack.

By 9 February 1945, the British and Canadians reached the Rhine at Nijmegen. Among the Allies, it became a rather unseemly scramble to see who could get across first, and, having done that, on to Berlin. The SAS thrust into Germany was called Operation Archway. B and C Squadrons were at Antwerp as the new year opened and had a taste of what civilians at home were getting, because the new missiles, the V2s, were pounding the area at the rate of four a day. The SAS found themselves doing what the police, the fire brigade and the ambulance service had done during the Blitz and were doing again – digging bodies out of the rubble. A and D Squadrons joined 2 SAS at Ostend, and the unit now came to be known as Frankforce, after Lt Colonel Brian Franks who commanded the second regiment. Franks was a great friend of the Stirling brothers and knew Ian Fenwick and David Niven of Phantom very well. Before the war, he had been assistant manager at the Dorchester, so knew anyone who was anyone on the London scene.

New jeeps were delivered with armour-plated glass windows two inches thick. The armaments were the same – twin and single Vickers – but one in three vehicles had a .50 calibre Browning and a searchlight. Each jeep had a Bren gun, bazooka and extra drums of ammunition. This was the vehicle that John Randall drove in Germany. The order came through – widely ignored – that the black beret of the Tank Corps was to replace the maroon of the SAS/Airborne. This was a sensible precaution. The enemy may have been in retreat but that made them dangerous and desperate. The SAS were notorious in Reich circles and could expect little mercy if any of them were to be taken prisoner.

The Rhine crossing began on 23 March, 21 Army group going across on amphibious landing craft known as 'Buffaloes', large enough to carry vehicles as well as personnel. Paratroopers of the

British 6th Airborne and American 17th were dropped further east, but a number of aircraft were lost or damaged in the process. John Randall crossed near the bridge at Wesel the day after the Americans. There were bodies strewn here and there and the bridge itself had taken such a pounding that it had to be rebuilt. He was in a Buffalo with Paddy Mayne and they landed on the far side at Bislich. There was now a parting of the ways as 1 and 2 SAS parted company and 1 SAS was reorganised internally. The squadron HQ was led by Harry Poat, but, as Randall's immediate superior was John Tonkin, by now a major, he was clearly in T Troop by this time. This unit was deployed on 8 April as the advance guard of the 11th Armoured Division. His old friends of the Inns of Court Yeomanry, they of the trout farm, were the reconnaissance regiment for the division, but Randall kept his cool and was prepared to let bygones be bygones. They were making for Neustadt. There were Waffen SS units everywhere, firing anti-tank bazookas from hedgerows and ditches. It was an unnerving business. The new jeeps were bristling with weapons and well armoured. Most of the men with Randall were experienced, some Originals from the desert days. But even so, around any bend . . .

Around one bend, a white flag was flying from behind a grassy hillock. Paddy Mayne made a point of joining as many troops as he could to boost morale and lend a hand, but technically he was in charge of Operation Howard. On that particular day, he was with T Troop and the column grated to a halt. This could have been a trap. The white flag was a universal symbol of surrender, but by now everyone knew that the rules no longer applied and it could mean anything. Mayne sent John Randall over to see what it was all about. Machine gun at the ready, the lieutenant crossed the open ground. In a ditch lay two soldiers, younger than he was, exhausted and dirty, in torn uniforms. This was no trick. These men were finished. Randall took them over to Mayne's jeep at gunpoint and the colonel drew his revolver. The SS men fell to their knees, terrified. They were going to die. Mayne winked at Randall and laughed. The prisoners joined the thousands who were being herded back to the Rhine where they would be interned in huge wire cages in the open fields.

All historians of the SAS admit that the detailed history of these days is almost impossible to put together. Bill Fraser was wounded in a gunfight in a village, which was typical of the many occurring on the east bank of the Rhine. The boys that Randall had taken prisoner were almost certainly Waffen SS who had recently been recruited from the *Hitlerjugend*, the Hitler Youth. It was a hint of things to come, when little boys were called upon by the increasingly deranged Führer to defend Berlin itself.

But there were other things to come too. One of the most terrible happened when John Randall and Corporal Brown took a side turning off a road in a forest near the village of Celle. An ordinary road. On a warm spring day.

13

A Miracle in Belsen

When John Randall was still struggling with the horrors of the curriculum at St Lawrence College Prep School, a little girl was born in the Hungarian city of Budapest. Her name was Mady Goldgruber, part of the small Jewish community that occupied an area of the city that straddled the Danube, and she was to meet Lieutenant Randall on 15 April 1945. That was the day his jeep rattled into the concentration camp at Bergen-Belsen. That was the day he saved her life.

Mady has very few memories of her early life and they are dominated by her beautiful mother, who would die of tuberculosis when her only child was seven. Two years before that, as John Randall was getting into his stride on the playing fields of St Lawrence, Mady had been sent to live with a great-aunt whom she called Gisi, but who was called Aunt Hoffmann by everybody else. Mady's new life began in the little town of Keszthely, 120 miles away from Budapest.

That was the year that the Wehrmacht started to build a military camp near the town of Bergen in the province of Hanover. Hitler had come to power two years earlier, and in quick succession made himself Chancellor and Führer of Germany. In keeping with his vow to tear up the Treaty of Versailles, he built up the armed forces, demanding a personal oath of allegiance from every serviceman and building aircraft for Hermann Goering's Luftwaffe in secret factories inside the Soviet Union. He came to an arrangement with the British, as the most powerful naval force of the day, and the Anglo-German Naval Treaty gave him carte blanche to build formidable new warships to replace those scuttled at Kiel and Scapa Flow at the end of the Great War. Those were the years of appeasement, before Hitler's megalomania became obvious and while British and French governments believed that he was controllable. The camp at Bergen was the largest training area in Germany, and was used primarily for tank corps deployment of the Panzer Divisions that would roar across France in a state of panic as John Randall was crouching behind hedgerows transmitting radio broadcasts back to base in Operation Haft.

Like many Jews in Europe, little Mady soon became aware that the 'them and us' dilemma was coming into sharper focus as the '30s wore on. A Jewish community had been set up in Keszthely in 1699, prosperous merchants with servants and status. That was to be challenged later, especially under the so-called Enlightened Despots the Empress Maria Theresa and her son Joseph II. Under them, Jews paid the patience tax. 'The Jew,' wrote the Empress, 'because we tolerate him, has to pay for our tolerance.' Even so, anti-Semitism in Hungary was not as marked as elsewhere, as Hungarian Jews were typical of the schizoid personality forced on them. On the one hand, they were the diaspora, the scattered children of Moses who had yet to find their promised land and were still waiting for their messiah. They had their own schools, synagogues, rabbis and cantors, and their holy day was Saturday. On the other hand, they were Hungarians, some of them joining Louis Kossuth in the Revolution of 1848, which overthrew the arbitrary government of Count Metternich, the Austrian Chancellor. And they fought in the First World War alongside Catholics whose holy day was Sunday, when they worshipped God and the messiah who had already come.

By the end of the 19th century, Hungary had lost its independence and was part of the over-large Austro-Hungarian empire of the

Habsburgs. Those creaking, lumbering giants – the Romanovs' Russia, the Ottomans' Turkey, even, arguably, George V's Britain – were blindly elbowing one another over an abyss.

No doubt, the majority of Hungarian Jews welcomed the country's independence in 1919; 40 per cent of the First World War casualties were Jewish. But things began to change. In 1920, the *Numerus clausus* reduced the Jewish university intake and there is some evidence that the rabid anti-Semitism of Adolf Hitler was present along the Danube too. The noxious little book *The Protocols of the Elders of Zion*, a fabrication that claimed that Jews planned world domination, was widely translated and widely read.

John Randall was scoring tries for the First XV by the time the army had finished the barracks at Bergen. The workers themselves, already the slave labour that the Third Reich relied on, were housed in huts near the barracks that became known as the Bergen-Belsen concentration camp. Within a year, with the army complex finished, those rows of quickly built 'Nissen' huts fell into disuse.

In the summer of 1937, a special honour was given to little Mady Goldgruber. There was an Ecumenical Congress in Hungary. Cardinal Eugenio Pacelli arrived, and walked along a red carpet. With her shining black hair and huge brown eyes, Mady was a 'natural' to present a bouquet to the great man. She was wearing a smart, blue double-breasted coat and curtseyed beautifully to the cardinal who 'looked down at me from a great height'.[1] This was the man, completely unaware that he was taking flowers from a Jewish girl, who would become Pope Pius XII in the years ahead. Many historians use a 'shorthand' term to describe him – Hitler's Pope.

By the end of 1938, war was looming all over Europe. Austria purported to be delighted when the *Anschluss* annexed them to Nazi Germany, and the film reels of the time showed ecstatic Viennese waving swastikas as the Führer toured their streets in his open car. They did not show the thousands turning away, staying indoors, watching events from behind lace curtains with a growing dread.

At Munich, on 30 September, a frantic deal was struck between the leaders of Europe that the area of Czechoslovakia called the Sudetenland would be handed over to Hitler's Germany. This was part of the Führer's foreign policy of *lebensraum* (living space), which he claimed he needed for his growing population. The Sudetenland was heavily populated with Germans – it was only right that it should become part of the Third Reich.

The British Prime Minister, Neville Chamberlain, came home with Hitler's promise not to annex any more territory, and, at Heston Aerodrome, then London's major airport, he held up Hitler's notorious written oath for the cameras. 'I believe,' he said, 'it is peace for our time,' although today most historians accept that secretly he believed no such thing. He was an old-fashioned gentleman who could not believe the duplicity of the new man in Berlin.

Hungary actually did well out of this new accord, gaining Czech territory to the north and east of Bratislava. By March of 1939, the scrap of paper that Chamberlain brought home was proved worthless. The Wehrmacht marched into Prague after the Czechs were presented with an ultimatum they could not possibly have accepted. By August, not only was there a 'Pact of Steel' in place between Italy and Germany, but also Hitler's foreign minister, Joachim von Ribbentrop, had signed a non-aggression pact with Vyacheslav Molotov, Stalin's man. This was a bizarre twist – Communist Russia cosying up to Fascist Germany – and it would result in the dismemberment of Poland, on which Hitler's steely gaze now turned.

None of this meant very much to Mady Goldgruber; like thousands of girls all over Europe, her own life went on. She enjoyed school and did well. In winter evenings, she sat with Aunt Gisi knitting and reading at a table. Gisi used to stick her spare knitting needles in her hair swept up into a bun so that she looked like a porcupine. In the summer, she joined other children at the lake at Heviz five miles from home, swimming among the lily pads and enjoying the hot springs there. Within a year, the solemn eleven year old had pledged herself to Steve, three years her senior. It all sounds a little odd today, but marriage was a serious business in pre-war Jewish communities, and the pair looked forward to their future lives together. He wanted to become a doctor and she an art historian. At that age, little things like wars don't make any difference. When she was 12 and John Randall was already in Tunisia with Phantom, one of Steve's friends, George Cziffer, asked her out. With all the sophistication and solemnity she could manage, she said, 'No thank you. I'm very serious about Steve and I could never be unfaithful to him.'

The German invasion of Poland on 1 September 1939 created thousands of prisoners within days. The September Campaign fought by the Poles exposed the inadequacy of poor, ill-equipped armies and was almost a showcase for the Blitzkrieg tactics of the Wehrmacht. The Bergen-Belsen huts that had been home to the camp builders now became a prisoner of war camp, known as Stalag XI-B. Over the next 18 months, as the war in the east was won and the Wehrmacht swung west, it became one of the largest camps in the Reich. As the Low Countries, Belgium and France fell, prisoners from those three nations joined the Poles.

Just as the concentration camps were growing in number and size to accommodate Poland's huge Jewish population, so prisoner of war camps had to grow when the Wehrmacht roared into Russia in Operation Barbarossa. Stalag XI-B now became XI-C and it was one of three huge camps in the area – Stalag XI-D was at Aberbke and X-D was in Wietzendorf. By the end of March 1942, an estimated 41,000 Russian prisoners had died in these camps, of starvation and disease. If Hitler's Reich had ever subscribed to the Geneva Convention, they certainly did not observe it in the breach.

For Mady Goldgruber, a creeping terror began to fill her life. Admiral Nicholas Horthy, the Hungarian Prime Minister, was married to a Jew so the more optimistic hoped that all would be well. Such things were not in his hands, however. Adolf Eichmann had already established a formidable structure to solve the Jewish problem. 'Resettlement in the East' was at first just that. The Lublin area of Poland and the island of Madagascar were hopelessly inadequate for any serious repatriation, and the camps were filling up. After the Wannsee Conference met in Berlin to discuss the actual mechanics of it, the SS were earmarked to continue the work of the *Einsatzgruppen*, the execution squads, in killing Jews in large numbers. Mass shooting was slow, bloody and expensive; converted army trucks that pumped gas into an enclosed space were inefficient. The answer, which was being devised during 1941, was Zyklon B, hydrocyanic acid pellets, which, when sprinkled into chambers and exposed to the oxygen in the air, produced cyanide gas, which could kill up to 2,000 people in 20 minutes.

For little Mady, all this lay in the future. In common with women and girls all over Europe, she gave away her clothes for the families of servicemen at the Front. Carried along by pressure from the Reich, Hungary had declared war on Russia in June 1941 and, by December, the country found itself at war with Britain and America too. Mady knitted furiously – mittens, scarves, balaclavas. By the end of 1942, clouds were gathering. One of Aunt Hoffman's best customers, a gentile, came into her shop one day with terrible news. 'All Jews are going to be taken away,' she told her. 'And no one knows where to or for how long. Of course, the *special* ones that everybody likes – like you, Aunt Hoffman – are going to be left alone.'

For the time being perhaps, but, throughout 1943, the stories of the death camps trickled through, and new names took on a terrible meaning – Auschwitz, Buchenwald, Ravensbrück. This should have been the year of Mady's bat mitzvah, but instead she was confirmed in the Christian tradition, even though the rabbi was involved in the preparation. Such was the shortage of teachers by this time that Mady, always a bright and able child, was called upon to teach Maths to a younger class.

This strange, walking-on-eggshells life came to an abrupt end on Sunday, 19 March 1944. John Randall was in Darvel with Paddy Mayne and 1 SAS preparing for a huge operation that was still highly hush-hush to all but the top brass. The Wehrmacht marched into Hungary. and terrified citizens hung their carpets over their balconies as symbols of welcome. Flowers were thrown under the wheels of motorcycles, armoured cars and marching boots; candles burned in windows. That was a day that Mady remembered very well; it was Steve's 17th birthday.

She finished her year at school, but every Jew now had to wear a yellow Star of David. Because of her skill as a seamstress and the material available in Aunt Hoffman's shop, Mady ended up making many of these herself. The pattern of Nazi occupation followed that was witnessed by thousands of communities under the jackboot; a scrimped, frightened existence, which turned into the nightmare of the ghetto. Valuables went first – jewellery, cutlery, crockery. In Mady's case, she said goodbye to her childhood – 14 dolls sat on Aunt Hoffman's dark-green rocking chair and leaving them all behind broke her heart. 'Who is playing with them now?' she wondered in the memoir she wrote years later. 'Does the girl who owns them know that there was somebody who also loved them, dressed them, looked after them and had to leave them behind, because she belonged to the wrong religion?'

The ghetto was made up of the cluster of houses around the synagogue where four to six people now shared one room. Jews who had once been neighbours living streets away now slept at the foot of the Goldgrubers' bed. It was a difficult time, the air electric with tension. Human nature being what it is, not everybody banded together against the common enemy. There was bickering, short tempers, frayed nerves. And, in June, even that grim life became grimmer.

Towards the end of that month, the Jews of the Keszthely

ghetto were rounded up and traipsed to the station, watched by the Hungarian townsfolk who were not sorry to see them go. All the racial tensions of the centuries were etched into those faces. One of those earlier centuries had given rise to the attitude 'You have no right to live among us as Jews.' Now it was 'You have no right to live among us.'[2] Soon, it would be 'You have no right to live.' Like the other undesirables of the Nazi state, the homosexuals, the gypsies and the Communists, the Jews of Keszthely were the *Untermenschen* and 'life unworthy of life'. Mady is not the only Jew whose memoirs draw a parallel with the Exodus, a nation on the march. Except that these particular Children of Israel were not being delivered out of bondage; they were going into it.

The little girl who was no longer a girl remembers the whimpering dogs left behind on the platform. Some tried to jump onto the moving train and were shot by the guards, the rifles cracking above the snort and hiss of the locomotive.

The first stop was three hours away, at Zalaegerszeg, and the exodus was housed in derelict buildings before moving on again, this time on foot to ramshackle tents in a disused quarry. The Nyilas or Arrow Cross, the Hungarian Nazi party, carried out interrogations in prefabricated huts here, and, one day, it was Mady's turn. She was 14, small for her age, with sad, dark eyes and she was terrified. The noise of earlier interrogations had echoed eerily around the quarry – the screams and the sobbing. The Nyilas wanted to know from the girl sitting bolt upright in the wooden chair where her family had hidden their valuables. Mady's family had no valuables and she said so. They made her kneel barefoot on the chair, her whole body shaking uncontrollably as one of them suddenly lashed out with his whip on her bare feet. She could not believe the pain. She tried to scream, but instead air came rushing from her tortured lungs and she just knelt there, too terrified to pray or even to breathe. Then the door opened and a rabbi, Solomon Halper, stepped in. He whispered something to the interrogator who dropped his whip and let Mady go. She never found out what the rabbi said because he did not survive what was to come.

Three days before John Randall dropped silently into the darkness somewhere over France, they made an announcement in Mady's quarry: 'You are all to be taken to a work camp. You are permitted to take only one piece of luggage with you.' This time, the exodus was by lorry, the wind whistling through floorboards and between door catches. At the station, there were cattle trucks, 40 or 50 people crammed into a space designed for perhaps 12 animals. The windows were high and small, crisscrossed with barbed wire, the universal symbol of hopeless imprisonment. For four days, this ghastly convoy rolled east, part of Eichmann's infamous 'resettlement'. Men, women and children stood for most of the journey, the living holding up the dying or the dead. The toilet was a tall bucket in one corner, soon filled to overflowing and, for most of the passengers, there was no means of reaching it. Food was a crust of bread. Water an afterthought. The journey through limbo ended on 8 July, almost the last date that Mady could keep in her head until life began for her again on 15 April 1945.

They took photographs of the arrival of the Hungarian Jews but Mady is not one of those caught forever on celluloid on their way to the gas chambers. KL Auschwitz-Birkenau was a vast, sprawling camp by July 1944; in fact, it was three camps rolled into one and was the most efficient of the extermination camps in the Third Reich. Because it has been preserved in all its stark horror, it has remained the most infamous. The chilling letters stood over the single railway track – *Arbeit Macht Frei*, Work makes you free – maintaining the fiction right to the end that this was just another work camp where undesirables 'did their bit' for the master race in exchange for a bed, food and the chance to live. But here, that chance was slim, and lives were measured in days or hours or minutes.

It was the noise that Mady remembered most. As the padlocks were broken open and the doors slid back, light hit her eyes like an explosion and with it came the snarling and barking of the dogs, the yelling of the guards in a language she understood all too well – *Raus! Raus! Schnell!*; Out! Out! Quick! Among the grey-green uniformed SS men on the Rampe were 'strange-looking people' scurrying about, wearing faded, ragged striped jackets that looked like pyjamas. They were Jews too, some of them wearing the Star of David. They helped the SS herd people into two lines. They hauled luggage off the trains and dumped it in piles. They dragged out the dead.

The two lines formed quickly, cowed people consigned to left and right at the whim of SS officers, one with immaculate doeskin gloves. Aunt Hoffman and Mady's sick cousin Margaret were flicked into the other line from her. She never saw them again.

The terrified 14 year old was herded with the other healthy ones into a dank shower room and told to strip. They had all heard stories about showers in camps but all that came out of the overhead nozzles was water, so cold it took their breath away. But not as permanently as Zyklon B. With no time to dry themselves, the women were given shoes, ill-fitting and without laces. Dead women's shoes. They were forced to sit, still naked, while hard-faced women clipped their hair and shaved them roughly under their arms and between their legs. The dress they put Mady in was three times too big for her, pink and blue calico that nearly reached the ground.

Out in the open again, Mady saw Steve for the last time. They had been segregated on the way and he still had his hair and his own clothes. To this day, she still feels the hurt that his last view of her was as some sort of fairground freak. 'Home' was Lager C, Barrack 8, a cell block housing 1,100 children between 13 and 15 years of age, and Mady soon learned the inverted hierarchy of prison life. The SS were remote and had more contact with the men in other barracks. It was the Kapos whom Mady remembered, large, fierce women like the Aryans she had read about, who spoke a guttural Yiddish patois she did not understand. These women were the favoured ones, as long as they did their masters' bidding. They had food, half-decent clothing and underwear. Life for teenaged girls was particularly harsh. There was no privacy. The toilet block had rows of seats and the girls sat back to back to relieve themselves three times a day. There was no toilet paper. Girls who were menstruating and asked for sanitary towels were met with a torrent of abuse or a slap around the face or both. The oddest thing to Mady was that the latrine buckets for night use, in the corner of the barracks, were emptied not by the girls themselves, but by gypsy women. And gypsies, she learned, were even lower than the Jews.

Food, served in huge pots hauled into place by four girls, was a warm liquid that passed for soup. It contained grass, tree-bark and small pieces of turnip. The rituals of the camp took over. The *Appel*, the roll call, happened twice a day and could last for hours. The dreaded selections happened every few days, especially as new girls arrived. The camp's medical staff watched as the girls paraded naked in single file through a room, their arms above their heads. 'For fourteen year olds,' Mady remembered, 'it was a special sort of hell.'

All things are relative and it may be that the women had an easier time of it than the men. That was not how it seemed in 1944. Mady saw people die on the electric fences trying to reach a loved one on the other side. She saw people committing suicide by provoking a guard to put a bullet through their head. In her book, Mady says she does not want to write very much about Auschwitz and we can understand why.

By October 1944 (Mady is naturally hazy about the date), John Randall had marched down the Champs-Élysées in the liberation of Paris and was preparing to cross the Rhine. Mady Goldgruber, along with dozens of others, was selected to be moved on. For the first time, the Germans were realising that they might lose the war, that the Reich might collapse, and nowhere is this sense of rising panic more obvious than in the attitude towards the Jews. At Auschwitz-Birkenau, the rate of killing escalated and, when the gas chambers and crematoria could not cope, bodies were burned in the open, in ghastly funeral pyres where the *Sonderkommando* threw corpses made bright pink by the effects of the gas onto the flames. The smoke and the stench drifted for miles. But Mady Goldgruber was not there. A new chapter of her life was opening, at Gruben.

Unlike Auschwitz-Birkenau, which was a killing factory, Gruben was a work camp proper and the 350 women and girls there operated in three shifts for the Lorenz factory in the town, making components for radios for the Luftwaffe. All over Germany, something of an economic miracle was being wrought under Albert Speer, once Hitler's architect and now his Armaments Minister. Today, some historians believe that he prolonged the war by 18 months because of the huge burst of factory production that he engineered. After Auschwitz, Gruben was a little piece of heaven. There was no mass murder here. The girls had their own underwear, and at Christmas were given a bonus of pickled shellfish and face powder, luxuries unheard of among most prisoners of the Reich. It was possible to have clogs repaired at the camp shoemaker's, and it was there that Mady, now 15, tasted wine for the first time in her life, smuggled in by the inmates. It was a taste she would never forget.

By the start of the new year, a new desperation became apparent among the SS. The Red Army had long ago halted the German advance in the east and it was payback time. Germany was paying the price for the old problem – the war on two fronts, which was the ultimate disaster for a country in the centre of Europe. That was the month that the death marches began; thousands of concentration camp prisoners prodded at gunpoint along the frozen roads of Germany, herded into barges along the Elbe, locked in open cattle trucks where they froze to death and drank water from icicles.

At Gruben, as elsewhere across the Reich, the sound of the Russian guns rumbled like distant thunder. Then, Mady Goldgruber was on the road again. They marched for fourteen days with occasional breaks of ten minutes. Mady learned to sleep leaning against a tree trunk, catnaps that probably saved her life. The snow froze to the soles of her wooden clogs, making them heavy to lift with each step. At night, the girls huddled in barns and the outhouses of farms, and some local Germans, moved to pity by the condition of the girls, gave them soup and bread, the first real food they had had for months. All along the route, the SS marched with them, three or four hundred women. When they stumbled through the towns, Mady noticed that the locals stared right through them, as though they were not there at all.

Many accounts of the camp at Bergen-Belsen use the analogy of hell. It is difficult to see it any other way. In April 1943, part of the camp was taken over by the SS Economic Administration Main Office, and it was then designated a civilian internment camp. By June of that year, the terminology changed and it became a holding camp. In the insane world of the concentration camp system, only certain camps were open to inspection by the International Red Cross under the Geneva Convention, and holding camps were exempt. Even so, Bergen-Belsen was always something of a special case. The Hungarian camp, to which Mady was sent, was one sub-section. The 'special' camp was for Polish Jews. The 'neutral' camp was for those unfortunates of neutral countries like Spain and Switzerland who had somehow been caught up in the madness. The 'star' camp was for Dutch Jews who were to be exchanged for German prisoners in Allied camps or for hard cash, something the Reich now needed with much greater urgency. By March 1944, while 1 SAS was still training at Darvel, the camp's function changed again and it became an *Erholungslager*, a recovery camp for prisoners too ill to work elsewhere. The theory was that, given medical treatment and decent food, these people would be returned to their original camps. In practice, this rarely happened, simply because medical treatment and food were not high priorities anywhere in the camp system.

By August of that year, while the Allies were fighting their way out of Normandy, Bergen-Belsen became largely a women's camp with an influx of 9,000 prisoners in November. Most of these were Poles interned after the failure of the Warsaw Rising,[3] but its most famous inmate, a girl only a little younger than Mady, died there in March. Her name was Anne Frank.[4]

After Gruben, Mady could not believe the hell that was Belsen. There were bodies lying on the open ground, piles of bones covered in skin the colour of parchment. The stench of decay was revolting. There were no bunks. The girls slept on hard wooden or concrete floors under a single blanket crawling with lice. Mady does not remember having a single bath or shower during her time at the camp. It was the worst of all worlds. While John Randall was feeding back vital information to the RAF in Operation Haft, the number of inhabitants stood at 7,300. By the time Mady arrived, there were 22,000 there, wrecks of humanity herded across Europe in the collapse of the Reich. Precisely *because* of that collapse, the command structure had fallen apart. SS Hauptsturmfuhrer Adolf Haas was replaced in December 1944 by Josef Kramer, who had himself come from Auschwitz-Birkenau. Kramer was a diehard Nazi known for his efficiency; he had been awarded the War Merit Cross First Class in the spring of 1943 as a result. By the time he reached Belsen, however, the situation was already hopeless and the camp was beyond the dwindling powers of the Reich. There was a constant shifting of senior SS personnel in the camps even before the writing was on the wall, but there seemed very little purpose to it at this stage.

For Mady and the new arrivals, there was nothing to do. Gruben had been a workplace and, for all it was slave labour under a vicious regime, there were elements of normality there. At Belsen, there was none. She lay inside or outside her hut, watching people die. They had nowhere to go and no energy to get there. She saw people go mad before they died of hunger. She saw the odd movement as a limb twitched in a pile of corpses. She noticed that the old lost touch with reality quicker than the young. A friend of her mother baked imaginary cakes every day, chocolate logs sprinkled with icing and leaves spun from invisible sugar. In her mind, her children danced around her, bubbling with excitement because it was somebody's birthday. The next day, she was a corpse on a heap of corpses turning black in the grey of winter.

Steve's cousin Susie had been with Mady since the ghetto at Keszthely and she ended up in the next hut at Belsen. They saw each other every day, both of them walking skeletons covered in lice. Their skin was yellow, covered in scabs and sores, and their eyes hollow in their skull-like faces. Even so, they talked and hoped and planned for the future, like 15 year olds do all over the world. Mady was still in love with Steve, and Susie still loved a boy they both knew from Keszthely. Then, one day, Susie was not in the hut any more. She was outside like a discarded mannequin on a pile of mannequins.

By the time Susie died, something strange had happened. The heavy guns had been getting nearer by the day, and one morning most of the guards had gone. There was an eerie stillness around the camp, and Mady swears that she knew the date. She does not know *how* she knew it but she did. It was a Sunday, 15 April 1945, and a jeep snarled through the open gates to come to a sudden, screeching halt. 'I saw a vision,' she wrote years later, 'through the filthy windows of the hut as I was sitting with my back against the wall. A British jeep appeared through the glass with two young soldiers . . . The miracle had happened.'

The miracle came in the form of Lieutenant John Randall and Corporal Brown of 1 SAS, and we have already read of Randall's disbelief at what he saw that day, a disbelief that soon turned to anger. Because of the independent nature of SAS work, he and Brown had no idea what had been going on in the previous days. Belsen was in the middle of a battlefield and, on 12 April, the Chief of Staff of the 1st German Parachute Army contacted the General Staff of British Eighth Corps. There was a prison camp ahead, he said, and typhus had broken out. The next day, a truce was called. The British would take over the camp and bring much-needed humanitarian aid. The camp itself was declared a neutral zone, which is presumably why the remaining guards did not open fire on Randall and Brown immediately. The SS camp staff were to remain, and the British could do what they liked with them.

In the aftermath of war, an astonishing number of men claimed to have been the first Allied soldier into Belsen. It is part of the 'What did you do in the war, Daddy?' syndrome, where otherwise anonymous people saw their chance for 15 minutes of fame. Others may have been genuinely sure they *were* the first. One man who makes the claim says that all the guards had gone, but that was never the case. When Randall and Brown got there, there was still a skeleton SS staff on duty. They were still fully armed and, bizarrely, even managed to shoot the odd prisoner after the arrival of the British.

John Randall has never contradicted these men because he does not have to and because of the kind of man he is. He is simply stating the facts. The official SAS report from Operation Archway does not mention the camp at all, and the pamphlet produced shortly after by General Miles Dempsey's Second Army gets it wrong: 'It is believed that Brigadier Glyn Hughes, Deputy Director of Medical Services . . . was the first to arrive. The first British Unit in was an Anti-Tank Battery of 63 Anti-Tank Regt.'[5] It is probably from this source that the confusion and anomalies arise. Glyn Hughes was indeed there, and his medical work to help the desperate inmates was nothing short of magnificent, but doctors do not spearhead patrols and he could not possibly have been the first man there.

Sergeant Duncan Ridler, of 1 SAS's Intelligence Unit, turned up in a jeep on the evening of 15 April, but he, like John Tonkin and Reg Seekings, got there after Randall. So did Johnny Cooper, who was one of several men inoculated against typhoid. Randall and Brown seem to have had no inoculation at all.

While Randall pointed his pistol at Josef Kramer and put him under guard in one of his own cells, the reinforcements referred to in the Second Army's pamphlet arrived. Photographs of Kramer taken that day show him in a boiler suit with several days' stubble on his chin. He looks well fed, as were all his staff, in contrast to the starving camp inmates, and he pretended to be one of the maintenance people, not a member of the SS at all. Duncan Ridler, who spoke fluent German, translated for Lt Colonel Taylor of the 63rd Anti-Tank Regiment, who assumed command temporarily, as the most senior officer there. Ridler was not in Belsen for long, any more than Randall was. There was a delousing station in one of the huts, and Ridler went through it, to be coated in white powder, before driving off again. 'In one minute we were back in the woods and there was no sound behind us in that horrible place. It might not have existed.'[6]

Rumours flew later that a number of SS guards were shot by the British, in a white-heat hatred at what they witnessed that day, but this simply did not happen. Reg Seekings, however, was beside himself with fury. As sporadic shooting still went on, he grabbed the nearest guard and beat him to a pulp with his fists.

Two journalists, Richard Dimbleby and Patrick Gordon Walker, reached Belsen the next day. John Randall had gone on to the next destination by then, Luneburg Heath, he and Brown praying they would not stumble upon any more camps like Bergen-Belsen. Dimbleby broadcast his famous and harrowing account via the BBC from the spot; a nation listened in disbelief:

This day at Belsen was the most horrible day of my life. I saw it all – furnaces where thousands have been burned alive . . . The pit – fifteen feet deep – as big as a tennis court, piled to the top at one end with naked bodies . . . The British bulldozers – digging a new pit for the hundreds of bodies lying all over the camp days after death . . . The dark huts, piled with human filth in which the dead and dying are lying together, so that you must step over them to avoid the sticks of arms that are thrust imploringly towards you.[7]

Dimbleby was the journalist whom Paddy Mayne had wanted to beat up in Cairo two years earlier. No doubt, if the colonel ever heard this broadcast, he changed his mind.

Patrick Gordon Walker saw the huge sign in red letters – 'DANGER. TYPHUS' – and gleaned most of his information inside the camp from officers of the Oxfordshire Yeomanry who were already there, driving the bulldozers and supervising, while the SS and Hungarian guards buried the dead. On the first night of liberation, Gordon Walker wrote, 'many hundreds of people died of joy'.[8] One woman came up to an Oxford Yeomanry officer with a baby in her arms. She was begging for milk, even though the baby, black and shrivelled, had been dead for days. He poured a little milk on the child's lips and the mother carried it away, crooning softly to it. She died moments later. At that time (20 April), Gordon Walker estimated there were 30,000 still alive at Belsen and 35,000 corpses. The guards were forced to cope with digging pits, so much so that some of them fell, exhausted, into the pits themselves, to be met with jeers and spitting from those inmates who still had the strength to stand and watch. Two guards committed suicide. Another was shot while trying to escape. It was the female guards who particularly horrified Gordon Walker and the Tommies who saw them. These were the Kapos that Mady Goldgruber talks about: 'more cruel and brutal than the men', according to the journalist. They were all in their twenties and the SS members were spearheaded by 22-year-old Irma Grese. Like Kramer, she had been transferred from Auschwitz, where she was known as the 'Angel of Birkenau'.

Gordon Walker ended his broadcast with these words:

To you at home, this is one camp. There are many more. This is what you are fighting. None of this is propaganda. This is the plain and simple truth.

John Randall knew that. And it has haunted his dreams ever since.

EPILOGUE

We Shall Remember Them

While 1 SAS penetrated deeper into Northern Germany, the Wehrmacht were surrendering in droves. On one occasion, a complete division tried to give themselves up to John Tonkin, travelling in a single jeep with his driver beside him. There was talk of a vicious rearguard group of diehards, the Werewolves, who, rather like the SAS, could live in the mountains for ever and wage a terrible guerrilla war. In the event, most of these units were scattered and disorganised, boys of the Hitler Youth who were quickly overawed by machine-gun fire.

Four days after Belsen, a number of SAS patrols hit Luneburg and drove out the remaining Nazis. The British posted photographs of the Belsen dead around the town, but the locals could not believe them. They were Allied propaganda, nothing more. For all the Reich was falling apart by the day, there was no sign of official surrender from Berlin, a city now besieged by Stalin's Red Army. So, various Wehrmacht and SS units fought on, depending on the mindset of their commanding officers or their specific situation. While Paddy Mayne roared off in a jeep to win his fourth – and final – DSO, casualties still mounted. Major Dick Bond was killed. Johnny Cooper was shot in the head. Lieutenant Gordon Davidson and some of his men were captured, almost certainly wishing they had abandoned their famous winged dagger beret badges, and were interrogated by the SS. Before the Germans had a chance to shoot their prisoners as promised, the Allied advance caught up with them and the SAS were force-marched eastward by the *Volkssturm*. Davidson and Trooper Albert Youngman escaped with the help of French prisoners and made a run for it through the forests. Three days later, exhausted and very hungry, they heard the distinct plummy tones of a British radio: 'This is the BBC Home Service.' It was background noise for the Guards Armoured Brigade while they had their breakfast!

The transcript of radio signals received from the time sounds grim, despite the fact that the end of the war was in sight. 'Squadron [actually A and D] now plodding along through bog and rain on their feet. Trooper Kent killed by mine. Nobody very happy.'

However, happiness of a sort reached everybody by courtesy of Hamburg radio on 1 May. Admiral Karl Doenitz announced to a disbelieving Germany that the Führer was dead, and that he was now running his Reich. 'It is my duty,' he said, 'to save the German people from destruction by the Bolshevists.' That threat, which would develop beyond Germany into the Cold War of the next 40 years, had been exactly what Hitler had been warning against since 1933 if not earlier. Ironically, his own megalomania had made the threat more tangible and more deadly. The day before Doenitz's broadcast, Adolf Hitler had said goodbye to his staff in the bunker, most of whom were thoroughly demoralised and drunk under the streets of Berlin, and had committed suicide along with his wife, Eva Braun. His Minister of Propaganda and Enlightenment, Joseph Goebbels, followed suit after poisoning his wife and six children. The Red Army would find their half-charred bodies the next day.

Even if the exhausted German people had had the will to fight on for Doenitz, they no longer had the capacity, and the admiral had no choice but to surrender. By coincidence, John Randall was at General Montgomery's headquarters on Luneburg Heath and witnessed the final act of surrender. The area of Luneburg had been captured on 18 April, and Montgomery had established his headquarters in a palatial villa in the village of Häcklingen. His tactical headquarters were in a carpeted tent on nearby Timeloberg Hill, and it was here that German staff officers arrived on Thursday, 3 May. Doenitz clearly did not have the power or the ability to surrender on behalf of every German fighting man simultaneously, especially since he had given orders for the Eastern Front to continue fighting to give him time to arrange the most favourable terms with the West. A stickler for protocol, Doenitz refused to deal directly with Montgomery as the man was a mere soldier and Doenitz was head of state. The man he sent was Admiral Hans-Georg von Friedburg, and there was much discussion in Montgomery's tent about the nature of the surrender. Monty said, in effect, it was all or nothing. The Germans went back to talk to Doenitz.

The next day, John Randall watched as von Friedburg came back with Colonel Fritz Poleck representing the Wehrmacht. The actual ceremony took place in Montgomery's caravan where the victorious general of 21 Army Group sat at a table with microphones in front of him. There were cine cameras rolling from Pathé News, which would show the black and white moment to ecstatic cinemagoers in the weeks ahead.

In a seven-point document, von Friedburg agreed unconditional surrender of all armed forces in Holland, north-west Germany, Schleswig-Holstein and Denmark, as well as ships still at sea in those areas. All this would take effect from 0800 hours, British Double Summer Time, on Saturday, 5 May. The details were written in English and German and the signatories were: von Friedburg, commander-in-chief of the Kreigsmarine, the German navy; General Eberhard Kinzel, chief of staff of the north German army; Rear Admiral Gerhard Wagner; Colonel Fritz Poleck and Major Hans Friedel. Randall had never seen so many high-ranking Nazis together before, but, even so, the moment was curiously anti-climactic. Millions all over Europe had hoped to see Adolf Hitler in that caravan, prior to a public trial in which he stood accountable for the deaths of millions more. Two of the men whom Randall saw that day would never get over the shame of their surrender; on 23 May, both von Friedburg and Kinzel committed suicide.

The day before that – and not many miles away from John Randall's position – a shabbily dressed man with an eye-patch and stubble on his receding chin tried to shuffle past a British command post at the bridge at Bremervorde. There was something about him that the sentry found familiar. His papers carried the name of Heinrich Hizinger, but the world knew him as Heinrich Himmler, Gruppenführer of the SS, the man who ultimately oversaw camps like Belsen; the man who was directly responsible for the deaths of millions and not least the near-murder of Mady Goldgruber. The next day, despite the British medical authorities' care, Himmler slipped a cyanide capsule hidden in his clothing into his mouth and bit down. He writhed on the floor for a few seconds and died.

Three days after Randall witnessed the surrender at Luneburg, he was with the regiment to celebrate the end of the war – Victory in Europe Day – 8 May. True, there were still pockets of diehard resistance, and, of course, Japan represented a different kind of war altogether. In Brussels, where the Belgian SAS joined them, Paddy Mayne's boys sang and drank with the best of them. Reg Seekings remembered old Belgian women in Poperinghe, smiling benignly on the Tommies who had helped liberate their country. '"They're just like their fathers; drink-drink-drink, piss-piss-piss."'[1]

On 1 October 1945, in a world suddenly at peace after so long, Lieutenant John Randall stood with the entire SAS on the parade ground at Hylands House near Chelmsford, their new base since November 1944, for the last time. In fact, by then, they were no longer 'entire'. There had been a brief stint for some squadrons in Norway, and there was some talk of sending men out to the

Far East in the war against Japan, although the bombs Little Boy and Fat Man had rendered that unnecessary when the terrible explosions at Hiroshima and Nagasaki broke the will of the Japanese to carry on. The Belgian SAS had returned to their own army on 21 September, taking with them good friends that John Randall had made in the two years he had served alongside them; particularly Lt Colonel Eddy Blondeel, 'the epitome of a John Buchan hero'. The French SAS went home on 1 October.

In front of 1 SAS that day stood Brigadier 'Mad Mike' Calvert, now in command of the SAS Brigade, having replaced Roderick McLeod in March. Everybody was wearing the maroon Airborne beret, except Paddy Mayne, who wore his old sand-coloured one from the early days in the desert. The night before, there had been a party, one of the many that John Randall had gone to during his war, but this one was tinged with sadness. Paddy Mayne drove a jeep up the staircase at Hylands Hall and got it stuck to such an extent that it had to be dismantled to get it down again. The Hall's owner, Mrs Hanbury, prepared to turn a blind eye to most of the regiment's celebrations, had finally had enough. 'Now, Paddy,' she said, wagging a finger at the huge Irishman, 'that's quite enough of that. You're keeping me awake. It's time you all got to bed.'[2] They did, but not before Harry Poat and Johnny Cooper got hold of the phone number of the secretary of the new Prime Minister, Clement Attlee, and told him his fortune: 'If you cut our bacon ration, we'll cut a slice off your arse!'[3]

Everybody knew the adventure was over. A lot of comrades had fallen on the way, but that was natural in war. Mike Calvert knew, as did Paddy Mayne and David Stirling, now back from Colditz, that the SAS were a unique fighting force with much to be proud of. And he was able to answer the critics who called for the regiment's disbandment blow for blow. In a memo written on 12 October, he rejected the early nonsense about the 'private army' (a criticism aimed at Phantom too). He rejected the notion that the SAS outfit wasted commanders' time; it was simply that too many of them did not understand its role. He denied that the SAS were only useful when the enemy was on the run and disorganised; this was not so in the desert, or in France in the summer and autumn of 1944. He refused to accept that the regiment's work overlapped or even clashed with that of SOE; in fact, they complemented each other. The SAS, he argued, was adaptable to all countries, although some had argued, stupidly, that it was not. He denied that the best men were skimmed by the SAS from conventional units (Montgomery's claim); a certain type of soldier was wasted in the other regiments – he could shine with the SAS. The expense of the SAS *was* worthwhile, Calvert contended; a single raid in North Africa had destroyed more enemy aircraft than six years of balloon barrages. As to the charge that *anyone* could do what the SAS had done, we can almost hear the exasperated hiss of steam escaping from the brigadier's ears.

However, the fact was that no one important was listening. Not at the time. It was a brave new world now, of atom bombs and a Cold War, not a hot one. The kinds of operations carried out by the SAS were thought obsolete and their old champion Winston Churchill had gone in the most surprising election result of the century. 'It was like the bottom dropping out of the world,' Reg Seekings wrote. 'You were lost.'[4]

Randall looked at the ranks ahead of him and alongside him that October day. He had lived with these men, laughed with them, fought with them and, if things had gone differently, he might have died with them. There would be no 'Lili Marlene' around an old piano now, no Padre McLuskey at the keyboard, no James McDiarmid doing his 'Puddle Dance'. Vera Lynn, the Forces' Sweetheart, might have offered dreams of 'Love and laughter, and peace ever after; tomorrow, just you wait, and see.' But now that tomorrow was here, some men were not so sure . . .

Michael Asher sums up that last parade at Hylands superbly. 'The RSM called the men to attention for the general salute. Four hundred hands snapped up to maroon-red berets. Then the men of 1 Special Air Service Regiment turned sharply and marched out of history, into legend.'[5]

John Randall was 25 and he was not a career soldier. The SAS would rise again, in the jungles of Malaya, in the torn streets of Belfast, on the balcony of the Iranian Embassy in London, in the sands of Afghanistan and Iraq. But all this would happen without him. He met a lovely girl, Jane, after meeting so many lovely girls during the war, but this one was different. He met her in Oxford Street and plucked up the courage to ask her out. The rest was history, and Mr and Mrs Randall went on to have three children, grandchildren and a long and happy life together, one that still continues. It was not all sweetness and light, of course – nobody's life is. John's son James developed serious kidney disease and John gave one of his own kidneys for the boy, only to be told at the last moment that it was not suitable. Thanks to dialysis, James survived. For years until his retirement, Randall Senior ran a very successful business consultancy, specialising in sales and management training. Later in his career, he became a senior course director at the Institute of Marketing College. He has always maintained links with his old regiment. He goes to their dinners still.

What of his old comrades whose names feature in his diaries and memories? Padre Fraser McLuskey, who joined the SAS on the same day that Randall did, remained a friend until his death in 2005. John Randall was at his funeral and remembers one time when he was less than kind to the man. Desperately worried about James, Randall said to McLuskey, 'See what your God has allowed to happen?' McLuskey smiled and wandered away. After he had calmed down, Randall followed and apologised. McLuskey – and his God – had heard such protestations before. He was Moderator of the General Assembly of the Church of Scotland and minister of St Columba's in London. He had a German wife, which must have caused some eyebrows to be raised at the time, and set up an army chaplains' training centre at Bagshot in 1950.

He wrote his autobiography *The Cloud and the Fire* in 1994.

After the war, Randall met up with David Stirling, the lanky Scot, several times. In fact, Randall's daughter, a successful estate agent, secured the purchase of Stirling's flat in Chelsea. There was talk, in the 1980s, of a movie based on his life but nothing came of it. He was knighted in 1990 and the man Rommel called the Phantom Major died later that year.

Johnny Cooper was demobbed in 1947 and returned to a post-war role in the wool trade. Unable, like many of the SAS, to slot back into peacetime, he re-enlisted in the new regiment, 22 SAS, with a short-service commission in 1951. He was soon deep in the Malayan jungle trying to prevent Chinese terrorists from spreading Communism to the local people. A hot warrior had become a cold warrior and he commanded C Squadron, followed by A and D. Defence cuts reduced the SAS in the 1960s, so he signed on with the Sultan of Oman's forces against President Nasser's Egyptian army. He died from tuberculosis as a lieutenant colonel in July 2002.

Eddy Blondeel had parachuted into the Ardennes at the end of August 1944, where the local Maquis were impressed by his coolness. As leader of the Belgian SAS, he had trained in Scotland and attended the same parties as John Randall. He and his men had another such party at Godesholt, having been instrumental in arresting not only the Doenitz government at Flensburg but also Hitler's Foreign Minister, von Ribbentrop. The unit was just about to go out on patrol when the cease-fire was announced, and Blondeel played the piano in the makeshift Mess and sang 'Auld Lang Syne' with his lads. 'We must now face,' he told them, 'the uncertainties and complexities of peace.' He returned to engineering in 1947, and stayed at the firm of Wiggins Teape until his retirement in 1981. Unlike the British SAS, the Belgian unit was never wound up but became the Amicale Nationale Para-Commando Vriendenkring, of which he became honorary colonel. When a reunion was held in 1994 at Loudon Kirk, near the ruined castle where the SAS spent many happy hours socialising with the Countess and her daughters, Blondeel was too ill to attend. John Randall read a message written by the Belgian, thanking the Countess's family (she had died by this time) for their hospitality 50 years earlier.

David Danger became a lieutenant colonel. The photograph in his obituary shows a 'geeky'-looking young man as he was when he served under Randall. He has 1930s spectacles, a Hitler moustache and a pipe. The radio operator in Operation Houndsworth, he had served with the SAS since L Detachment days. He transferred to the Parachute Regiment and served in Palestine until 1947, left the army and became totally bored. He took a commission in the Royal Army Ordnance Corps, serving in Hong Kong and Cyprus, and was promoted to lieutenant colonel in 1965. He left the army for the last time in 1978 and died in 2009.

'Mad Mike' Calvert (his friends never referred to him as that) had been a Chindit with Orde Wingate in the Burma jungle, and his efforts as commander of the SAS Brigade at the end of the war had a great deal to do with the regiment's revival later. His brigadier rank was only temporary (he was just 33), and he was posted after the war as a major in a civil affairs job in Trieste, a position he loathed. His military career came to an abrupt end when he was convicted on three counts of gross indecency, but he went on to lecture at Manchester University. He died in November 1998.

Tony Marsh, one of Randall's friends in 1 SAS, stayed on in the army until the late 1950s when he joined the Trade Development Board in Bermuda. He died on the island in 1984.

Reg Seekings, whose fists had served him well before and during the war, emigrated to Rhodesia (now Zimbabwe) and became a tobacco farmer. The bottom may have dropped out of his world in 1945, but he kept his hand in by helping police with anti-terrorist operations. He died in England in 1999.

And what of the colonel, Paddy Mayne, the troubled legend regarded by many, John Randall included, as the very embodiment of the SAS? He went back to Belfast and the law after the war, but he missed the action more than anyone knew. He became Secretary of the Law Society of Northern Ireland, but the drinking and the fights were increasing and he was clearly an unhappy man. There was a lot of alcohol in his blood when he crashed his red Riley Roadster on 10 December 1955. He was 40 years old. The memorial service for him at his home town of Newtownards was the biggest ever seen in the area, and Fraser McLuskey said at his graveside, 'The gift of leadership and the ability to inspire complete devotion and loyalty were his to an exceptional degree.' Earl Jellicoe, who had first met the man in L Detachment, wrote in a memorial service to him years later: 'His favourite book [was] that lovely anthology *Other Men's Flowers* by Field Marshal Lord Wavell. He loved his roses. He loved his family, above all his mother whom he adored. And he cared with deep feeling for those under his command.' Over the years, a campaign has been mounted to obtain a posthumous VC for Mayne. Several men who have been awarded it did far less than he did, but somehow the shadow of his temper and the drinking binges have always hovered over his achievements. The Paddy Mayne Association has 7,000 members and there were petitions to the queen during her Golden Jubilee year and three early-day motions in the Commons, signed by 105 MPs of all parties: 'This House recognises the grave injustice meted out to Lt Col Paddy Mayne.' That injustice has still not been put right.

John Randall's other regiment, Phantom, survived the war but not with the élan of the new SAS. By 1951, it had been subsumed into Princess Louise's Kensington Regiment, part of the Territorial Army, but technology passed it by and it became obsolete. The regiment's historian, R.J.T. Hills, got it partly right, however, at the end of his book *Phantom Was There*: 'The Englishman in uniform must still be an individualist. At his best he will be an artist in war. Hence the Commandos, hence the Chindits and the

SAS – hence Phantom and all Private Armies. We shall see them again should the need arise.'[6]

Tam Williams, Randall's actor friend, continued in movies after the war, and his son Simon followed him into the acting profession, appearing regularly in films and on television. His grandson Tam is now a heart throb just like his grandfather. The original Tam died in December 1969. The philosopher Michael Oakeshott lived on as a respected academic until December 1990; Robert Mark made his name as a Commissioner of the Metropolitan Police in the 1970s; and the most famous of them all, David Niven, made nearly 90 films during his career, before his death aged 73 in Switzerland. He once told his sons to tell people, 'My father's a lousy actor, but he absolutely loves doing it.' He quite enjoyed his starring role in Phantom too.

Of all the incidents that befell John Randall during the war, none affected him as much as Belsen. He recalls with a quiet sense of justice the fate that befell Josef Kramer and Irma Grese. The camp itself was totally destroyed by flame throwers, and bulldozers levelled the ground, but a number of the SS staff who worked there were put on trial in Luneburg between September and November 1945. The total number was at least 480 but only 45 of those ever faced retribution. Some of those were charged with crimes against humanity at earlier camps, and the media coverage ensured that horrific details emerged, which would otherwise have been buried with the victims of the Holocaust. Eleven of the defendants were sentenced to death, including Kramer, Grese and another woman, Elisabeth Volkenrath. Fourteen were acquitted and the rest served sentences that were often reduced on appeal. European society was trying to draw a line in the sand after the horrors of the war and to rebuild a shattered continent. Men like John Randall and anyone else who had seen Belsen at first hand did not see it that way. All those sentenced had been released by 1955.

The man who would hang the 'Beast of Belsen' was Albert Pierrepoint, a quiet, unassuming professional who carried out more judicial sentences than any other British executioner. In all, he hanged nearly 200 war criminals in Germany shortly after the war. He admits to feeling sorry for the 11 about to die from Belsen, despite the enormity of their crimes, which no doubt he had seen on grainy black and white newsreels. When he said as much to a young soldier nearby, the man said, "'If you had been in Belsen under this lot, you wouldn't be able to feel sorry for them.'"[7] Unusually, Pierrepoint had to measure each of the condemned to get the 'drop' right. This was done in Britain by prison staff, but not at Hameln. And he had to get it right. Too long a drop and a man's head could come off; too short and he would slowly strangle to death. Kramer came out first. Pierrepoint had seen cartoons of this man, portrayed as half man, half beast. His ears were flat to his head, his hair close-cropped and he was of a powerful build. Pierrepoint knew that two days before John Randall had arrived, Kramer had fired at random with his Schmeisser gun out of his office window and killed twenty-two people, just for fun.

Irma Grese seemed 'as bonny a girl as one could ever wish to meet'.[8] She came out of her tiny cell laughing, a 22 year old responsible, according to trial testimony, for up to 30 deaths a day.

On Friday, 13 December 1945, Pierrepoint went about his business with his usual cool professionalism. Irma Grese was called first and he pinioned her arms behind her in the corridor outside her cell. She followed the hangman to the execution chamber, looked at the trap and the officials standing around and stood on Pierrepoint's chalk mark. He placed the white cap over her golden curls and she muttered, 'Schnell,' before he pulled the lever and avenged those who had had the misfortune to have known the 'Angel of Birkenau'.

Kramer hanged alongside Fritz Klein, one of his staff. He had lost two stone since John Randall had pointed a pistol at him at the gates of Hell but he was still strong. The execution of them both took 25 seconds and the Beast of Belsen made no sound at all.

In 1968, Alan Bennett wrote *Forty Years On*, a nostalgic and affectionate look at the cultural history of Britain since the turn of the century. One entire section of the play revolves around an MP, his wife and old nanny living out the war in the basement of Claridge's Hotel. It is riotously funny, but it also has a message. At the end, various characters come together and stand, facing the audience with a sad comment on the state of things as they had developed by the end of the '60s. For convenience' sake, I have run the various parts together:

> In our crass-builded, glass-bloated, green-belted world Sunday is for washing the car, tinned peaches and Carnation milk. A sergeant's world it is now, the world of the lay-by and the civic improvement scheme. Country is park and shore is marina, spare time is leisure and more, year by year. We have become a battery people, a people of underprivileged hearts fed on pap in darkness . . . The hedges come down from the silent fields. The lease is out on the corner site. A butterfly is an event . . . Once we had a romantic and old-fashioned conception of honour, of patriotism, chivalry and duty. But it was a duty which didn't have much to do with justice, with social justice anyway. And in default of that justice and in pursuit of it, that was how the great words came to be cancelled out.

Much of what was John Randall's world has gone. Phantom is no more; the SAS is a different animal, albeit one with new imperatives and a new charisma of its own. The London he knew has vanished. It gleams with shiny architecture in shapes that give Prince Charles the vapours, but at least it is not still full of sandbags and bomb craters. Most of the clubs he took his ladies to have changed beyond all recognition. Few people still take tea these days. The castle he knew at Loudon where he danced away the early hours with the pretty girls from FANY became one of Scotland's major theme park attractions but is now a ruin, unable to pay its way. His family home, Donnington Manor in Sevenoaks, is part of the Great Western chain of hotels and, since the storm of 1987, Sevenoaks has only one oak left.

However, there are memorials. At Belsen, where so many died, there is a memorial to the sisters Anne and Margot Frank, the Star of David in white on a large black stone. Over one of the mass graves a sign reads, 'Here lie 5000 dead. April 1945'. And there is another memorial too, one copied from the obelisk at Darvel where the SAS trained before D-Day. This one is on the clock tower at Hereford near the current headquarters of the SAS:

> We are the pilgrims, Master, we shall go
> Always a little farther, it may be
> Beyond the last blue mountain buried with snow.
> Across the angry or glimmering sea . . .

On the morning of Sunday, 10 April, 2005, Mady Gerrard was sitting having coffee before her favourite programme of 'Golden Oldies' started on BBC Radio Wales. She lived in Cardiff and, over many years, had gained a huge reputation in the fashion industry. She was thumbing through the *Sunday Telegraph* and she screamed. There, on the 60th anniversary, was an article on the liberation of Belsen. It was called 'The Gate of Hell' and it featured a young man whose face Mady had carried in her head for all of those 60 years: the face of 24-year-old Lieutenant John Randall, 1 SAS. He described in the article that he had entered a hut and had come face to face with girls who could have been no older than 15 and who believed they had only days to live. She had been Mady Goldgruber then, a hopeless waif whose life had been all but taken from her. She immediately dashed off a letter to the *Telegraph*, explaining the link and saying she would like to meet John Randall again, to thank him for what he had done all those years before.

Randall rang her and took her to lunch at the Special Forces Club in London. They talked non-stop for three hours and became firm friends, staying in regular communication from that day on.

He wrote the Foreword to her book *Full Circle*, and it ends with a letter he wrote to her on 5 May 2006: 'Congratulations – I am proud to know you and I am lucky to have played a tiny part in your survival.'

Another Belsen survivor, Susan Pollock, wrote to Randall in April 2010, enclosing photographs of herself before and after the camp:

> You came on the 15th of April and not on the 16th. Thank God. I would not be here. You came, strong, determined and selfless with all Goodness in your heart to liberate us wretches. I could not walk or move or talk and was totally emaciated ready to be thrown on the heap of corpses with the rest.
>
> But you came and helped me. Put me in a clean bed, gave me food and lifted my spirits beyond the imagination of my hopeless mind. How brave and noble. The best – whose kindness will live on forever in my mind. You planted a new vision of the world and now I want to thank you . . .

Susan Pollock, like Mady Gerrard, carries in her head and in her heart the handsome face of the young SAS lieutenant, in his maroon beret and his camouflage Denison smock. 'I hope he's going to live forever,' Mady says. The historian George Santayana famously said that those who cannot remember the past are condemned to repeat it. Those who cannot remember the horrors of war are in danger of being drawn into another – remembering people like John Randall and his comrades will perhaps ensure that Mady Gerrard's wish will come true.

Notes

CHAPTER 1

1. It was not until the 1870s that the interior of Africa was explored by Englishmen like Burton, Speke and Baker.
2. Conversion to modern values is always tricky, but, using the most popular method, this equates to around £66 today.

CHAPTER 2

1. The Mass-Observation Unit was a socio-anthropomorphological organisation set up in 1937 to study the habits, attitudes and opinions of the British people.
2. 'Never in the field of human conflict has so much been owed by so many to so few.' – Winston Churchill, House of Commons Debate, vol. 364, col. 1166, 20 August 1940.
3. Women over 30 had first been given the vote in the 'Coupon Election' at the end of the Great War, but that was a cynical ploy by the government of the day because they knew it was likely that older women would be more likely to vote as their husbands told them. It was not until 1928 that 21-year-old females got the vote, giving them real equality for the first time.
4. The use of phosgene and mustard gas in the Great War was, rightly, viewed with horror by everyone. It was silent and unpredictable, with horrific results for those affected by it.
5. Although the Lewis gun was largely supplanted by the Bren

gun in the Second World War and was taken out of service completely in 1946, training was still given on it and just as well – when much of the British equipment was lost after Dunkirk, the stock of Lewis guns were reissued to troops and the Home Guard.

6. Churchill, Winston, *Hector Debates vol. 361, col. 796, 4 June 1940.*

7. Quoted in South, Godfrey (ed.), *How It Was in the War,* 1989, p. 71.

8. For two reasons: he hated his time there and would hardly have linked his most famous victory with a place he detested, and because Eton had no playing fields in the late 18th century!

CHAPTER 3

1. The Dardanelles campaign in 1915 was Winston Churchill's least fine hour and he had been forced to resign from the Admiralty as a result. The idea was to hit Turkey, the 'soft underbelly' of Europe, and capture Istanbul. Turkish resistance, backed by German troops, proved too stubborn, however, and the casualties, of British and ANZAC troops at Gallipoli, were appalling. The campaign achieved nothing.

2. Viscount Gort was a distinguished soldier who won the VC in the Great War. His work of modernisation of the army in the run-up to the Second World War was essential, but still underway on the outbreak of war.

3. Hills, R.J.T. *Phantom Was There*, Edward Arnold, London, p. 15.

4. *Ibid.,* p. 14.

5. *Ibid.,* p. 14.

6. America did not officially enter the war until 8 December 1941.

7. This was, of course, several months before the Blitz started, when such men would be very busy indeed.

8. Quoted in Hills, *Phantom*, p. 29.

9. This error has been compounded by Hills, *Phantom*, p. 297.

10. All quotes from Niven are from his 1977 autobiography: Niven, David, *The Moon's a Balloon*, Penguin, London.

11. Hills, *Phantom*, p. 134.
12. *Charpoy* = Hindi for bed. *Schlafen* = German for sleep.
13. Calder, Angus, *The People's War: Britain 1939–45*, Pimlico, London, 1969, p. 413.
14. Such an attempt – badly bungled – had been made in 1798 when rebel Wolfe Tone's United Irishmen were supposed to liaise with a French warship, which eventually landed by mistake in Pembrokeshire!
15. Hills, *Phantom*, p. 55.

CHAPTER 4

1. Our Sea.
2. For example: How many gears does an Italian tank have? One forward and four reverse.
3. Churchill, Winston, *The Second World War*, originally published Houghton Mifflin, 1959, this edition Grange Books, 2003, p. 95.
4. Churchill, *Second World War*.
5. Churchill, *Second World War*, p. 104.
6. Churchill, *Second World War*, p. 109.
7. Churchill, *Second World War*, p. 117.
8. Montgomery, Bernard, *The Memoirs of Field Marshal Montgomery*, Leo Cooper, 2005, p. 71.
9. The term comes from General Francisco Franco's attack on Madrid during the Spanish Civil War (1936–9). He led four columns but believed there was a fifth column working against him as an army of spies inside the capital.
10. In the older sense of happy.
11. Lefebure, Molly, *Murder on the Home Front*, London, Grafton, 1954, p. 103.
12. Hills, *Phantom*, p. 66.
13. His wife Dr Han Suyin became an outspoken critic of Mao Tse-Tung's Communist regime in China, and, among many books she wrote, her novel of an East–West romance was turned into a Hollywood film, *Love Is A Many Splendored Thing*.
14. Quoted in Hills, *Phantom*, p. 40.
15. Hills, *Phantom*, p. 102.

16. Niven, *Moon's a Balloon*.
17. Churchill, *Second World War*, p. 163.

CHAPTER 5

1. In the slang of the Second World War, a 'type' was an officer, e.g. Army type, Air Force type, etc.; for Other Ranks it was 'bloke'.
2. The Bookmark of St Teresa of Avila 16th century.
3. Quoted in Hills, *Phantom*, p. 106.
4. The cages were fences made into pens on open territory to house the sudden influx of prisoners.
5. Quoted in Churchill, *Second World War*, p. 178.
6. Quoted in Churchill, *Second World War*, p. 178.
7. Sergeant Major Loy Smith, of the 11th Hussars in the Crimea (1854–6), collected a button from a soldier of the Russian 11th Hussars, which he wore on his jacket for the rest of his career.
8. Things had improved in this context over time, however. When the Coldstream Guards arrived at the docks to sail for the Crimea in 1854, the officers had to leave all their personal crested china and silverware behind as there was no room aboard the troopship.

CHAPTER 6

1. Churchill, *Second World War*, p. 182.
2. *Daily Telegraph*, 8 June 1943.
3. The brilliant espionage ploy *Operation Mincemeat*, later filmed as *The Man Who Never Was*, was used in this deception.
4. A Yeomanry regiment originally raised in 1902.
5. Originally raised to defend hearths and homes in 1794.
6. Throughout most of his wartime career, John Randall was called by his second name because of the large numbers of Johns in various units.
7. No pun intended!

CHAPTER 7

1. The generation who went into teaching after 1945 needed no specific qualifications. Two of my teaching colleagues in

the late 1970s had served as young officers in Operation Overlord.

2. Batmen, attached to officers, usually looked after uniforms. Brass button 'sticks' were used for cleaning purposes. The electro-plated 'staybrite' button, which required no cleaning, was not in widespread use until 1950.

3. Comparing money values from other points in history is always difficult because there are so many variables, but, taking inflation and other factors into account, this is the equivalent to around £27 today. By comparison, the GI's wage is the equivalent of £133.

4. There is still a debate about the meaning of this. General Infantryman? Or General Issue, stamped onto equipment the men carried?

5. The going rate, by June 1945, was £5 for a 'quickie', Commando style, i.e. up against a wall.

6. At the time of going to press, the Berkeley Hotel in Knightsbridge provides rooms *from* £660 per night.

7. Frederick John Westcott (1866–1941), best known by his stage name Fred Karno, was an English theatre impresario of the British music hall. Among the young comedians who worked for him were Charlie Chaplin and Stan Laurel; the group became known as 'Fred Karno's Army', a phrase still occasionally used to refer to a chaotic group or organisation.

8. Hills, *Phantom*, p. 220.

CHAPTER 8

1. Although, as we shall see, the general was not particularly anxious to assist the SAS in their recruitment of the best men in 1943.

2. Asher, Michael, *The Regiment: The Real Story of the SAS*, Penguin, London, 2008, p. 32.

3. The phrase comes from Henry Newbolt's poem *Vitaï Lampada*, which in itself was based on the shattering British defeat at Abu Klea in 1885.

4. Stirling was probably playing Uckers, a strictly Forces version of Ludo, which is still played today. Feelings can run high – an insult to a careful player is that he is 'a Ludo player';

beating someone before they have any pieces home is called an 'eight-piece dicking'.

5. Waugh, Evelyn, *Letters*, quoted in Kemp, Anthony, *The SAS at War 1941–5*, Signet (Penguin), London, 1993, p. 2.

6. Quoted in Mortimer, Gavin, *The SAS in World War II*, Osprey, Oxford, 2011, p. 11.

7. Quoted in Trow, M.J., *Swearing Like a Trooper*, Constable Robinson, London, 2013, p. 54.

8. When Captain Louis Nolan of the 15th Hussars wrote his book *On Cavalry* in 1854, it was widely ignored by senior officers, despite Nolan's huge experience of cavalry tactics in India.

9. Later reduced to four or even three.

10. A huge and lumbering organisation which was already too cumbersome to operate effectively. In part the SAS circumvented it.

11. Stirling *Memorandum*, quoted in Kemp, *SAS at War*, p. 12.

12. Apart from anything else, white is a particularly obvious colour at a distance, even in the desert. Virtually the entire Austrian army wore white uniforms in 1866, the year they were thoroughly trounced by the Prussians.

13. Riley, Pat, quoted in Mortimer, *SAS in World War II*, p. 23.

14. The father of the future mountaineer, Chris Bonington.

15. That said, it is surprisingly difficult to engineer dust in the desert when you need it. I appeared in a television documentary filmed in Egypt in 2009 called *Dust Cloud Warriors* in which we used twenty Arab horses galloping at full stretch and it took us three hits to get the desired effect.

16. Blackman, Mike (ed.), *The Paddy Mayne Diary*, unpublished, 1945, quoted in Mortimer, *SAS in World War II*, p. 37.

17. Kemp, *SAS at War*, p. 25.

18. Similar buildings were erected at Leptis Magna, the vast Roman city in today's Libya. They have largely collapsed, whereas the Roman buildings are still in relatively good condition.

19. Quoted in Mortimer, *SAS in World War II*, p. 44.

20. A tiny unit made up of German-speaking Jews recruited in Palestine. They eventually disappeared because of the difficulty in finding new blood.

21. James [Pleydell], Malcolm, *Born of the Desert*, Collins, London, 1945.
22. Pleydell, *Born of the Desert*, p. 91.
23. From 'folding boat', the collapsible rubber dinghies used by these troops.
24. John Hackett later became a general and was the principal of my college in the late 1960s. I remember him cutting a cake in honour of the college's 140th birthday with his Mameluke sabre. He said he was glad to have found a use for it at last, as so far he 'had just kept tripping over the damn thing on the parade ground'.
25. Quoted in Mortimer, *SAS in World War II*, p. 79.
26. Kemp (Author interview), *SAS at War*, p. 95.
27. Quoted in Mortimer, *SAS in World War II*, p. 109.

CHAPTER 9

1. All quotations from McLuskey are from McLuskey, J. Fraser, *Parachute Padre: Behind German Lines With the SAS France, 1944*, Spa Books, Stevenage, 1985.
2. Using a basic calculation to include inflation, this is the equivalent of around £15, quite a useful sum to be given as a book token.
3. The famous shop Marshall and Snelgrove, based in Oxford Street since 1837.
4. None of these is very likely. When William Wallace was executed at Smithfield in 1307, his body was cut into four pieces. Only one of them was sent to his native Scotland.
5. Reg Seekings of the SAS could not stand the man. Neither could my own father, a corporal in the 8th Army. Many years later, he was telling his war stories to his doctor, especially about his time in the Western Desert. The doctor, tongue-in-cheek, asked whose side he had been on.
6. Quoted in Wellstead, Ian, *The SAS with the Maquis*, Greenhill, London, 1997.
7. Quoted in Ross, Hamish, *Paddy Mayne*, Sutton, Stroud, 2003.
8. Transkei, an area set aside for Xhosa speakers, was given autonomy in 1963 but previously was part of South Africa.

9. These units, totally separate from the Local Defence Volunteers (Dad's Army), are still rather shadowy and under-researched.

10. Quoted in Mortimer, *SAS in World War II*, p. 141.

11. Quoted in Mortimer, *SAS in World War II*, p. 144.

12. Graham, James, Marquis of Montrose (1612–50) *I'll Never Love Thee More*. As a principal supporter of Charles I in Scotland, Montrose was executed by the Covenanters who opposed the king.

13. As we have seen, the Sicily landings involved more men in the initial phase, but the *overall* commitment of troops in Normandy was far greater.

CHAPTER 10

1. Pleydell, IWM Documents 337, 15.2.43.

2. Colditz was a medieval fortress that, by 1942, had become a prisoner of war camp for 'undesirables', Allied officers who were likely to cause as much disruption as possible. Thanks to one inmate, Pat Reid, stories of escapes from Colditz became synonymous with boys' own yarns. There were about 130 such escapes.

3. RSM Graham Rose's letter, quoted in Mortimer, *SAS in World War II*, p. 148.

4. Kemp, *SAS at War*, p. 156.

5. See next chapter.

6. Quoted in Mortimer, *SAS in World War II*, p. 157.

7. Quoted in Mortimer, *SAS in World War II*, p. 167.

8. Violette Szabo (1921–45) was brought up in London by her French mother and English father. After the death of her husband, a Hungarian who was an officer in the French army, she was recruited into SOE and became known as one of the bravest and most effective agents. She was captured during her second mission and was executed at Ravensbrück concentration camp.

9. See next chapter.

10. Quoted in Kemp, *SAS at War*, p. 150.

11. Quoted in Kemp, *SAS at War*, p. 152.

CHAPTER 11

1. Top Secret Report on Operation Haft 702, 1944.
2. Haft Report 1944.
3. Presumably on microfiche contained in the aluminium capsule fastened to a leg.
4. Radio transmitters are beacons and their location can be easily detected by the enemy.

CHAPTER 12

1. The alleged question screamed down the phone from Hitler to Dietrich von Choltitz, commander of the Nazi garrison in the city.
2. Various sources from eyewitness accounts, quoted in Calder, *People's War*, p. 559.
3. Waugh, Evelyn, *Unconditional Surrender: The Conclusion of Men at Arms and Officers and Gentlemen*, Chapman and Hall, London, 1961, p. 245.
4. West End eyewitness, quoted in Calder, *People's War*, p. 560.
5. Model, quoted in Lucas, James *Hitler's Enforcers*, Arms and Armour Press, London, 1996, p. 99.
6. Alfred Dreyfus was a captain in the French artillery. He was also a Jew. In 1894, he was wrongly convicted of selling military secrets to the Germans (the actual guilty party was uncovered later) and was imprisoned on the brutal Devil's Island. The case hinged on Dreyfus' Jewishness and 'l'affaire', as it came to be known, split France down the middle.
7. Source unknown.
8. Army slang for the gold braid on senior officers' dress caps.
9. Quoted in Ross, *Paddy Mayne*, p. 164.
10. Ironically, because of the contrasting fortunes across the Channel, the British Home Guard was disbanded the following month.

CHAPTER 13

1. All quotations from Mady Goldgruber are from Gerrard, Mady, *Full Circle*, privately published, 2006.

2. Raoul Hilberg, the Jewish historian and political scientist (1926–2007).
3. The Warsaw Rising was a gallant but hopeless attempt by the inmates of the city's ghetto to break free of Nazi control. It failed, with considerable loss of life.
4. Anne Frank is the most famous Holocaust victim because of the diary she wrote before her deportation to the camps. The exact cause of her death is unknown.
5. *Belsen Concentration Camp* 2nd Army pamphlet, May 1945.
6. Ridler, Duncan, 'On a spring evening in 1945' Mars and Minerva.
7. Dimbleby, Richard, BBC Broadcast, April 1945.
8. All quotes from Gordon Walker are courtesy of the US War Department.

EPILOGUE
1. Quoted in Kemp, *SAS at War*, p. 223.
2. Dillon, Martin and Bradford, Roy, *Rogue Warrior of the SAS: The Blair Mayne Legend*, John Murray, London, 1987, p.147.
3. Stevens, Gordon, *The Originals: The Secret History of the Birth of the SAS: In Their Own Words*, Ebury, London, 2005, p. 231.
4. Stevens, *The Originals*, p. 30.
5. Asher, *Regiment*, p. 320.
6. Hills, *Phantom*, p. 333.
7. Pierrepoint, Albert, *Executioner: Pierrepoint*, Coronet, London, 1974, p. 143.
8. Pierrepoint, *Executioner*, p. 145.

Select Bibliography

Ailsby, Christopher, *SS: Roll of Infamy*, Brown Books, London, 1997.

Asher, Michael, *The Regiment: The Real Story of the SAS*, Penguin, London, 2008.

Badsey, Stephen, *D-Day*, Color Library Books, Godalming, 1993.

Bennett, Alan, *Forty Years On*, Faber and Faber, London, 1969.

Calder, Angus, *The People's War: Britain 1939–45*, Pimlico, London, 1969.

Churchill, Winston S., *The Second World War*, Houghton Mifflin, London, 1959.

Dillon, Martin and Bradford, Roy, *Rogue Warrior of the SAS: The Blair Mayne Legend*, John Murray, London, 1987.

Gerrard, Mady, *Full Circle*, privately printed, 2006.

Hallows, Ian S., *Regiments and Corps of the British Army*, Arms and Armour Press, London, 1994.

Hills, R.J.T., *Phantom Was There*, Edward Arnold, London, 1951.

James [Pleydell], Malcolm, *Born of the Desert*, Collins, London, 1945.

Kemp, Anthony, *The SAS at War 1941–45*, Signet (Penguin), London, 1991.

Lefebure, Molly, *Murder on the Home Front*, London, Grafton, 1954.

Lucas, James, *Hitler's Enforcers,* Arms and Armour Press, London, 1996.

Lucas, James, *Last Days of the Reich,* Guild Publishing, London, 1986.

McLuskey, J. Fraser, *Parachute Padre: Behind German Lines With the SAS France, 1944,* Spa Books, Stevenage, 1985.

Morgan, Mike, *Daggers Drawn: Real Heroes of the SAS and SBS,* Spellmount, Stroud, 2012.

Mortimer, Gavin, *The SAS in World War II*, Osprey, Oxford, 2011.

Niven, David, *The Moon's a Balloon*, Penguin, London, 1977.

Pierrepoint, Albert, *Executioner: Pierrepoint*, Coronet, London, 1974.

Ross, Hamish, *Paddy Mayne*, Sutton, Stroud, 2003.

Seymour, William, *British Special Forces*, Pen & Sword, Barnsley, 2006 (orig. Sidgwick and Jackson 1985).

Shortt, James G., *The Special Air Services*, Osprey, Oxford, 1981.

Snyder, Louis L., *Encyclopaedia of the Third Reich*, McGraw-Hill, London, 1998.

Sommerville, Donald, *World War II Day by Day*, Bison Books, London, 1989.

Stevens, Gordon, *The Originals: The Secret History of the Birth of the SAS: In Their Own Words*, Ebury, London, 2005.

Trow, M.J., *War Crimes*, Pen & Sword, Barnsley, 2008.

Trow, M.J., *Swearing Like a Trooper*, Constable Robinson, London, 2013.

Waugh, Evelyn, *Unconditional Surrender: The Conclusion of Men at Arms and Officers and Gentlemen,* Chapman and Hall, London, 1961.

Wellstead, Ian, *The SAS with the Maquis*, Greenhill, London, 1997.

NEWSPAPERS AND PERIODICALS
Daily Telegraph
Sunday Telegraph

SELECT BIBLIOGRAPHY

Yeomanry Despatches – Official Newsletter of Oxfordshire Yeomanry Association 2012

ORIGINAL MATERIAL

Diaries of Lt John H. Randall 1942–44

'Wladimir Aksakov's Adventure with the SAS' (from Belgian SAS Veteran News)

Report of Operation Haft 702 Captain MJDA Blackman 1 SAS Regiment 1944

GHQ Liaison Regiment Officers' Addresses 1939–46

Mentioned in Despatches citation Army Form W.312 1944

Belsen Concentration Camp 2nd British Army, May 1945

After his wartime career, **John Randall** ran a highly successful business training school and is now happily retired. Adored by his wife, children and grandchildren, he still has passionate feelings about the events he witnessed at the end of the war and is the quintessential English gentleman – a quiet man of integrity with a steely resolve that has carried him through his long and fascinating life.

Mei Trow is a military historian and the author of sixty books, his output covering detective fiction, true crime and historical biography.